# FROM BEHIND THE CHAIR

## A Soul Seeker's Journey to Freedom

Jeri Brown-Roraback Ph.D Cht

FROM BEHIND THE CHAIR

Copyright © 2020 Jeri Brown-Roraback Ph.D Cht. All rights reserved. No part of this publication may be reproduced, distributed, or transmitted in any form or by any means, including photocopying, recording, or other electronic or mechanical methods, without the prior written permission of the publisher, except in the case of brief quotations embodied in critical reviews and certain other noncommercial uses permitted by copyright law.

Your Inner Power
3451 Harmony Lane
Sacramento, California
95821
Yourinnerpower.com
Jeri Brown-Roraback.com

ISBN: 978-0-578-70964-2

Design by Transcendent Publishing

Printed in the United States of America.

# *Dedication*

This book is dedicated to anyone who has been sexually abused in any way, to anyone who has lost a child or any loved one, to anyone who has survived a divorce, to any family dealing with transgender issues, and to anyone suffering with depression and thought there was no way out of the darkness.

This book is for anyone searching for a different version of themselves or a different way of life.

I welcome you with an open heart.

# Contents

Foreword . . . . . . . . . . . . . . . . . . . . . . . . . . . . . . . . . . . . . .vii
Preface. . . . . . . . . . . . . . . . . . . . . . . . . . . . . . . . . . . . . .xv
Chapter 1    The Beginning of What . . . . . . . . . . . . . . . 1
Chapter 2    Miracles In the Hospital . . . . . . . . . . . . . .14
Chapter 3    Continue to Uncover . . . . . . . . . . . . . . . . .38
Chapter 4    Fake It 'Til You Make It. . . . . . . . . . . . . . .51
Chapter 5    Homecoming of Questions . . . . . . . . . . . . . .54
Chapter 6    Stop the Auto Accidents. . . . . . . . . . . . . . .64
Chapter 7    There is Always More . . . . . . . . . . . . . . . .68
Chapter 8    Molestation and the Inner Child . . . . . . . . . .72
Chapter 9    Karma and Past Lives . . . . . . . . . . . . . . . .79
Chapter 10   Magazines in Hawaii. . . . . . . . . . . . . . . . .81
Chapter 11   "Break a Leg," They Say. . . . . . . . . . . . . . .85
Chapter 12   My Babies . . . . . . . . . . . . . . . . . . . . . .90
Chapter 13   Angels and Ghosts. . . . . . . . . . . . . . . . . .96
Chapter 14   Magic of Peru . . . . . . . . . . . . . . . . . . . 110
Chapter 15   A Love Meeting with Lessons. . . . . . . . . . . . 121
Chapter 16   The Magic of Greece . . . . . . . . . . . . . . . . 159

Chapter 17  Shampoo, Indians, and Life Between Lives . . . . . . . 179

Chapter 18  Another Trip to the Indian and a Ph.D. for Me. . . . . 195

Chapter 19  Climbing the Mountain . . . . . . . . . . . . . . . . . 203

Chapter 20  Return to Panama . . . . . . . . . . . . . . . . . . . 225

Chapter 21  See Your Power and Keep Your Light On . . . . . . . 228

Chapter 22  Miracle on the High Seas . . . . . . . . . . . . . . . 238

Chapter 23  Seventy Unforgettable Years . . . . . . . . . . . . . 256

Chapter 24  Seventieth Year . . . . . . . . . . . . . . . . . . . . 264

Chapter 25  The Unexpected . . . . . . . . . . . . . . . . . . . . 270

Chapter 26  Discovery . . . . . . . . . . . . . . . . . . . . . . . 274

Chapter 27  The Last Hurrah . . . . . . . . . . . . . . . . . . . . 280

Chapter 28  The Healing Begins . . . . . . . . . . . . . . . . . . 291

Chapter 29  A Pandemic, A Broken Arm and Jack's Back . . . . . . 301

About the Author . . . . . . . . . . . . . . . . . . . . . . . . . . 305

Acknowledgments . . . . . . . . . . . . . . . . . . . . . . . . . . 307

# Foreword

*What happened for me, and I hope will happen for you, is an awareness and appreciation that all our experiences leave their unpredictable imprint on the feelings and beliefs that decide the path we choose to follow — or escape. We do not know how the life we live can impact or touch not only ourselves, but also others. The elemental residue always remains.*

When I was offered the position at a hospital in Sacramento, California, it immediately felt different. As a travelling Registered Cardiovascular Invasive Specialist (RCIS) with a BS in Cardiopulmonary Sciences, I take short assignments in hospitals to fill human resource shortages in Catheterization and Electrophysiology Labs. I stand beside the physicians, preparing equipment and assisting them through many types of cardiac procedures. I fix broken hearts. My intuition told me to take this assignment and motivated me to drive the three thousand miles. This took me five sixteen-hour days. I felt a presence, much bigger than anything I had ever known, leading me onward, and even when my car broke down in the Mojave Desert, I just found a way and kept on driving. I just knew that this assignment was not like previous ones, though I had no idea that the broken heart I'd fix this time was my own.

Two weeks after arriving in California, I still had this odd feeling that I hadn't yet reached my destination. Once again inspiration took the wheel, and I began looking for another room to rent. My search yielded several possibilities; one, however, was different. It included a bio: "I am a hypnotherapist for over 20 years, a hairstylist for over 45 years, author, speaker and teacher." The location was Jeri's Harmony Lane Beauty Salon. Harmony Lane sounded like the place for me. I was desperately searching for harmony and realized that my new necklace, purchased at a Cherokee Trading Post in Oklahoma on my drive westward, was the symbol for harmony. Coincidence? No, for there is no such thing. If we open our hearts, we find that reason connections exist. I felt this is where I needed to be, so when after a few days Jeri had not responded to my email I was very disappointed.

I was still thinking about Jeri and her salon the following Saturday evening when I decided to resume my search for a new place to live. This time, the response was overwhelming, and within minutes I had received texts and emails from fifty or more properties. Some people were wheeling and dealing for me to stay at their home and some were just not the right fit. I was in the middle of trying to respond to all these messages when my phone rang.

"Hi. This is Jeri Roraback."

Thinking one of the people texting me had called through, I said, "But I just sent you a text telling you the rent is too much for me."

The woman said she had never spoken to me and that she did not even know how she knew to call me or where the number had come from.

As I listened to her voice, it dawned on me that this was the person I had emailed more than a week earlier and thought about almost continually since. When I mentioned that I had reached out, she said she had received no email from me; she also reiterated that she did not know where my number had come from. Right there, my instincts told me that *she* was the reason I had come to California. I didn't know why yet, but I knew.

We agreed to meet the next day, and when we did we both knew it was a fit, but it was oh so much more than that. I walked into her home feeling as if I already knew her. She stated she had searched her computer all evening for the email, and it did not exist. How did she know to call me? How did she find my number? Though the feelings were strong, I said I would leave and let each of us think about it. I also told her I don't make immediate decisions because regrets sometimes come up later. (Later she would tell me that she thought she would never see me again. I left not knowing whether she would choose me, as she had other applicants as well.) The truth was, I knew what I wanted, and it was to rent that room from Jeri. I gave it about forty minutes, then, unable to wait any longer, I sent her a text. At the instant I pushed send, a text from her arrived, and I do mean the very instant. We both agreed that there was going to be more to this than just a rental agreement.

    I moved into the room and soon found that Jeri was one of the most positive people I had ever been around. I thought, Jeri must have lived a beautiful, perfect life. How else could one be so at peace with themselves? I, on the other hand, was not at peace, but rather depressed and sad as I went through cycles of excitement for a new place and job, fear of the unknown, and loneliness from missing my family. Jeri saw these stages in me. She said that she had channeled visions of me and explained what she did in her Life Between Lives Hypnotherapy® sessions. Jeri told me to be positive and put the energy out there that I wanted to experience. I feel that she already knew there was a lot of escaping hidden in my broken heart, but she did not force the issue and just dealt with the person before her. Jeri did tell me that she was writing a book about the life she had survived. Survived? What could she know of survival? I knew everything about surviving and escape had been my only way out. She still never forced the issue of hypnotherapy on me, even though once I was hypnotized to stop smoking and it had worked beautifully, for a time. Hypnosis for smoking cessation and Jeri's Hypnotherapy sessions are not the same.

    Jeri's book was revealed to me in stories as we sat on the patio together. We were so much alike, and like mine, her heart had also been hammered to a nearly flattened, lifeless form. I realized she really had survived, and though I found myself wanting to break open my broken heart and reveal the pain of my life to her, I stayed in my shell, even as I tried to do the positive work she was asking me to do. Then the hospital began to cancel my shifts and I found myself on that patio, near to her and the energy she gave to me, a lot of the time. My depression had deepened, as did my awareness that this precious time was wasting and I had to use it wisely. When I told Jeri that I wanted to start hypnotherapy sessions with her, she agreed; then said she never would have asked me. It was a decision each person must arrive at on their own.

We have thus far completed two two-hour sessions and a four-hour session. In these sessions I have been able to reveal the book of my life, and the life before this life, in a setting of control and ease. Each time, emotion has poured from my eyes and ran down my cheeks as tears, but with no weeping or drama. I saw how people and events had taken my power and I felt so grateful to have the past come up and escape my broken heart. Also, I saw Jeri and I together in the life before this life and in the time not lived yet. I witnessed places that I never imagined, and we have connected so much of what I saw with what exists in this time.

Before we began the sessions, I asked her, "Why do I have to learn a lesson in this life?"

"Because," she replied, "we repeat it over and over as our souls come in and out of the lives we live."

I can tell you now, it was more than a lesson. In fact, I wouldn't call it a lesson at all. Instead, I will attach the labels "acceptance" and "freedom" to those moments when I realized that none of the things that had broken my heart — and there were many, and they were tragic — were caused by me. Those in my life who have blamed me for their own actions are the lesson I learned. People who hurt me chose to do so because I am an empath. Hurt hits me like arrows and later dissipates. It was revealed to me that my path is to be the one to show kindness so that people, patients, and even angels might know that there is goodness, and not everyone has the capacity to hurt others. I fix broken hearts and allow them to be free. That is my role in the hospital and in life. Jeri is the medium of healing that comforts you and allows those freedoms to exist. She is the angel of Freedom.

Read the life she has lived and know that the person that survived this is an amazing messenger. You too will realize that you are not alone in the search for escape. You are not to blame for the actions of others. You will survive to love and live the life you want. Inspiration is speaking to you. Read it in her words and feel the inspiration that led me to find Jeri. Don't be afraid. Freedom awaits.

Angela E. Murphy, BS, RCIS

Our misconception of "self"
Is all that separates us from true
Love and Abundance.
~Jeri Roraback Ph.D

I feel the breeze and rain and know the snow is melting
I think of the fun and beauty of it all
It's white, its pure, it's clean, it's soft
Then I remember the destruction it's creating all around me
The mud, the pain, the price we are all paying
That's my life
The polarity I've created
I started this life pure, clean, soft and open
I've created
The mud and muck, the pain of my experiences and the loss
And the price I've paid to maintain the wall
The time is here to clean it all up
Create a new road
And enjoy the ride

~Jeri Roraback

(Many years ago!)

# Preface

*"The secret of change is to focus all your energy, not on fighting the old, but on building the new."*

~**Socrates**

Did this book start the day I was born? Did it start when a psychic told me, "You have three books in you that have to come out?" Did this book start that day I stood in my beauty salon and said, "Self, you have to write about this"? Or did it start lifetimes ago, as my soul evolved? I will leave that up to you to decide as you read about my journey.

However it began, that first installment of my journey became the book *The ABC's of Never Having Another Bad Hair Day!* It was during that time that I realized there was more to my story. And, eventually, I would realize that this story had to be told in service to others.

As I searched for and attended numerous classes, seminars, and anything I could find to be certified in or learn about, more of my path unfolded before me. One day, one of my teachers asked me, "When are you going to take your knowledge and help people?" This got me thinking, and I soon found myself in hypnotherapy school. Next, I was blessed with an invitation to the Michael Newton Institute, where I learned the incredible process of Life Between Lives® hypnotherapy sessions. Then I was off to college, attaining my Doctorate in Metaphysical Sciences.

More miracles than I could imagine began to take place as I traveled the world doing private sessions, teaching classes and helping the many people that awaited me, just like I had seen in my classes. I found I did have an essence for my life. I had a Soul Journey to continue living.

This is when I began to understand, *You don't know, that you don't know, what you don't know.* Breathe into that statement. I pondered this for months before I realized I really didn't know much about this life I was living or why I did most of what I did. Up to this point I thought I was pretty much okay; now I found I was living in such a little space on this planet.

This is my story. I am sure the people who appear in it see things differently, which brings me to a crucial point. Never judge anyone's life, because you don't know how they saw or understood a given circumstance or event. Nor do you know what that person is living out as part of their Soul Journey. When I discovered that I didn't know why I did the things I did, I began to work very hard at not judging anyone. I also changed the names and some of the locations in this book, I guess to protect the innocent.

I do not name specific classes and or teachers, for a couple of reasons. One reason is that some of the classes and teachers are not even around any longer. The big reason, however, is this is *my* Soul Journey, and mine alone. Your Soul Journey is different, therefore, trying to walk my path would not be beneficial to you. That said, I do know I can help you discover your soul and its journey using the combination of healing modalities I offer.

As you read the following, my hope is that you discover that no matter how bad you believe your life is right now, it can be different if you are open to change. I hope you decide that it doesn't matter how old or how young you are; you can start today to unfold your own Soul Journey.

I've lost count of the people who have said to me, "You have been doing this stuff for years. Why isn't your life perfect?" It's a valid question! However, as you read these pages you will see how one situation must unfold before another one will be shown to you. When I first began my journey of exploration, I didn't know it was going to be a journey. After each class or seminar, I would say, "Thank God I am healed now," and indeed, I had resolved that particular hurt. Soon, though, more questions, issues or challenges would arise and off I went.

Along the way, I found the meaning of the adage, "Life is a journey, not a destination." I also realized the differences between faith and trust and knowledge and wisdom, and so much more. I hope you do as well.

## Chapter 1

## *The Beginning of What*

I ran into the bathroom, slammed the door and screamed, "I hate my mother!"

I was shocked to hear those words leave my mouth. Where had that come from? I was not a child having a tantrum, or a teenager in rebellion. With tears streaming down my face, I stared at myself in the mirror. Who was this person and what was going on? I had no answers, only more questions. My heart ached, along with my head and every other part of my body as I slumped onto the closed toilet, crying uncontrollably. There were more tears than I could ever remember shedding. I hadn't realized anyone could cry this hard.

Jack yelled through the door to let him in. Instead, I opened it and made my way to the stairs outside the bathroom with my face in my hands. I was shaking and didn't want Jack to see my face. My insides were screaming, *Hold me, hold me, protect me, don't leave me, just love me*, but my mouth was yelling, "Leave me alone!"

"Jeri," he pleaded, "what is wrong? Jeri, what did I do? Jeri? Just answer me!"

He tried to get me to look at him and stop crying long enough to tell him something, but I couldn't; what's more, I didn't even want to try. I just wanted to collapse and never get up. I couldn't go on any longer. Jack held me close in his strong arms, and though they felt good I froze inside. I had always wanted a tall man, big and strong, but now that I had one I was afraid. Why did I pull away from the strength? And when he drew up to full height, why did I tighten up inside? Why did part of me want to run, run away from it all?

After a while I got a few words out through my sobs. "I can do anything myself, I don't need anyone, especially you, so go ahead and leave. I'll put on my own license plate."

Jack's head whipped up. "Damn it, Jeri!" he yelled as he stamped his foot. "It was you who told me to leave! I'm not the one who constantly wants me gone. I love you. What do you want me to do?"

Watching him, I was suddenly transported back to our teenage years, when the stomp of Jack's size thirteen cowboy boots had an electrifying effect on my whole body. With that flashback, my overpowering emotions calmed down somewhat. I was able to sit on the sofa and try to talk about what had just happened.

"Jeri," he said, "I was just trying to show you how to put the license plate on your new car before I left. You know you are the one who told me to leave. What do you expect? I can't stay where I'm not wanted."

While he said this, I was thinking, *If you hadn't wrecked my last car, we wouldn't be having to put a license plate on a new one. I don't want a new car or a new license plate, and I certainly don't want car payments I can't afford. You don't even think about that, with all your money.*

As he continued to talk, my thoughts ran away with me. Yes, I hated that new car. I wanted my old one back. It had meant so much more to me than a way to get from A to B. Why couldn't I have anything I want? I didn't want much. Right now, I just wanted my life back. I wanted to be happy. *My God, what is going on?*

And what about my screams of "I hate my mother!"? Yes, my mother had always been a mean rageaholic, but what made me say that now? The questions ran through my mind like water over the dam. Why had I gone over the edge when Jack was just showing me how to put on that license plate?

Most of all, I wanted to know about the voices I'd been hearing in my head. Where were they coming from? And why were they now talking to each other? Was I losing my mind? All I knew was that I couldn't tell anyone about them. They would lock me up. Even Jack would think I'd flipped.

*No, I don't need help— I can do it myself. I don't need anyone or anything. I can pull this together and the crisis will be over. It will be okay. I can make it work. I have made a lot of things work and I can do it again.*

Or could I? Suddenly I wasn't so sure.

I thought back to the day Jack got here, over a year earlier. That morning I was upstairs getting ready for work when I heard his truck pull into the driveway. I ran down to open the garage, then, as I saw him bend under the rising door the voice in my head said, *What have you done now?* Shocked to hear those words, I pushed the thought away and ran to him. But as he hugged me, I couldn't get it out of my mind. I told myself, *Shoot, it will be okay – I can make this work*. And I had, though now I was not so sure what it was that I had made work.

After my outburst over the license plate subsided, we made up and tried to be normal as we went about our daily routine. Yet all the while my mind kept going with all the questions. By evening we could make love and I could try to make him forget all that had happened. At least I thought I could. After sex I was alone with my thoughts again, well, alone with the voices that kept talking to me.

The next morning in the shower, the voices started again, even more of them. Yes, I was definitely losing my mind. What was I going to do? Where did I go from here? *If I can get Jack to leave I will be okay. That's the answer. If he leaves, I will be okay. I was okay before and I'll be okay when he leaves.* Truth be told, I wasn't really okay before; I hadn't been okay since Luke and I broke up, but only a couple of friends knew that. Even now, I still missed Luke. But I couldn't think about that now. I had to come up with a way to get Jack out of here without hurting him or making him mad.

I headed to the salon, grateful for the distraction work would bring. At some point in the day I had a little time between clients, so I grabbed a magazine and settled into my chair. Funny, it was the same magazine that I had put on my desk at home, I had taken it out of my bag the day before. As I began to flip through it, I saw ads for psychics and all kinds of things that I had never heard of before. I wasn't interested in psychics, not even a little bit. My mother had gone to psychics, paying huge amounts of money to them, as well as numerologists, and it never made her happy. They wouldn't help me either. I also knew that talk therapy didn't work because my mother had taken us many times, only to leave when the therapist inevitably told her she had to do something in order to change her circumstances. Was there anyone or anything that could help me now?

As I looked at the ads, one telephone number jumped out at me. It had the same prefix as my home number. *Oh well,* I thought, *at least this person is close to the house.* And before I knew it I had picked up the telephone and was dialing the number.

"Inner Words," I heard a woman say.

I took a deep breath. "I don't know who you are or what you do but I need help."

"Would you tell me about it?" she asked.

"Okay, well, I am hearing voices and I think I am losing my mind. I don't know what to do or where to go."

As the conversation went on, she acted as if this was no big thing and that I certainly wasn't crazy. She then told me of a man who did a "process" on people. I hadn't heard of anything like that and I didn't even know if I was hearing her right, but I said, "Make me an appointment."

"Don't you want to know anything about him or what he does?"

"No," I replied, "just make me an appointment."

"The cost is one hundred dollars."

I didn't care how much it cost, so long as he could help me.

After setting up the appointment, the woman told me he was doing an introductory speech on Sunday at a church about forty-five minutes away. I took down the directions but knew there was no way I could go. Jack and I were going camping with a motorcycle group and he would be upset if I didn't go with him. He was upset when I did anything without him. This thought was on my mind the rest of the day, right up until the moment I went home and announced that I had other plans that weekend.

As I'd thought, he was not happy. He also didn't understand what I was telling him, which wasn't surprising as I didn't understand it myself. I just knew I was going to hear this "process" man. That Sunday, Jack was camping without me and I headed to the talk. Where I got the push to go through with it I'll never know, especially since going to church for any reason, let alone to hear some random person speak, was not exactly my cup of tea.

When I arrived, I sat at the back so I could leave whenever I wanted. Instead, I listened for two hours. I didn't understand anything he was saying; in fact, I wasn't even sure I *heard* what he was saying because he used words I didn't know. Everyone else seemed to know them, though, because they kept nodding their heads and even applauding. They also asked the man questions and he answered them. At the end, we were all invited to go up and speak to him. I went and stood in line with the others, watching and listening to them and trying to act as if I knew what it was all about.

Finally, the woman in front of me stepped toward the man. I heard her choke up as she asked, "How should I deal with death?"

The man looked at her, held her hand and said, "I know how I deal with death. I don't know how *you* should deal with death."

My first thought was, *What? This woman is crying and asking this supposed "expert" for help and he doesn't know?*

My second thought was, *Here's how you deal with death — you just buck up and get over it. That's what I did when I lost my dad and my twins.*

Suddenly, it was my turn. And because I had no idea what to say to him, I responded to his friendly greeting with, "Hello, I'm Jeri, your nine a.m. appointment tomorrow."

With sparkling eyes and a cute smile, he shook my hand and said, "Happy to meet you, I'm Mark."

I don't remember what, if anything, else I said to him; I just remember wanting to get out of there. As I walked back down the aisle, my mind returned to the woman who had asked about dealing with death. *I did it and lived through it and no one feels sorry for me.* It was the same thing I thought whenever anyone complained about losing someone.

Once alone in my car, however, I was sure I was going crazy. I hadn't understood one word that man said and yet I would soon be forking over one hundred dollars of my hard-earned money so he could do I-didn't-know-what. At that moment, the voices seemed to be my only friends.

Adding to my reluctance was Mark's inability to answer the woman's question. If he couldn't do that, what made me think he could help me? I told myself I couldn't think of that right now; my only task at the moment was smoothing things over with Jack. I still couldn't believe I'd had the nerve to let him go camping without me. I always did what Jack wanted because I had to make him happy. I had to be the perfect one.

The following morning I travelled the few blocks from my house to the home of Ronney, the publisher of *Inner Words* magazine. As I walked inside, she peered at me and said that I looked very familiar. A few moments of back and forth about where we could have met yielded no answers, then I headed upstairs, where Mark was waiting for me in a cozy master bedroom with a table and a couple of chairs. There was also a massage table set up, and as he greeted me with the same warm smile I'd seen the day before, I thought, *What is that for?*

We chatted for a few minutes, then he asked me to lay down on the massage table. *Okay,* I thought, *I'm fully dressed, I'll go along with that.* As I got settled, he explained what was going to happen. Okay, I told him, though I felt self-conscious because I did not understand what he was talking about. How could this work if I didn't know what was going on? He then proceeded to pull and push my arms, legs and head while, at his direction, I repeated different things he said. Sometimes he stopped talking and just held his hands over a part of my body. Suddenly, he asked me to close my eyes and visualize how I wanted the essence of my life to be. *What the hell is the essence of my life?* I thought, *I just want a life.* But I closed my eyes anyway, and to my surprise, I saw myself standing in a pink suit holding a folder and lecturing to a big crowd of people. Deeply shocked, I thought, *I can't tell him that! He'll think I'm stupid, or worse. He'll think I'm nuts.* He talked to me for a while (again, about concepts I didn't understand), then we went to sit at the table and he started explaining what had just happened. Yep, you got it — I didn't understand that part either. Yet suddenly I heard myself telling him that I wanted to learn to do what he had just done.

"Just be with this for now," he said kindly, "and let me know what comes up for you. Then we will talk about you learning what I do."

He then wrote some words on a paper and told me to recite them three times with my eyes closed and three times with my eyes open. I was to do this in the morning and in the evening for two weeks. This sounded completely ridiculous, and even as I agreed I was laughing inside and very happy no one I knew could see me. I surely wasn't going to tell anyone that I paid the guy a hundred dollars for this!

I thanked him, then chatted with Ronney for a few minutes before getting into my car. All I could think was that Jack was going to be livid that I'd wasted the money. Then I decided that since I wasn't going to get the hundred back I would recite these sayings as many times a day as possible — in the car, at work, in bed, in the shower and anywhere else I could.

For the next couple of weeks I did just that, repeating the words religiously even when I didn't feel like it. Then, one morning while sitting in traffic and in my usual hurry, I found myself slowing down to let someone in front of me. Wow, that got my attention. I had let someone in, something I wouldn't normally do. What did that mean? I was still thinking about this when another person slowed down to let me in. Wow, see how this works! Before I knew it, I had arrived at work, and in a good mood. That day flew by, in part because all I could do was think about how, by using Marks words, I had experienced a very different commute. The voices in my head were still there, but for some reason they didn't scare me anymore, at least, not for now.

I maintained things at home and at work, but now I had a new awareness of certain boundaries at home, boundaries I couldn't step out of.

Next question, who had set these rules? And were they really "rules" at all? These questions led to more questions until my mind was teeming with them. The questions about me were hard enough, now I had to deal with all these questions about life as well.

As I lay in bed one night, experiencing the tightness I always felt in my body at that time, I tried to remember the saying I had repeated so many times over the last couple of weeks. Only I couldn't. Jack was sleeping next to me in the darkness, and as I wracked my brain I was careful to remain still so he wouldn't get any ideas about touching me. Why couldn't I remember?

Just as I was ready to risk moving to get the paper out of my purse, the little voice in my head said, *He said to do it for two weeks.*

Oh, okay, it's been two weeks. Now what?

*Go to the next step,* the voice replied.

What is the next step?

*Go find out what he was talking about and how this works.*

I fell asleep thinking about this, and when I woke up the next morning I knew another visit to Mark was in order. I called Ronney and found out where he was speaking next. It was as simple as that.

I started going to talks every chance I got, and each time I would understand one little part of what he said. I also met other people at these gatherings, and they always seemed to know so much about the concepts. Now, in addition to my confusion, I was dealing with the feeling of being stupid.

I also had to deal with Jack, who sat home drinking every night and was angry when I came home. Finally, I persuaded him to come to one of the meetings with me, thinking things would be easier if I could get him involved. Well, that was a mistake! Not only was Jack completely uninterested in what Mark had to say, he accused me of wanting to have an affair with him! This soon became a constant theme in our arguments, but I didn't care. The more I understood, the more I wanted to understand. I had become addicted to learning.

Then came the books. I hadn't read an entire book in years, but I bought the ones Mark recommended and I read them. When I told him I didn't understand ninety-nine percent of the information, he didn't make me feel stupid. He just told me to keep reading, that the information was going "somewhere into my body." Read and re-read it, he told me, and I listened. Some of it got easier, some of it still eluded me.

I started learning how we hold memory in the cells of our body. These cellular memories never go away, even though our conscious mind forgets about them. Some of these memories cause pain or disease. I also started understanding pheromones – chemicals secreted by our bodies that affect the behavior of those around us without them even realizing it. One of the most important things I learned, though, were the differences in growing spiritually, emotionally, physically and mentally. All of these are necessary aspects of our life. They are like the legs of a table – if one leg is missing the table is off balance and won't stand for very long.

I found myself considering how these areas were playing out in my own life. Before meeting Mark, I'd thought I had this spiritual stuff figured out. I thought it meant going to church, and I wasn't having any of that. Now I was learning that "spirituality" was different than religion, which, to my surprise, brought me relief. Physically, I'd had my share of illnesses and pain, and mentally, well, just a month or so earlier I had been ready to commit myself. Now I was ready to listen.

Every time I went to a talk, I heard someone speaking about something new – things like incense, stones, crystals, aromatherapy, essential oils, feng shui, and breathwork sessions. I also learned about the inner child and past lives, as well as how our expectations, focus and choices create our reality. For the first time in my life I was reading books that fascinated me and having real conversations with people, rather than just bitch sessions. I realized that there was an enormous world, so much bigger than the one I was living in, and it was filled with knowledge. All I wanted was to soak it all in.

With all of this to learn I didn't care what Jack thought or what he wanted from me. I soon discovered that I didn't even want to go home, and it was my house! What I felt as I walked into the house or even driving toward home was not good. I recalled feeling this way so many times in other relationships before I ended them.

I started learning about the energy people carry and give out, and that there was a way to protect myself from that energy. As I was learning how to do this my insides were screaming, *I want a life in which I do not need protection!* Wow, what would that be like? I had no idea, because I had never had that kind of life. I was always protecting myself from my mother, my sisters, my daughter or my husbands. Could I really have a life that I could relax into and let my guard down? Just the thought of it motivated me to keep going.

At times this all sounded like hogwash. Other times experimenting with energy felt so good it put on me on a natural high. When I felt doubt, I asked myself, does it work? Yes, it does. Am I and these other people as crazy as the world says we are? Nope, it all feels too good, too real, to be crazy. Besides, these answers made sense. For the first time I had a glimpse of how to take control of my life, rather than just bouncing off everyone else. At least, that was what these people were telling me.

They didn't care if I hated my mother, didn't go to church, had been married four times, had a baby out of wedlock, or was financially or emotionally broke. They didn't judge me or what I had been through. They just wanted to help me find ways to feel better and grow. Wow, I felt so good around them.

Whenever we were together, these new friends and I played an interesting game: we would call each other out on any negative things we spoke. Well, pretty soon I was afraid to say *anything*. We all caught a glimpse of how negative we were. No wonder we had attracted such undesirable experiences into our lives! Or at least that was how Mark put it. I realized how seldom, if ever, my thoughts were about what I wanted to create. I didn't even know what I wanted to create – I just knew what I wanted to get rid of.

How many of us hear that alarm in the morning and say to ourselves, "Crap I don't want to get up and go to work"? We shuffle into the bathroom, look in the mirror and tell ourselves how tired we look and how awful our hair is. Then it's back into the closet to find something that fits or looks good, only to settle for something presentable because we are running late. By then we have torn our body apart for how it looks and feels, all the while complaining to ourselves about how bad the morning is. The weather is either too hot, too cold or too rainy. As we're driving or riding to work we complain about the traffic and the other drivers. When we arrive at work, we start in on how bad our coworkers and clients and bosses are. After we put in our hours there, we complain all the way home about everything that needs to be done before we fall into bed, exhausted, and complain that we can't sleep because our mind won't shut off.

Now, do you suppose this attitude is at least part of the problem, part of the reason that our lives and dispositions are a shambles?

- *Do you ever hear the alarm go off and spring out of bed saying, "This is one great day!"?*
- *Have you ever looked in the mirror in the morning, stared straight into your eyes, and said, "I love you"?*
- *Are you thankful for having a bed and a home to sleep in? Are you thankful for having a car or transportation to a job that pays you money for your wants and needs?*
- *In fact, how often are you thankful for anything you have or are? How often are your thoughts about what you want to create? How often are your thoughts positive?*
- *Start a list of the things you're grateful for. Start a list of your positive thoughts. Write down your negative thoughts and figure out how you could make them into positive thoughts or emotions.*
- *Play the game mentioned above by noting how often you express negativity or hear it from others. Your subconscious picks it ALL up – every little bit of it – and that's what it will set out to help you get.*

Money is a similar story. If we complain, put down, envy and talk badly about people with money, how or why would our subconscious help us get money?

- *How do you feel about having money? Or not having money?*
- *How do you think, feel or speak about people who are wealthy?*
- *How do you think, feel or speak about people without money or who are homeless?*
- *What were you told about money as a child?*
- *What have you taught your own children about money?*

What is inside our body, our thoughts, our memories, the decisions we made early in life, and our dramas and traumas is what shapes our subconscious and our lives.

I started taking this new knowledge outside of the classes. I started really listening to my friends, clients, coworkers and anyone else around me. I noticed how negative people were. It didn't take long before my old friends started to get tired of me, and I of them. I just couldn't take the time to hash and rehash everything that was going on in my life. I couldn't sit around, putting everyone down. I just couldn't listen over and over to how unhappy they were with men they had been with for years. I also realized that the news was one of the most depressing things I listened to, and I quit watching it. Things were really changing.

I learned that silence is golden. I stopped telling my customers what I was doing because when I did, they would either laugh or tell me how stupid it was and to "be careful." Besides, I had a new tribe of people I could talk to who would support me and help me learn more.

Each time I watched one of Mark's demonstrations, I felt more motivated to start sifting through my past. As I heard him explain others' lives, my own started to look different. Little by little, different questions arose. When, where and how come? With each class or talk, something else would be revealed to me.

# The Beginning of What

After three and a half months of changes, it was time to go to a class where Mark would teach us to do what he did. I was so excited and scared. All my insecurities reared their ugly heads – how stupid I was; how I wouldn't be able to do it; shoot, how I didn't even know what "it" was. I had been reading and listening and still didn't understand most of it. Then – bam! – I was stopped in my tracks. Jack's mother passed away and I had to go with him to the funeral, a plane ride away.

People told me to take care of myself, but they just didn't understand my circumstances. Nope, Jack would be way too upset with me if I didn't go; just as importantly, I would be way too upset with myself. However, I did have the guts to tell him that I was flying home immediately after the services were over so I could go to the class. Where these ideas, and the courage to follow through with them, came from was a true mystery to me, but I did it.

This class was pretty much a blur. There was so much to learn, yet at the same time it felt like all the information was springing up from somewhere inside me. Knowing this, I began to feel better about myself than I ever had before. Where had this information been hiding all this time?

At this point I was still hoping and believing that somehow all of this would help change or fix my mother, sisters, daughter, Jack, and a lot of others in my life. If they were all okay, then I would be okay too.

Mark would tell me that the only one I could help was myself. As I changed, my world and the people in it would follow suit. Then one day he said, "Look at your life like a baseball game. You are the pitcher. Every day, you and your family play the game. Some days there is a strikeout, some days there is a homerun. Sometimes someone makes it to first base and other days they make it to third, but the game goes on. Now, remove yourself as the pitcher. There is no game. Everyone will change somehow and probably there will be chaos."

Nope, didn't understand that either, but I had learned (to some extent) to just be with it and wait to see what happened next.

## Chapter 2

## Miracles In the Hospital

Despite all the drama with Jack, I still believed our relationship was heaven-sent and that I had to make it work. We knew everything about each other from our years in Montana, back when I was in junior high and he was in high school. Later, I would often tell people the story of how, after three decades apart, Jack and I had gotten back together. I told myself I wanted others to understand that we were meant to be, but sometimes I wondered whether I was really trying to convince myself.

We reconnected while I was skiing in Vail with Richard, a gay man from Los Angeles whom I had met on a dive boat in Turks and Caicos. There, among the sweaters and long johns I had packed for the trip was Jack's home phone number, though I wasn't sure why I had decided this was the time to finally put it to use.

That Saturday, I took a few breaks from the slopes to call the number I had for him, but got no answer. On Sunday morning I called again, and this time he picked up. My God, I still remembered that voice!

"Is this Jack from Montana?" I asked, my heart pounding.

"How did you get this number?"

I almost hung up then, because it sounded like he was annoyed. Instead, I asked him if he knew who it was.

"Of course, I do," he replied, "I would know your voice anywhere." He asked me where I was staying and said he would call me Monday evening after work.

My emotions went wild all that day. The night was interminable, and even the hours spent skiing on Monday seemed to drag. When evening arrived, I sent Richard off to dine alone while I stayed in the room and waited for the call. By that time I was so keyed up that when the phone did ring it actually startled me. That night, Jack and I had one of those marathons conversations that you know you'll never forget. After all, we had a lot of ground to cover.

Thirty years earlier, his mother had moved him to Denver after his father died of a heart attack. Later that summer my mother and stepfather moved me to San Francisco. Jack and I wrote each other, a fact we kept from our mothers because they were dead set against our being together. I mailed my letters to Jack's sister's house, and he sent his to a friend of mine who lived in a nearby apartment building. It would have worked, too, if I hadn't made the mistake of hanging onto them. One day Mom found the box of letters hidden in my closet and confiscated them, along with their envelopes containing Jack's return address. Around the same time, the girl who had been receiving my mail moved away. Jack and I lost contact, but I never forgot him.

I had reached out to him a couple of times over the years. The first time was back in 1974, when I got his number from information. Jack was already married but we spoke to and wrote each other regularly; that is, until his wife found out and put a stop to the exchange. When my divorce was final, I moved to Sacramento, met someone else and forgot all about it. Another lifetime passed before I decided to get in touch. I called his work number this time, only to learn that he'd left the job. A friend later gave me the home number, but by then my nerve had faded and I tucked it away for safekeeping. There it remained for the next six years, until this trip to Vail.

After talking for hours, we arranged for me to meet him in Denver on my way to the airport. The following night I waited by a phonebooth at a gas station, hoping he would show up. My friend Richard was mad that I wasn't going to the airport with him so I knew he wouldn't come back to get me.

Suddenly, there was Jack, standing in front of a big Cadillac. He was thirty years older and had a full beard but I would have known those eyes anywhere. Long-buried emotions rose up in me like a sudden storm, then he grabbed me and kissed me and my world stood still.

It was such a surreal feeling as we got into the car and started driving; I was sitting beside someone who had been made a stranger by time and distance, yet I knew him to the core. I only had a couple of hours before I had to be at the airport, so I asked him to take me to Mile High Stadium, home of the Broncos. After years of watching them on television I could finally see where they played their games.

Jack stayed with me until I boarded my plane. We exchanged telephone numbers and addresses. Still riding high on the time we'd spent together, I wrote him a long letter on the plane and sent it off the next day. I had no sooner dropped it in the mailbox when I began to second guess myself. Maybe I shouldn't have sent it.

During our catch-up session I had learned that Jack was married. It was a road I had gone down before and had no desire to do so again. But it wasn't a happy marriage; in fact in a couple days he moved out of his house and in with his mother. *And besides,* I told myself, *he's JACK.*

I headed to work, hoping it would distract me from my dilemma. Instead, I was confronted with it head-on when the florist delivered a bouquet of thirty long-stemmed red roses, one for each year we were apart. It was the type of romantic gesture I had never experienced before, and apparently not a lot of others did either because everyone — stylists and customers alike — were abuzz. How could I answer their questions about me and Jack when I didn't have the answers myself? All I knew was that I couldn't wait to get home to talk with him.

We were on the phone all night, and I don't think there was a topic we didn't cover. One particular thing that stands out was Jack's insistence that I was not a virgin when we first got together. No matter what I said he remained unconvinced. We finally moved on, though it wouldn't be the last time he brought up the issue. Each time, as I blew it off, I'd ask myself, *At this point what does it matter?*

Mostly, though, the conversation was magical, and it was only the beginning. Soon we were on the phone all night every night. I was running on adrenalin. I told him the good, the bad, the marriages, the children, and he told me how awful his marriage had been since we'd last talked in 1974.

Much of the time was spent reminiscing about our escapades back in Montana in the sixties. I was just twelve when we started dating, and Jack was fifteen. We talked about how hard our mothers tried to keep us apart. They had seemed like cruel oppressors back then; now, after raising our own children, we understood their concerns. Both women had no doubt worried that I would get pregnant, and it's a miracle I didn't.

We reminisced about sneaking out at night, and the time we were caught by John, my stepfather, while my mother was in the hospital. Jack had snuck in through my bedroom window in the middle of that night and John heard us and opened my door to find us in bed. Jack jumped out the window, but my stepdad was too fast for him. He raced around through the kitchen and onto the glassed-in porch that Jack was now trying to run through, then picked up a roaster pan with a cooked turkey in it and threw it at him. Bam! Right in the face. For days afterward Jack had a black and blue nose and eye, and I was in a lot of trouble when my mom got out of the hospital. She told Jack's mother what had happened, thus enlisting her in the battle to keep us apart.

We talked about the freezing nights when we snuck out and how he would steal his parents' car for us to ride around in, the summer nights at the park under the big sky. It was all beginning to come back to me.

He filled me in on so much information that I either didn't know or had just forgotten, like the times I would just disappear with my mother and sister because Mom had decided it was time for another move. We had always come back, though, until August of 1962 when he returned to Montana to visit me and found out I was gone and no one knew where I was. He was devastated.

I told him about our move to San Francisco and how I was both excited and upset about leaving Montana, though it hadn't been the same for me once he left. I told him how we had driven through Nevada and Sacramento Valley and it was so hot I could not wait to get to the beach. I had envisioned us living somewhere like Los Angeles, with sandy beaches, tanned bodies and beach parties. Boy, was I wrong about that! As we drove across the Bay Bridge during the evening rush hour, the fog dropped over us, the temperature dropped about fifty degrees, and my mood dropped right along with it. I remember saying to myself, "I hate this place and I am going to be miserable." Writing Jack made it tolerable for a while, but once my mother put a stop to it I felt lonelier than ever.

I was surprised to hear that in the late seventies, a couple of years after his wife had put an end to our letter-writing, Jack had come looking for me. Actually, he had come to California on vacation with his family but had spent much of the time sneaking around trying to find me, only to learn that I had moved to Sacramento. He couldn't get any other information.

Now, for the first time in our lives, we were free to speak with and see each other anytime we wanted. Within two weeks we were making plans for him to fly out to California for a visit. While we were on the telephone, my girlfriend Judy started talking with his friend, Jim, and he decided to come out and meet her as well.

They flew in on the night of April 9, a significant date for me because it's my granddaughter Brittany's birthday and the date my dad had died. It would also turn out to be the night my daughter Loni met her next husband. After a Friday night out on the town with Jim and Judy, Jack and I spent the rest of the weekend either on the go or in bed. Amazingly, after thirty years I still remembered his body. Now much wiser, and having raised a daughter myself, I could see why my mother had been so opposed to our relationship when I was fourteen.

Sunday night, as we stood at the airport waiting for their flight to board, I noticed Judy had tears in her eyes.

"I really love him," she said, "and I should be with him." I looked at her in surprise. I had seen her in many relationships and had never known her to have feelings like that.

And she was serious. That night and the following day the phones were ringing off the hook as the four of us called each other about when we were going to get together next. I figured Judy and Jim would spend some time seeing if their feelings were indeed serious, so imagine my shock when on Tuesday Judy announced that she was moving to Denver to be with him. She was leaving her entire life behind for a man she barely knew! Before the end of the week, she was on a plane to Denver. In truth, I would have loved to do the same, but at the time I had obligations and had to stay put.

When she arrived, Judy called and said that Jack was planning on flying back out on Friday night to surprise me. The rest of the week dragged as I went about my business and counted the minutes until I saw him again.

Finally Friday arrived and I started getting ready for our weekend. I hadn't heard from Jack that day and figured he was on his way, by but midnight, I was still waiting for a call or to hear him walk in. I was listening for those sounds as I dozed off. When I awoke and saw the sun shining through the blinds I knew that something had to be wrong. I tried calling Judy, but she and Jim had already left the hotel they were staying in and I had no idea where they were going. I called Jack's mother's house but there was no answer.

As the hours went on, I became more convinced that something was wrong. I even called his job but no one picked up. Finally, his mother answered the phone. Jack was not there, and his bed had not been slept in. She started asking questions, and I could tell that she didn't know about me. I wasn't going to be the one to tell her. I then tried to contact Stan, another friend of Jack's, but couldn't reach him. By one p.m. I was truly frantic and sent Stan a telegram through Western Union asking him to call me. Three more nerve-wracking hours later, my phone rang.

"Oh! My God, what's wrong?" I gasped when Stan told me Jack was in the hospital.

He told me that Jack had collapsed at work about four on Friday and had been brought to the hospital by ambulance. He was in Intensive Care and though the doctors weren't sure yet they suspected a brain aneurism. I knew what this could mean because my nephew had had one.

While I was crying and asking questions, Stan told me I couldn't call the hospital because Jack's job had called Jill, his wife, and she was in the hospital room all the time. He would go back and find out what he could.

I then heard from Judy, who said she and Jim had been looking for Jack. When I told her what had happened, she said they too would go to the hospital and keep me posted.

The next couple of hours were sheer hell, and to make matters worse I had to work. The poor people that got haircuts during that time left in pretty bad shape, not that I noticed. I only found out later when they came back in and told me.

When I didn't hear back from Stan, I started calling all the hospitals in Denver to find out which one Jack was in. After about ten or twelve calls, I hit the right one. They said Jack was in ICU and no calls could be forwarded, but I could talk to the nurses or the family. I couldn't do that, because how could I explain who I was? I just said thank you and hung up. I now knew where he was, but what good did that do me? And where was Stan? Judy?

Finally, I said to hell with it, I had to know something. I called the hospital again and asked for the nurses' station. When the nurse reiterated that I could talk to one of the family, I explained who I was and why this wasn't possible.

She paused, then said, "Please hold for a moment."

I didn't know whether to hang up or hang on. I didn't know who she would tell. I heard her talking to someone, then a man's voice came on, saying, "Hello, I'm Jack's doctor."

I started crying so hard that I couldn't even speak. He waited patiently until I regained my composure, then, after I briefly explained who I was, he told me that Jack was very sick and he would do what he could for me. He then asked a peculiar question.

"Do you know anything about a plane he was supposed to be on?"

When I told him that he was supposed to come to California that weekend, the doctor said Jack had been asking for me and talking about the flight he had to catch. The doctor then told me to hang on, and I heard him tell the nurse to somehow get the wife out of the room and let Jack talk to me.

"Do anything you have to do," he said.

I couldn't believe my ears! I was happy, scared, crying, laughing – every emotion at once. I waited for what seemed hours and finally I heard the nurse telling Jack there was someone on the phone to talk to him.

When I heard his weak voice, I wanted to cry. He kept saying, "Jeri, I've got a plane to catch. Tell them to let me out of here."

I tried to make him understand that he needed care, but he kept talking as if there was nothing wrong and the hospital staff were holding him hostage. Judy and Jim were there, he said, and he wanted to leave with them so they could take him to the airport. He then told me he loved me but that he had to go.

The nurse took the phone and told me they had to hang up because his wife was coming back into the room. Also, Jack was getting very agitated and that was not good for him. She then assured me they were working to get his blood pressure down and get him stabilized and said I could call back in the morning.

The next day was Easter Sunday, and I had plans to spend the holiday with my mother, Loni and Brittany at Bob and Pat's, Brittany's paternal grandparents. I went, but my mind was consumed with Jack and when I would be able to speak to him again. I called the hospital, only to learn there had been a shift change. No one knew the story and none of the nurses wanted to give me information. The day passed without a word, and it wasn't until late that night when I finally got Stan on the phone. He said that there had been a lot of family in and out all day and Jill had not left the room. Jack had been awake most of the day and was tired.

Monday morning, I asked Judy to go back to the hospital for an update. I would be at work, I said, so she could reach me there. Fortunately, Jill wasn't there, so they were able to give my work number to Jack. I was thrilled to hear from him, but scared that he still didn't seem to know what was going on or why he was there. He just remembered that he had planned to come out for a visit but then he got this awful headache. It kept getting worse and worse, then everything went blank.

"Jeri, it's killing me not being able to see you or talk to you."

"Just get better," I said, my heart melting, "and you can go home."

While I wanted Jack to get out of the hospital, I couldn't help but wonder where he would go when he did. I'd heard through the grapevine that Jill was saying she was the only one who could take care of him. Jack, on the other hand, was saying no way, he was not going back to that house. While I was happy to hear he didn't intend to return to her, I knew there would be a fight. What if he was too sick to argue? Doubt began to set in, followed by panic. Would he go home and forget all about me? Had he meant everything he said? What if I'd finally found Jack only to have the relationship come to an end before it started? Had I been a fool again? My mind went on and on all day, playing out every scenario to its logical end. I must have come up with at least fifty of them, one more depressing than the next.

That night I called the hospital and talked to the nurse on duty. She said that Jill was there and I couldn't talk to him. She also said that Jack was agitated, restless, and asking for me. There wasn't anything I could do except ask Stan to go to the hospital and give Jack a message. But of course, Stan wasn't home.

When I reached Stan on Tuesday, he said he'd been there the night before and Jack kept telling him to, "Make a call for me, call Jeri," but with Jill standing there he could do nothing but pretend he didn't know what Jack was talking about. Stan said Jack didn't look as good as before and wasn't making a lot of sense. What's more, Jill was now giving Stan a tough time about being there. Judy said much the same when she and Jim went to the hospital to see what they could find out for me. She also said that Jack kept telling them to call me, and that they had pled ignorance in front of Jill. I called the hospital a couple of times that day, but it was the luck of the draw. Some nurses would talk to me and some wouldn't.

By Wednesday, my nerves were shot. Jack was not getting better; in fact, he was getting worse. A lot worse. What's more, Judy had called to tell me that she and Jim were moving back to California as soon as possible. Then all I would have was Stan, and half the time I couldn't even find him.

I knew it was time to start seriously considering a trip to Denver. The problem was my friend Martha and I had already booked a vacation to Kauai, Hawaii for the following week. When I'd first told Jack about it he had asked me to cancel and come to Denver instead, to which I'd replied, "I don't cancel trips to Hawaii for anyone or anything. I'm going." He wasn't too happy about that but there wasn't much he could do. Now, with his health at risk, everything had changed.

"Jeri, go to Denver," Martha said when I told her about my dilemma, "Kauai will always be there and he needs you now."

The truth of these words would soon bear out. On their way to the airport, Judy and Jim had stopped by the hospital, only to find that Jill was no longer allowing any visitors. They had, however, looked through the glass into his room and could tell he was rapidly deteriorating. He looked terrible, and the doctors had hooked him up to even more machines. The nurses who would talk to me said they'd had to tie him down to his bed because he was so agitated, and that his wife now only stayed in the room part of the time.

I also learned why Jill had forbade any visitors. Apparently, Jack's boss, who was coincidently was named "Jerry," had gone to see him, and Jill must have figured out that he wasn't the person Jack had been asking for. After that, she didn't trust any of his friends.

By Thursday I couldn't take it anymore. All I could think about was Jack sick in that bed, with no one allowed to see him except the person he dreaded most. He was calling out for me, and I couldn't do anything. Was he thinking he'd been abandoned? Why was he getting worse so fast? Why couldn't the doctors do anything?

Telling myself I had nothing to lose, I called the office of Jack's main doctor and was told he was with a patient. I left a message, figuring I had hit another dead end, but an hour later he called me back. He confirmed that they really didn't know what was happening or why Jack's condition had deteriorated so badly. They couldn't find where in his head the bleed was located, but there was a lot of pressure and now he was paralyzed on the left side. The doctor also confirmed that Jill had ordered no visitors and there was nothing he could do about that. We talked for a while, and then I told him how Jack had said on Monday that it was killing him not being able to see me. The doctor's response: "It probably is." That set me back for a while. I decided I had to do something, but what? I thought again about going to Denver, but with his wife standing guard over his hospital room I wouldn't be able to see him anyway. If only I could talk to Jack and ask him what he needed and wanted.

After a night of crying I headed to work, my mind still running on a loop. Stan and his friend had been to the hospital and from what they could see it didn't look good. They could also tell that his wife was getting very nervous and scared.

Just as I was about to head home for the day, Sandy, a long-time friend of mine, stopped by the shop to see me. She took one look at me and knew something was very, very wrong, I gave her the abbreviated version of the story, and she immediately said she was coming home with me. At the house she listened as I told her everything in detail, then she said, "I can help you. I'm going to get you an appointment with someone who can tell you what's going on there."

By that time I was so frazzled I didn't even think to ask what she was talking about. I just wanted an answer. I told her to set up the appointment.

I then made my usual phone calls looking for information about Jack. The news was terrible. They were taking him into surgery to put in a mainline into his heart. Now frantic, I called my oldest sister, Bobbie, who was a nurse; she told me that it didn't sound good at all. I waited a few hours, then called the hospital and luckily got a nurse who was willing to speak with me. She said he had just gotten back from surgery and was resting well; they were monitoring him closely.

Then, before I knew it, the words, "Could I please speak to his wife?" had flown out of my mouth. What had I just done? I didn't have long to panic, though, because a moment later the nurse put Jill on the phone. Thinking fast, I pretended I was my friend Judy. I said I had returned to California and I just wanted to know how Jack was doing. Instead of answers, however, Jill started firing off questions: Who was I, really? How did I know Jack? Had I grown up with him in Montana? Had Jack recently gone to California to see me? And the big one: did I know a woman named Jeri? I must have answered to her satisfaction, because she told me that Jack had just come back from surgery and wasn't doing very well. Then she told me that I had better be telling the truth when I said that I didn't know Jeri. When we hung up, I was physically and emotionally drained.

"Come on," Sandy said, "It's time to leave for your appointment."

I don't even remember driving to the address Sandy gave me; it was as if I just suddenly appeared there. I walked into the building and sat in a waiting room, crying and praying for someone to help me.

"Please help me decide what to do," I begged, "I can't let him die without him knowing I care."

I also continued to ask why I would find him after thirty years, only to have him taken from me again. Could I ever forgive myself if I didn't do the most I could? What was "the most?" What would Jack say if he could talk to me? What would he want me to do? I felt like I was losing my mind. Suddenly I realized I was sitting in this strange place, with no idea who these people were or how, if at all, they could help me.

A woman walked through a door and asked me to fill out a paper. Yeah, right, I thought, because I couldn't even see it through my tears. I was also having a hard time breathing, as the stress had set off an asthma attack. The woman then asked if she could ground me. I didn't know what that meant so I just nodded yes. She put her hands over my head and closed her eyes and just stood there. I wanted to scream, *What is this? Why aren't you doing something to help me!*

Suddenly I realized the sobs weren't coming as hard and that I could breathe. She started talking to me about taking some deep breaths, closing my eyes and relaxing. I started feeling small and light, and though I didn't understand what was happening, at that point I didn't care. I felt better. After a while she stepped back and asked if I thought I could fill out the paper. To my amazement, I could. As I finished up a group of other people came into the waiting room and began talking with her. I tried to listen, but the few words I could hear I couldn't understand anyway. A few minutes later they asked me to follow them into another other room.

In this room there were only chairs, one turned to face seven others. Of course, they put me in the one facing them. I felt like I was sitting before a firing squad. But instead of interacting with me, they turned to a woman standing behind them and began talking to her. They spoke about the different colors, size and shapes of my auras, whatever the hell they were. They spoke of various energy patterns I had, all different things they said were going on around me. I thought, *Oh, shit, I did it this time.* I wasn't hysterical anymore, but I was a bit scared and wondering how quickly I could escape. After about forty-five minutes of this I asked whether they were going to answer any of my questions. They said we would take a ten-minute break and then they would tell me what they could. As I headed out for a cigarette, I debated just leaving altogether.

Yet there was something that made me return. Maybe because I knew all that awaited me at home was more worry and more unanswered questions about Jack. When I returned to the room, one of the people asked, "What is it that you want to know about this sick person in your life?"

I was shocked. How could she have known this?

Somehow, I managed to say, "What should I do or how can I help him?"

"He is out of his body," another said, "watching what is going on. He left his body because of the pain and the drugs he is being given."

Still another said, "He has three days to make up his mind if he is going to live or pass on."

I sat there, my mind and heart racing. What did they mean? He has to make up his mind about whether he would live or die? This was unreal. Things were happening so fast I couldn't even think. They said I could go to Denver, or stay here and communicate with him through soul travel and he would know; it would be the same as being there. *Yeah, right.* What were they talking about? I wanted to run out and yell at Sandy. Was she out of her mind, or was I, for being here? But there was no denying these people knew a lot about our relationship, things that went far beyond guessing. As I stayed and listened and questioned, I felt a calm come over me. Suddenly, I knew I was alright and that they were helping me. I didn't know how it all happened, but I just knew I felt okay.

In about an hour they said they had told me what they could and now I had to decide what to do. Great, now what? My session was over and I still didn't have an answer.

After leaving the building I headed to my daughter's. I was spaced out and perhaps not in my right mind, but somewhere between the two places I knew I was going to Denver in the morning. I was at total peace with the decision. When I walked into Loni's I found my mother and Sandy there was as well.

"Let's get going," I said to them, "I've got a lot to do and I'll tell you about it on the way home."

Loni started crying. "Mom, what is going on? What are you going to do and where are you going?"

I pulled her into a hug. "Please don't worry. I'll be all right, just take care of you and Brittany. I'll be back real soon but I've got to do whatever it takes to help save Jack."

As soon as we got to my house I called Martha, who was a travel agent, and asked her to get me on a flight around one o'clock the next day. We then stayed up almost all night getting my things ready and making a list of what they could take care of while I was away. After grabbing an hour's sleep we got up, called my clients and took care of last minute details, then I headed upstairs to take a shower.

The hot water felt so good, I just stood there for a while, trying to relax. Suddenly, I got the distinct feeling I was being watched. Thinking it was Loni or Sandy coming to tell me something, I opened my eyes and looked around but didn't see anyone. Then I looked up and there, above my shower curtain, was what I could only describe as a "puff," like a small cloud. Without thinking or analyzing it, I just said, "Jack, hang on, I'm on my way." I then closed my eyes again and knew it was Jack coming to see what I was doing.

*Shit, I'm losing my mind. I must get out of here.*

After I got dressed I talked to Stan, who gave me Jack's sister's phone number. It was an odd conversation to say the least — she didn't know me or what had happened between Jack and I — yet somehow she wasn't all that surprised. I told her I was coming to Denver and we talked about her going to the hospital that night to try and get Jill out of the room so I could see Jack. I started to feel that maybe I had some help, though she sounded hesitant to go up against his wife.

Reality, and panic, hit when it was time to leave for the airport. What was I doing? What was I going to do when I got there? I was running on fumes and didn't want to think about how hard I was going to crash. When I checked in for my flight, I discovered that Martha had put me in first class, and I was filled with gratitude for my friend.

I was even more grateful when I realized no one else was sitting there because I cried the entire flight. The stewardess kept asking me if there was anything she could do, and I kept her busy bringing me glasses of water. As I looked out the window, I once again saw the "puff" that had been above my shower curtain; it was following the plane! I wanted to talk to it, but I knew someone would see and think I was insane. I wouldn't have disagreed with them. Still, I started speaking with it under my breath. Somehow, I knew it was talking to me. I knew Jack knew I was on my way and that he wouldn't die.

The flight went by quickly because I was in such deep thought and conversation with that thing outside the window. As I was landing in the Mile High City for the second time in a month, I started to worry again. Where would I go from the airport and how would I get there?

In this case, at least, I didn't have to worry for long. I was barely off the plane when I heard a voice say "Jeri." There stood a short, grey-haired guy.

"Stan!" I dropped my bag, threw my arms around him and cried, "Take me to Jack!"

He returned my hug, then said, "If you want to see the big guy, let's get going."

On the way to the hospital, he went over all that had happened that week; some of it I had heard before and a lot of it I hadn't. Apparently Jill was even worse than Stan had let on over the phone, at least with regard to how she treated everyone who wanted to see Jack. Looking back, if I'd had any smarts at all I would have gotten on the next plane back home.

Stan turned into the hospital parking lot and pulled into a spot that gave us a clear view of Jill's car. It was like we were on a stakeout. We watched and waited, but she didn't leave and Jack's sister didn't show up. Nothing was going our way and it was getting late. In the meantime, my bladder was about ready to burst. Stan drove down the street to a gas station and I ran to the ladies room. When I came out I saw Stan talking to a cute, twenty-something guy on a motorcycle. Turned out it was Danny, another one of Jack's friends. Stan introduced us, then Danny parked his motorcycle and rode with us back to the hospital. By then it was after nine o'clock and they convinced me that I wasn't going to see Jack that night. Finally we left and went to a bar, where Stan and Danny soon tired of holding me and listening to me cry. We went to a couple of different places but never stayed long because some guy would inevitably ask how Jack was, setting off another crying jag and putting Stan and Danny in a very uncomfortable position. They didn't know how to explain me.

It was about one in the morning when we pulled up to Stan's apartment building. I was exhausted but when Stan pointed and said, "There's the big guy's truck," I suddenly perked up. Something was pulling me toward it. Stan handed me the keys, but only after I reassured him, I would not go anywhere. I just wanted to be close to something that belonged to Jack.

I climbed into the truck, laid on the seat and cried, "Why me? Why now? Please live."

In that moment, the enormity of what I was doing washed over me again. I had traveled all this way with no idea how I would help Jack or if I would even get to see him. I was also about to sleep in the apartment of a man that, aside from a few phone calls, I really didn't know. As I finally sat up and got out of the truck, I told myself it was just another thing I had to do, and that it would be all right.

Morning came so fast I don't even know if I went to sleep. We went to breakfast and then to the hospital to begin round two of our stakeout. This time we were only sitting there for a little while when Stan said, "There she goes."

Jill was leaving!

As soon as her car disappeared from sight we headed in. The hospital was enormous, and it seemed we were walking down the hall forever before we saw the sign for the ICU. Stan approached a nurse and explained who I was and what was going on, to see if she thought Jack could take the shock of seeing me.

She looked from him to me, then said. "I don't see a thing."

Stan went in first, while I stood at the door in shock. I couldn't believe how bad Jack looked, or that someone could be hooked up to that much stuff.

I was even more shocked a moment later when Jack opened one eye and said, "Hey Bud, you gotta make a call for me. Call Jeri."

It was one thing to hear his friends say he was asking about me, it was quite another to hear it right from the horse's mouth. My heart swelled.

Stan replied, "I got one better for you. Jeri's here with me."

With that, Jack sat up in bed, put both arms out and smiled the biggest smile you ever saw.

Stan and I looked at each in amazement, then I rushed to the bed. Jack wrapped those arms around me and laid back, pulling me over the guardrails and onto the bed. My ribs felt like they were breaking, but I didn't care. It felt so good to be with him.

"I'll be back," Stan said as he slipped out of the room.

Not wanting to be seen lying in his bed, I eventually slipped out of his arms and stood. Jack drifted in and out of sleep as I talked to him and played Vanessa Williams' "Save the Best for Last," a favorite song of ours, over and over again on the little cassette recorder I had brought with me. Occasionally, nurses would come to take his blood pressure and vitals, and they just smiled but didn't say a word. When Jack was awake I asked him simple questions, trying to gauge his condition. I asked him where I had gotten my jacket and he told me that it was his and he had left it in California with me. I asked him if he knew where I'd gotten the gold chain I had on. He said he'd bought it at Tiffany's for me. Then he opened one eye and said, "Why, did you forget where you got it?" I laughed as he went back to sleep.

Before I knew it, Stan returned. "It's been two hours," he said, "and you better get out of here."

On our way out we gave a nurse Stan's phone number and told her to call if Jack needed anything. I would be back in the morning.

The rest of the day went by in a blur. We saw some of Denver and hung out with Danny, just killing time. Sunday night, they wanted to teach me to play pool so I could surprise Jack when he got out of the hospital. At some point I took a break from playing to call and see how he was doing. This time I got a male nurse on the phone, one I had never spoken to before. I never knew who would give me the time of day and who wouldn't – I would just explain who I was and let the chips fall where they may. This time, after telling my story for the hundredth time, I was shocked to hear him ask if I would talk to Jack. He was agitated, so much so that they'd had to tie him to the bed, and his wife would not stay in the room. Apparently, Jack kept giving them a phone number that didn't make sense, and he was calling for me.

I said of course I would speak to him, but by the time the nurse got a phone into his room, he was asleep again. I gave the nurse Stan's number again and told him I would be there in an hour; if Jack woke up he should call me. About three a.m. the nurse called, but once again Jack passed out before he could put him on the phone. I told him I would be there about seven a.m. to see the doctor. My nerves were shot. What could I do with Jack's wife in and out of the room?

I had barely closed my eyes when the alarm went off. It was five a.m., time to take Stan to work so I could use his truck to go to the hospital. I didn't know how I was functioning, or where I got the guts to go inside, but a few moments later I was marching toward the ICU. I stopped when I saw the buzz of activity by Jack's door. Doctors and nurses saw me standing there, but said nothing. They would just glance my way, then talk amongst themselves as they went in and out of the room.

*What is going on?* I wondered, my stomach in knots, *And why won't anyone come talk to me?*

Finally, a doctor approached me. He told me that Jack was very seriously ill and that *if* they could stabilize him and *if* he made it he would need months of rehabilitation; he would need to learn to walk and talk again, and still he may never be the same. I was still reeling from this when the doctor asked if I was ready to commit to taking care of him. Without thinking, I told him I would.

The doctor told me to wait there, then he headed back toward Jack's room. The next thing I knew an attractive young woman dressed in street clothes was asking me to come with her. I followed her into a room and once again repeated the story, abbreviated version, of me and Jack – how we had known each other thirty years ago and had recently reunited. I showed her the pictures we had taken in Sacramento and at the airport when we'd first met up in Denver.

The woman, a hospital administrator named Ms. Hill, listened to everything, then told me to wait there. It seemed like forever before she came back to tell me Jack's wife had left the hospital for an appointment and that I could go in to see him. She walked me down the hall into Jack's room, where I was greeted warmly by the nurses. Jack was tied to the bed and not moving, and as I as leaned over to talk to him I heard a voice say, "WHO THE HELL ARE YOU, AND WHAT ARE YOU DOING HERE?"

My heart stopped as I looked up and saw this big woman shooting daggers at me with her eyes.

I had just come face to face with Jack's wife.

I just stood there like a deer in the headlights as two nurses ran into the room.

"Please step out of the room," one of them said, but as I passed them, she said "It's okay. It's not you. We will send for someone."

Jack's wife kept asking me who I was. I kept saying, "Wait, someone will be here to talk to you."

Thank God Ms. Hill came around the corner and led her out. The nurses asked me if I was alright, then told me I could go back in to Jack. I was in there for a while when Ms. Hill returned and told me she had told Jill what I was doing there. She then said that Jill wanted to speak with me. I said I would do anything to help, and Ms. Hill assured me that she would be right across the hall from the room we were going to be in. Security would also be close by if I needed it.

The first thing Jill said when I walked into the room was, "You are a very beautiful woman; no wonder Jack wants you."

I was so shocked I had to sit down. She then started firing off questions, just as she had on the phone when I pretended to be Judy. I tried to answer, though it wasn't very often that I got a word in edgewise. When she started asking me about sex, I drew the line, telling her I didn't think it was any of her business and she would have to ask Jack.

Finally, I'd had enough, so I leaned over and opened the door so someone would come in. Ms. Hill appeared, and as I stood up to leave with her, Jill put her hand out to shake mine and said, "May the best woman win."

I was horrified.

"That man may be dying, this isn't the time for a contest. Let's get him well and then we will see what happens."

Once again, I turned to leave, and that's when Ms. Hill announced that we would have to take turns seeing Jack; we would each get ten minutes every hour. The patient's wellbeing was the utmost concern to them. The staff had decided I would go first, then Jill could take her turn the following hour.

As I left and started down the hall, Jill ran past me, yelling, "She is not going to see my husband first!"

By the time I got back to ICU, she was already in his room with the curtain pulled closed across his door. I was looking around for a nurse when I heard Jack yelling for help. Shocked, I stood there not knowing what to do, then nurses and doctors came running from everywhere. They even got stuck in the door trying to all get there at once. I couldn't believe my eyes.

I dropped into a chair outside his door, put my head down on the table and started praying.

"Please don't let him die, please don't let her do anything to make him die. God, did I do the wrong thing by coming here? What is going to happen?"

There was so much running through my head. I was scared, mad, worried and trembling so bad that when someone started shaking me I didn't feel it at first. They were saying, "Are you alright?"

I looked up to find people all around me. One of the nurses gestured to a woman, told me she was a reverend, and asked me if I needed her; another told me that Jack was very sedated but that I could go see him. Still another was telling me something else. There was so much going on I don't think I really got any of it.

Finally I asked, "Where is she?" and was told that they had removed Jill a while ago. I was shocked and in disbelief because I hadn't seen or heard any of it, though they had to have walked right by me. The reverend asked if she could do anything, and I said, "Go see her, I think she needs you more than I do. I just want to go in now and see Jack."

As I walked through the door, two doctors looked up and nodded to go to the other side of the bed. They were still watching him very closely. One by one they all left, except one nurse who kept taking his vitals and putting information into the computer. I stayed for a while, but I knew I had to get a hold of myself, stop shaking and get my asthma under control so I could breathe. When I tried to move I realized I was frozen; my hands hurt as I tried to unwrap my fingers from the rail of the bed and my knees hurt as I tried to move them. In fact, every bone and muscle of my body hurt as I tried to move. I looked up to find the nurse watching me with concern.

We walked out of the room, and when I said I had to go for a while she told me that if I left the hospital to be very careful because there had been threats on me. She also explained how to call for help if I did stay in the hospital; security had been alerted and they would walk me to my car when I left.

I didn't know how much more I could take, but I had to know what had happened when Jill ran into the room earlier. The nurse said the staff had found her shaking Jack and yelling at him.

I didn't think I had any more tears to cry. I was wrong.

I didn't leave the hospital; in fact except for a short break I stayed with him the rest of the day, until it was time to get Stan from work. After we ate, we went to see Jack again and were relieved to find him resting comfortably.

The next morning, I walked into Jack's room and was shocked to find him sitting up in bed eating breakfast. How could this be? The nurses were amazed also. I stayed at the hospital all day with him. When he was awake, we would talk some.

The morning after that I walked into his room and heard him trying to convince the doctors to let him out long enough to go for a ride with me. He promised them he would come back. Laughing, they told me how amazed they were at his recovery. In fact, they were even going to disconnect him from most of the machines that day.

His wife had not returned, and while everyone was curious as to where she was no one wanted to go out of their way to find out. I think mostly they were relieved to not have to deal with her. Still, security stayed around me when I was there, and I was very careful when I was out.

Thursday, they moved Jack to a regular room. He was now making sense most of the time and could remember different things. All he wanted was to get out.

Friday when I showed up at the hospital, I found out they were releasing him. A couple of hours later he walked out of the hospital carrying his balloons and a teddy bear I had bought him.

It had been an amazing journey and homecoming. Well, sort of a homecoming because we were at Stan's house. Then the unbelievable happened. We had no sooner walked through the door when Jack started accusing me of messing around with Stan! It felt like an arrow to the heart, but I gave him a pass because he had been so sick. I didn't want to upset him, and besides, I knew nothing had happened.

Stan, however, was shocked and more than a little angry. After everything we had done for him, this was how he acted? And to make matters worse, none of us got much sleep because Jill had called the house all night screaming at us. Mentally, physically and spiritually exhausted, I told Jack I was heading home. We would make our plans for the future, but in the meantime I had to put my life in California back together.

We continued talking on the phone every night, and Jack was getting better every day. Before long I went back to Denver to see the new him. He had lost so much weight I barely recognized him. We spent most of the weekend on his motorcycle, just riding around and enjoying each other's company. The most exciting part of that weekend was when Jack presented me with a beautiful ring and asked me to marry him! Of course I said yes, and as I wrapped my arms around him all the memories from when I was fourteen and we talked about growing up and getting married came flooding back.

A little over a month later, Jack packed up and moved to California with me. The morning he arrived was when I heard the voice in my head say, "What have you done now?"

Before long, we began settling into a daily routine; Jack found a job and I told myself that everything would be alright. But though we had our good times, there were other times that let me know, somewhere inside me, that this was not going to work. There was a battle raging within me most of the time, but I had done all I could to make that square peg fit into that round hole and now I would have to live with the consequences.

We drove out to Denver a few times to get more of his things and to help his mother. On one of our return trips to California a blizzard struck. The roads were closed, and we had to spend the night. The following morning was beautiful, new snow and blue skies. I played on the CB radio as we stopped for gas. Before we drove away I asked Jack to go in and get me doughnuts and milk. As he got out of the truck, I saw an image out of the top of his head. I was shocked and didn't know what to make of it, but I said, "We need to put on seatbelts." He pulled the seat up and got the belts and we put them on.

Twenty-one miles down the road I heard over the CB, "Shoot we got one in the ditch." As I looked around, I saw the snow flying by, and I realized we were the ones in the ditch!

I still wasn't sure what had happened, but someone or something had warned me that day. Something was protecting us.

## Chapter 3

## *Continue to Uncover*

> *"I am convinced that you can actually do what you want to do as long as you don't place impediments in your own path. Success is not an accident. It is the collision of events brought about by effort, stamina, and a wholehearted belief in yourself and the people around you."*
>
> **~Given to me by a great friend many years ago**

During our long separation, there were many times I imagined how different my life would have been if Jack and I had both stayed in Montana. There were also times when I'd thought that if I could find him again he would save me.

Just as I'd suspected when we first crossed the Bay Bridge, I truly hated San Francisco. Not only was I lonely and lost without my friends, I also hated the climate. It was cold, even in August, and I stayed home alone every day until school started. School was like going from one prison to another.

Finally, in March of my ninth grade year a girl invited me to go to a dance at the Presidio. That night changed my life. I made a couple of friends and soon met Marty, the brother of one of the girls. We started dating, which drove my mother crazy because he was Filipino. Once again I was sneaking around with a boyfriend, determined not to let her take this one away from me.

I caught a break when my sister Bobbie left her husband in Montana, took two of her three children and moved in with us. My mother was so busy with them that she had little time to micromanage my life. My freedom was short-lived, however, because my brother-in-law soon moved to San Francisco with my other nephew. When they all moved out, the attention was back on me.

For months, I snuck out at night to be with Marty. I also cut school to be with him. Then he graduated, and though he was going to college and working at a service station, we still saw each other every chance we got. By the next year I couldn't stand fighting with my mother any longer and ran away to be with him. Eventually I went back home, only to run away again. I ran away so often and missed so much school that I was placed on probation. Mrs. Merriell, my probation officer, was a wonderful woman so I didn't really mind having to check in with her.

Marty wasn't the only reason I wanted to leave. My mother and John didn't have the most stable of relationships; when they were getting along she let him live with us, when they weren't he got his own apartment. Money was tight, and when I was finally old enough to get a part-time job I had to turn my earnings over to Mom to help pay the bills.

One day, Mom announced that we were going to Bakersfield to live with someone. This was to get me away from Marty. The joke was on her, though, because on his days off he would make the five-hour trip to see me, and I would cut school to be with him. It wasn't long before she found out, and one Sunday afternoon she abruptly told me to pack up the car because we were leaving for Montana that day. She didn't have to ask me twice – I was so thrilled to be heading home again. We had gone back there once before, and even though it was to a different town than where I grew up, I was devastated when after only a month or two we returned to California. Thinking this time would be different, I eagerly gathered up everything we owned, put it in the car and we set off. Turned out I was wrong again. When we stopped for dinner, Mom revealed that we were not going to Montana, but to Virginia to visit my middle sister Billie; she had moved there with her husband, who was in the Navy. It had been in a couple of years since I'd seen her so that took some of the sting out of my disappointment.

We drove for five days and nights, stopping only to sleep in the car for a few hours before moving on. I often felt sick to my stomach as we went from one-hundred-ten-degree weather in Bakersfield to blizzards in Flagstaff to tornados in Oklahoma, then headed south. It was 1965, and the Deep South was very different than it is today. Segregation was alive and well, and there were dilapidated houses and a level of poverty I had never seen before. All of it made me very uncomfortable.

It was Good Friday when we finally pulled up in front of my sister's home. I got out of the car and went to the front door, thinking I'd surprise her. She was surprised alright; in fact, she didn't even recognize me. I didn't recognize her either. The swinging sister I remembered from California had become a housewife!

Our reunion was a short one. By the afternoon of Easter Sunday Mom and my sister had a huge blowout and before I knew it I was packing up the car again. We drove to Washington, D.C. over the Chesapeake Bridge. It was so amazing to be on a bridge one minute and in a tunnel the next, and then the bridge, the tunnel and the bridge again. Later I learned that this was so big ships could go over the tunnel, instead of having to make the bridge high enough for them to go under.

We then drove past the White House, the Capitol, the Lincoln and Washington Memorials, and finally to Arlington National Cemetery to see President Kennedy's grave. His assassination a couple of years earlier was still an open wound, and to see the eternal flame burning in his honor was very moving. We might have stuck around to do more sightseeing, but it was cherry blossom time and Easter break and every hotel was booked solid. Mom had to drive a hundred miles out of town before we were finally able to rest.

The trip back to San Francisco was just as torturous as the drive east had been. I was often sick to my stomach and could not eat. Even the smell of food made me sick. When we arrived we picked up right where we had left off, with me fighting with Mom and John and them fighting with each other. This time, I didn't even consider going back to school; it was time for me to find a job.

I was thrilled when I was hired by Pacific Bell. This meant I would be making enough money to move out on my own and finally be free. All I had to do was pass the physical. Piece of cake, I thought. Guess again. As I was still a minor, my mother had to be present at the appointment, so she got to hear the shocking news of my pregnancy firsthand. I was three months along, which solved the mystery of why I had been so sick on our car trip.

That night, a huge fight broke out at home. I don't know who was screaming the loudest – me, my mother or John; All I knew was I couldn't stay there any longer. She was not going to take my baby from me. The next morning while she was in the shower I packed a few items and left everything else, including my little poodle. I ran. I never wanted to see that woman again.

I called Marty to give him the news, and he got me a room above a store on Upper Market Street where I could hide from her. It was a vast improvement from the previous times I had run away and hid out in his car or on the streets. After talking about it for while we decided to run to Reno and get married, only to find out that I had to be eighteen. My birthday was still six months away, and I didn't want to wait because by that time the baby would have already been born.

Not knowing what else to do, I turned to Mrs. Merriell, and with help from her and some others we got a letter of consent. They realized that after years of battling with my mother I really needed to get away from her. Little did we know she was gearing up for another round.

Marty and I returned from Reno married, happy and free. As we parked our car in front of Marty's dad's house, two men in suits got out of a car across the street, arrested me for running away and took me to juvenile hall. It was a weekend, so nothing could immediately be done to get me out. I spent the first few nights of my married life in a tiny room crying and hating my mother for doing this to me.

On Monday morning, Marty, Bobbie and I met with Mrs. Merriell, then they called my mother to tell her I was being released into Bobbie's custody. Mom had left for Montana as soon as she found out I was arrested, under the mistaken belief that if she was out of town they would have to keep me in custody. Instead, her last-ditch effort to control my life had failed. I was out of juvenile hall and the matter would be kept out of court until I was eighteen. I was finally free of this woman.

Or so I thought.

We stayed with Marty's father until we could get an apartment of our own. We had nothing but we didn't care; we were free and waiting for the baby. The next two months were the happiest I had even known.

One Thursday evening, I suddenly began having pains. The baby wasn't due for another eight weeks! I tried not to panic as we rushed to the hospital, then nearly lost it when we went to Admitting and saw none other than my mother sitting behind the desk. She had found out what hospital I was going to and got a job as a clerk there.

I don't remember the next few days, but when I woke up on Sunday I learned I had delivered the twins the night before. Yes, twins. I was still reeling from the shock of learning there were two babies when I was told one had passed away a few hours after birth. The other was in the NICU. I went to see her, my tiny little baby girl. The next thing I remember is Marty telling me how both of them were going to be buried. The second baby had died a couple days later. We named them Katherine and Rhonda.

Those first days after losing my babies remain a blur. I do remember Billie telling me I could go live with her and her husband in Virginia. I found out later my mother had told her to call me; I also learned that while I was in the hospital she had caused so much confusion and fighting that she was banned from the maternity floor.

It was a long time before I wanted to leave the house. My first outing was an airshow at the Air Force base in Fairfield, just outside San Francisco. We had to leave when I saw a woman with twins in a stroller and could not handle it. (Jack was in the Air Force at that time, and when

I told him this story years later I learned that he was probably in the parade I was watching.)

My sister Bobbie convinced me to get a job. She said I should tell potential employers that I could do anything they asked.

"You can learn on the job," she said.

I took her advice and before I knew it I had lied myself into my first full-time job at a wholesale grocery outlet. It only took my boss a couple days to say, "You have never done anything like this before, have you?" I couldn't lie any longer, I had to admit it. He told me that if I would work Saturdays and stay after work, he would teach me everything I needed to know.

I did stay and worked very hard and he did teach me everything. Way too much, in fact. It started subtly enough, with touches I felt uncomfortable with but tried to ignore, then went from there. Before long he was sexually abusing me on a regular basis. I didn't know what to do. Back then these things just weren't talked about; women assumed, and rightly so, that they wouldn't be believed, or worse, that they'd be blamed. I didn't want to get fired, so I just went along with it.

At the same time, Gary, a manager of one of the grocery stores we dealt with, began flirting with me, both on the phone and when he came to the main office for meetings. It wasn't long before we were going to lunch, then out for a drink after work. I wasn't even twenty-one but it didn't matter as long as I was with Gary. He had the hot car, money, personality, and was so much fun. I felt important and grown up just being around him.

Soon Marty and I were going to Vallejo and spending time with Gary, his wife Rita and their three children. We waterskied, partied, drank and partied more. Gary and I got to spend more time together, and Marty and Rita had no clue about our affair. I later heard that Gary was also having an affair with a friend of his wife, but I didn't want to believe it, so I didn't.

Eventually Marty figured it out and left me, but I didn't care. I was free to spend time with my new love and have more fun. I moved to

Vallejo and it wasn't long before I was pregnant. I was thrilled. After losing the twins, my doctor had told me I would probably never be able to get pregnant or carry a baby to term. All I wanted was a child.

I spent that summer getting ready for my baby. My coworkers threw me a shower so I had everything I needed. I also reached an uneasy truce with my mother. Apparently she had hit the roof when she first learned I was pregnant again, but Bobbie told her if she wanted to be included in this she had better behave. On the other hand, my relationship with Gary was rapidly deteriorating; in fact, it was awful, but even that couldn't put a damper on my excitement of my baby.

On August 15 a woman at work convinced me to see the doctor before I left to drive home to Vallejo. Good thing too, because the next thing I knew I was being admitted to the hospital. I called Gary and my mom but told them not to hurry because I didn't have any pain and didn't know why the doctor was keeping me. I no sooner got into bed when they took me off to the delivery room. By the time I woke up, everyone was in my room, holding my beautiful daughter. I was amazed that she had come so quickly. I spent the next few days in the hospital, in total bliss and disbelief that I had a healthy little girl. I named her Loni.

I wish I could say that this joy continued once the baby and I got home. Instead I would spend the next year fighting, running and trying to maintain sanity without being hurt or killed by her father. The charismatic, charming Gary I had met was gone, and in his place was a monster.

One night, when Loni was only a few weeks old, Gary took us up in the hills, pulled out a gun, and said if he killed us they would think the Zodiac, a serial killer in the area, had done it. After a terrifying couple of hours he decided he couldn't shoot a baby and wouldn't know what to do with Loni if he killed me.

My mother, who knew what was going on, called his wife. When Rita saw that Loni looked just like Gary, we got together and cornered him. Then the unbelievable happened: I moved in with them. We were now one big not-so-happy family.

We had more visitors than you could imagine. Everyone wanted to see if this was for real, and I couldn't blame them; I could hardly believe it myself. One night while I was at work Rita called me and told me to come home because Gary had tried to commit suicide and was being taken to the hospital. The stress of it all became too much for Rita. She got sick and had to have surgery, leaving me alone with all four children. I took care of them until she came home from the hospital; then, deciding I had had enough, I moved to Los Angeles with my aunt and uncle.

For a few months I had a good job, a new boyfriend and peace before Gary found me. Rita had divorced him, and he said he wanted us to be together. Eventually I gave in, and we moved to Santa Rosa. I was twenty-two years old and married for the second time with four children. Rita didn't fight for custody because she knew I would take care of them. When I look back, I am still astounded at how special I felt when I heard this "compliment" from her. In truth, despite all Gary had done, I did not want my daughter to grow up without her father like I had. I was going to make this work for her.

And over the next four years that's exactly what I tried to do. I went to beauty school and did everything I could to provide the kids with a loving home. I also endured Gary's controlling ways, feared for my life when he pulled a knife on me, and learned he was stealing my disability checks (I had been sick and underwent a hysterectomy at age twenty-six); I also witnessed his cruelty to the girls, because in his mind only the boys counted.

The day I knew I had to get my daughter out of there was the day I watched her sit in the driveway, waiting for Gary to return with the boys and the candy bar he'd promised her. When they drove up she jumped up and ran to him, only to find out the boys had candy and he had forgotten hers. She came to me, trying not to cry, and as I held her and told her I would get her a candy bar, my mind was made up. It wasn't long before we were driving away from hell with a U-Haul behind us.

That was 1974, the same year I found Jack again and we talked and wrote letters until his wife found out. Then I moved to Sacramento, where my sister Billie was now living and a good friend was going to move. I found a job at a wholesale florist and had a cute little one-bedroom apartment, but my freedom and peace were once again short-lived. My sister left her husband and moved in with me and Loni. Then Gary found me and was soon making regular trips, trying to rattle me. It worked.

It was through Loni that I met Ted, the nice man who lived upstairs. I thought he was my savior because he stood up to Gary, who was threating to kill me or take Loni. Twenty-three days after we met, the two of us ran to Reno and got married, but unfortunately, my "savior" turned out to be just another man I had to fear. Thankfully, I had the help of family and friends, who came over after he had left for work and moved me out. Eighteen months later, I was divorced for the third time and starting a new life yet again. Part of this new life was running my own beauty salon, which I had acquired through an amazing opportunity. It even came with a built-in clientele.

One of the people who had helped me get away from Ted was Pat, who I had met through a mutual friend. Pat was a former sheriff who had moved to Sacramento to help his mother. In the days following my divorce we became very close and started dating. Pat also had a daughter, and as our relationship progressed we got the girls together to see if a blended family would work. Though his mother was always working against us, there were more good times than bad.

Pat and I had been living together for a few months when we were invited to go to my cousin's wedding in Atlanta. By then things were going so well between us that we decided to get married the following day. My uncle was overjoyed for us to have a ceremony and even for us to have a ceremony in his living room. It had bothered him that we were living "in sin" and had even refused to let us sleep in the same room of his house.

I was still basking in this happy event when I learned that Pat hadn't yet divorced his wife! Though I was devastated, I found I wasn't willing to let go of what we had. He got the divorce by bargaining with his ex over child support and visitation.

The next twelve years were mostly fun, living in our new home and building our family. We had show dogs, went scuba diving in many parts of the world, drove new cars, skied, had good jobs, lots of friends, parties and a life I never believed I could have. During one of our diving trips to Jamaica Pat and I broadened our horizons in another way by going to nudist communities. There were more friends, fun and parties. My mother was in and out of our life (this after a period of estrangement when she accused me of sleeping with my stepdad), while my sister Bobbie and I remained very close.

When Pat realized his dream of being accepted into the academy for correctional officers, I thought life couldn't get much better. He went away to the academy and never came back emotionally. In the months to follow I found out he'd had three affairs in six months. I was totally devastated.

On top of this I was dealing with the trials and tribulations of raising a teenage daughter. When I learned Loni, who had a turbulent relationship with her boyfriend, was pregnant, I felt like my entire world was falling apart. I was pulled in so many directions that I didn't know what to do and sought help in therapy.

I didn't know it at the time, but I was about to begin one of the most exciting times of my life. I started going to bartending school after work. Everyone told me I would never find a job just working four or five hours on Friday and Saturday nights, but I didn't care; I just thought it would be fun. Then a friend introduced me to someone who owned a small restaurant and bar down on the river and he hired me for the weekends. And just like that, I left my sewing, house cleaning and domestic life behind me.

I started doing things for myself, just because they made me happy. One day at work I decided I needed a four-wheel drive car to go skiing, so I went out and bought myself a new Subaru. In doing so, I traded in the Pontiac Fiero Pat and I had bought the day after he got out of the academy, which I now knew was a "guilt gift" for his infidelities. Getting rid of it signified that that part of my life was over.

When I took my new car in for service, Luke, the service manager, did all types of extras for me for free. I took him out for a Friday afternoon beer to thank him, then he started bringing me lunch and morning coffee and donuts. Before I knew it, my heart was aflutter and we were meeting regularly for lunch and sometimes at my friends' homes. Like me, Luke was still technically married, though he had moved out of his house and was splitting his time between his houseboat and his mother's.

Suddenly, life was crazy good. I was spending long summer weekends with my friends at the nudist resort, doting over my new granddaughter Brittany, running the beauty salon and tending bar on the weekends. I also had my new car, a new boyfriend, and was planning a big beautiful wedding for my daughter. And if that wasn't enough, I had decided to go back to school to get my real estate license. Pat and I were still living together, but I was so busy that what was going on at home no longer mattered.

In the middle of all of this my friend Martha the travel agent asked me to go to Hawaii with her. We stayed in a new resort in Kona, the most beautiful place I had ever been. One of the first nights there I was swept off my feet by a beautiful specimen of a man. He was a very important figure, but because I didn't understand the impact he had on so many lives I was not impressed. I was surely fascinated with him, though, and in the coming months I would continue to meet him when he traveled for work. I always had to wait for him to contact me because he was such a big deal. He loved being with me because I didn't fawn all over him like everyone else did.

Finally, it was time to officially end things with Pat. I moved into my own apartment, but I wasn't there for long. I was working part-time as a real estate agent and full-time at the beauty salon and within a year had enough money to buy my own condo. Now that I was settling down a bit, I wanted more of a commitment from Luke, but he was unable or unwilling to make it.

I decided to get together with the amazing friend I'd met in Hawaii and who was always in the background. We made plans to meet in the

Bahamas, and when he cancelled a couple of days before I decided to go alone. On my layover in Miami I was asked to give up my seat in exchange for another flight, money, and a free ticket anywhere that airline flew. I took them up on it and had a wonderful trip, hanging out with a couple of girls in the timeshare next to mine and diving with dolphins. Later, friends and I traveled to Guatemala to see another friend who was the director of an orphanage there. Life was good.

One of the things Luke and I shared was a love of motorcycles, and we spent a lot of time on his Harley. On one of the rides to Carson City I won seventeen hundred dollars. With the money and the free airline ticket burning a hole in my pocket, I told Loni to pick anywhere she wanted to go. She chose Barbados and off we went. As soon as we got there she met a guy who worked in the diving shop at the hotel. When he offered to take us snorkeling in the bay to see the seahorses, I thought he was nuts. Seahorses, really? Aren't they a myth? After playing with these creatures and seeing that they were indeed real, I swam back to the dock in the middle of the bay. Just as I was thinking, *Okay, how do I get back on this thing?*, help arrived in the form of a good-looking man with his hand outstretched. The rest of the week was spent with him, having dinners, drinks and sightseeing. Loni and I also went scuba diving, took boat tours, went shopping, and hung out on the beach. Though on the surface this vacation was all about fun, I now know that it totally changed the direction of my life. (That is, if my life could have been seen as having any direction at that time. In truth, I had never given "direction" much thought at all.)

When I came home I knew it was time to leave my relationship with Luke. It was fun, but that's all it ever would be. I realized that as much as I loved being free, deep down what I really wanted and needed was a committed relationship.

Just because moving on was the right thing didn't make it any easier. One morning, as I was battling with my emotions, these two "beings" (actually they looked like a cloud or smoke in the form of a person) appeared in my bedroom. At first I thought I was going nuts. Of course

I had heard of ghosts but I had never seen them before and certainly not in my house! When a moment passed and they were still there, I started screaming and chased them down my stairs. As soon as they disappeared I called my friend and blurted out what had just happened, but she thought I was saying there were "beans were on my stairs." Laughing with her brought me out of my hysterics. Much calmer now, I called one of my friends/clients who had told me about all kinds of weird things for years. She matter-of-factly explained that the beings I had seen were Luke and his mother. He was there because he did not want to leave me, and I guess his mother was just tagging along for the ride...? I didn't know what to think about the experience; all I knew was that for days after that I felt like I was being watched.

Between the ghost sightings and my emotional upheaval over the breakup, I was grateful for the busyness of the holiday season. When I got lonely, I reminded myself that I still had my businessman, as well as the man I had met in Barbados. In fact, we already had a diving trip in Turks and Caicos planned for January.

A few weeks later, I found myself on a dive boat, surrounded by the most beautiful water I had ever seen and a crowd of really nice people. As for my date, the two of us had diving in common and not much else. He was kind and attentive but he just didn't do it for me, and I found myself spending a lot of time with Richard, a gay man from Los Angeles. He and I had so much fun and so many laughs. Since we were both from California we talked about going skiing when we got back. We ended up going to Vail, Colorado, which brings me back to that fateful trip when I reunited with Jack.

## Chapter 4

## *Fake It 'Til You Make It*

One day, while I was taking all these spiritual classes, I got a call from Sheila, who used to live down the street from me and Pat. Sheila and I were casual friends, meaning we would speak occasionally or see each other at bingo and when she came into the salon to get her hair done. Her husband Jared also had an interest in scuba diving, and they had even joined me and Pat on a diving trip to Jamaica. Yet Sheila and I had never been very close because Jared was hard to be around. In fact, I had always wondered how she put up with him, as she seemed so nice and he was always bouncing off the walls. On this particular day, however, she opened up about her life with her husband. She told me she had collapsed from all the stress and was off work and on a lot of medication. She couldn't even go out of the house. She then asked me about the "stuff" I was doing. She needed help, she said, and wanted me to do a session with her. She had seen how much I had changed and she wanted some of that.

Whoa. First, I didn't know she had realized I had changed. Second, *I didn't know I had changed.* I knew the inside of me was more peaceful, but I surely didn't see how the outside looked any different. Plus, my home life with Jack was still a mess.

I gave her Mark's contact information and thought that was the end of it. Then I got a call from Mark saying he was traveling and would be unable to do the session. I would have to do it. What? Me, do a session?

I wasn't ready for that! When I said this to Mark, he said I had taken enough classes to do it. He then gave me a couple of instructions and reassured me that I would be fine. After talking with Sheila and another friend who had a space for me work in, I set up the appointment for the next evening.

As the saying goes, "Fake it till you make it," and that is exactly what I believed I was doing. From the moment Sheila got in my car she started telling me about everything that was going on in her life and how she hadn't been out of the house in over a week. All I could do was keep myself together so I'd be able to do the session.

I did everything Mark had taught me, and when it was over I felt an overwhelming sense of relief. Then Sheila asked me to channel for her, something that up to that point I had only done for people in class. Yet, in the peace of this room, I was able to get into that space and receive the answers Sheila was looking for.

All the way home I thought about the experience. I thought it was amazing, but had it really helped Sheila? I got my answer a couple of days later when she called to thank me. She was off the medication and had been able to go for a long drive with her husband. She was grateful, and I was astonished. *My God,* I thought, *does this stuff really work?*

She then surprised me again by asking if I would take her to some classes. It would be great, I thought, to have someone who knew me there, and who I could confide in about how bad things were with Jack, how I was constantly walking a tightrope to keep him happy and keep the peace between us.

One evening, Sheila and I went to a metaphysical bookstore that held all kinds of classes. The original class had been cancelled and someone was going to do a group "breath session."

Sheila and I shrugged our shoulders and said, "Why not? We are already here."

After an explanation of what it was and how it worked, which of course I didn't understand, the leader told us to lie on the floor. *Okay, this is weird, but everyone else is doing it.* Music began, and the lights dimmed.

While the drum sounds in the music reverberated in my head, the facilitator began talking to us, telling us to breathe. Breathe deeper, longer, and more and more.

As the drums got louder and changed pace, so did my breath. Soon I began seeing things, hearing things. It was so beautiful that I lost time and space. I was just there. For once, I wasn't trying to figure anything out or remember anything; I wasn't angry, sad or scared. I was just peaceful and floating.

As the drumming slowed down and everything got quieter I noticed the facilitator was still talking.

"Just relax and be with yourself," she told us.

Oh my God, what had just happened? What was that? As I lay on that floor, I thought I was another person because the one who walked in here had surely never felt like this. I felt clean and light inside and out.

After that, breathe sessions became my new thing to do. I found out who else held them and began going to classes once a month. I saw, felt and heard things that one just must experience to believe. One evening on my way home, I suddenly began to yell and scream at the top of my lungs. It was dark and the windows were up, so no one could hear or see me. For days after that my throat was sore, but I felt so light and clean.

## Chapter 5

## *Homecoming of Questions*

*You don't know, that you don't know, what you don't know.*

I was so focused on my classes that the drama at home became my second priority. I began to worry less about making Jack happy and spend more time delving into the experiences that had led me to this place in my life. Oftentimes this was painful, especially when we began investigating mother-daughter relationships. Every time something came up about my mother, it would bring me to being my daughter's mother. When I thought about my mom I would wonder how my daughter interpreted how she was raised. This was not easy to process.

As I listened to others share in class, I began to realize how many times my actions could have affected my daughter negatively. But how could I undo a lifetime of trauma? At the same time, I was listening to others with really crazy mothers, yet they loved them and seemingly could not do enough for them. Still others told stories about good mothers whose kids wanted away from them nonetheless.

These stories brought up so many thoughts, feelings and issues I wasn't sure which one to handle first. It was time, I realized, to go deeper into my childhood. *I had discovered in these classes that our childhood and our inner child can and does make us our adult self.* I began by asking myself these questions:

- How do you think and feel about your childhood?
- Do you know your inner child?
- How do you feel about your parents?
- How do you feel your childhood affected your adult life?

Shortly after my meltdown over the license plate, Jack and I decided to take a road trip to Montana. It would be the first time we were together there since we were separated as teens, and my chance to put the pieces of my childhood together once and for all. I told everyone during a weekend class.

On the way home, I stopped at a red light. Suddenly, before me I saw a little girl crouched down in a small closet. Somehow, I knew that little girl was me, hiding in the closet of the bedroom I shared with my sisters. That vision stayed with me all night, as well as many questions, like "Why was I hiding in that closet?" I couldn't wait to ask Mark about it.

When I got to class the next morning I rushed up to Mark. "You won't believe what happened to me on the way home last night!"

I told him what I had seen while stopped at the light and was shocked to see not a trace of disbelief or surprise on his face. He explained that when we commit to doing something, the energy, our guides – the whole Universe – goes to work setting things up for us. I might even have more insights before we left next weekend. Well, soon after that I was watching him write on a white board when the entire board suddenly changed into the wallpaper that was in the dining room of the house my mother and stepdad bought a few years before we moved to California. I blinked several times to make sure I wasn't seeing things. How had that happened, and – an even bigger question – how did I remember that wallpaper? I certainly had never thought about it. Again, Mark wasn't surprised, nor did he make me feel stupid. He said it was going to be a great trip to Montana because they were setting it all up.

"Great," I said, "Who are 'they'?"

"They are your guides, Jeri."

With these simple answers, Mark had sparked a whole host of new questions. What was "the energy" and how did it set things up? Who were my guides, where were they or where did they come from, and what about these angels everyone talked about? Were they always with me? Had they always been there? If they had been with me all time, then why hadn't they set things up better for me? Why would they let me grow up without my dad? Why did they let my twins die? Why did they allow me to have a crazy mother? Why did they put these husbands in my life, only to have the relationships not work out? Questions, questions and more questions; it seemed every time I thought I was going to get an answer, more questions sprung up instead.

- Do you know that your guides are around you?
- Do you know who they are?
- Do you believe in angels?
- Do you know how they affect your life?

These thoughts were still racing around in my mind the following weekend when Jack and I left for Montana. We drove through the night, stopping only for short breaks, and though I was exhausted by the time we pulled into town I didn't want to rest. Instead, I told Jack to head to the farm where my family lived when my dad was killed when I was eight. As we drove into the yard, I was stunned to see how small it was. I had remembered it being so big. I had remembered the long walk to the big red barn with the outhouse, the chicken coop, the root cellar, the garage and the huge yard. Now everything was so close.

I spotted a tractor in the field and got out of the car to approach it. When the driver pulled up I asked him if he lived there. No, he said, he just plowed the field for Phil, the man who owned the place. I drew back in surprise. Phil was still alive? I then told the driver that I had grown up there.

He immediately jumped off the tractor and said, "Oh my God, are you one of the Brown sisters?"

"Well, yes, I'm the youngest."

Just last week Phil's sister had told him the story of the Browns, and that the place was called the Big Red Barn because that was what they called it. He then told me to get in his truck and come see Phil – he would be so happy to see me. Off we went, with Jack following in the car.

Phil was wonderful. He greeted me warmly and we had a long chat. He even told me to take anything I wanted off the property. As we spoke, I could remember helping him deliver a calf, riding on his tractor and doing chores with him. I also remember thinking he was an old man, but now I realized he was probably only in his forties.

I told Phil I just wanted to walk around the farm for a while. I wanted to experience what I was feeling, even though I wasn't sure what those feelings were. It seemed everywhere I turned, memories I had forgotten or had never been aware of came flooding back. I even went inside the house and was once again amazed by how small it was. The linoleum my mother had put down was still on the kitchen floor. How had she raised three girls in this house? I couldn't believe how tiny the bathroom really was. Sure it had been small, but *that* small? There were only two bedrooms, and as I walked into the one I'd shared with my sisters, there it was, the closet in my vision. Why had I been hiding in there, so scared?

Out in the tall grass of the yard I found the remnants of the outdoor stove my dad had built out of bricks. I started picking up bricks and putting them in the back of my car. I also took the black iron stovetop. Jack was having a fit, saying I couldn't put all those heavy bricks in the car. Oh yes, I could. And I did.

I walked around the yard, looking at everything except one corner behind the garage I couldn't make myself go to.

*Oh well,* I told myself, *that is okay.* I also kept thinking that whoever this energy and these guides and angels were, they had sure done their job setting this part up.

When I was done I thanked Phil then Jack and I headed off to find a place to stay. As we drove into town, shock and confusion ran through me again. It was so small. The buildings were so much smaller than I recalled, and everything was so close together. The streets were narrow with no traffic, a shock after living in California for all these years. What shocked me most, though, was the size of hospital where my mother worked after Dad died. How many patients could it possibly hold? I rode through town with my mouth wide open. It was if the whole place had been frozen in time.

The next day was more of the same: driving around looking at the places where I used to live and being able to go into some of them. Jack was an excellent resource, answering my questions and telling me story after story to help fill in the blanks.

Bobbie and her husband were also there on vacation, and that evening Jack and I headed to the house where they were staying. They told me more stories while we soaked in the hot tub. After a while Jack and I became hungry and decided to go out to eat.

"Where?" my sister said, "There isn't anything open this late."

*This late?* It was still light out! That's when I realized it was almost ten p.m. No wonder our mother put us to bed before dark. For years I had thought she was so mean, making us go to bed so early when it was still light outside. Now I realized that being farther north, it stays light later during the summer months.

Again I wondered, how did my mother do it? I had hated that woman all my life and now I just wanted her to love me and be the mother I wanted so I could love her. She had been erratic and unpredictable, to say the least. How did she survive? Her mother had left her and her two brothers when they were three, four and five years old. They were raised by different aunts and uncles. When Mom was fifteen she met my dad, who was twenty-eight years old. Dad had been driving through town when he had an auto accident. He found a local job to pay for his car repairs. (She always said a car accident brought him to her and a car accident took him away.) A year later they got married, and in another year Bobbie was born. Three years later Billie came along, and four years after that was my turn. He was a god to my mother. Then, sixteen years after they married, he died in an auto accident, leaving her with three girls to raise and a chicken farm to run.

I remembered the night my dad was killed like it was yesterday. He had taken me to school that morning. I was in the second grade and my mother had just started working outside of the home at the mental institution. The story was that my dad had been out drinking and was going to surprise my mother at work when she got off about ten p.m. On the way there he missed a curve in the road, rolled over his new car and died instantly.

At home the phone rang, and I ran to answer it, knowing it was going to be my dad. It turned out my mother hadn't even worked that night and was home with us. When I heard an unfamiliar voice on the phone, I went and got my mom. She started crying and told us Daddy had been in an accident and she had to go to the hospital. A short while later she returned with her aunt and uncle and told us Daddy had died. Everyone was crying and making phone calls.

I remembered being wrapped up in a blanket in a big chair by the window. Suddenly, I turned around to see a man's hand pulling back a big knife before it stabbed me in the back. It was my first vision, at least the first I could recall, and it was very scary. I couldn't remember whether I told anyone, but I did have the feeling that no one cared.

The next few days, all our relatives came for the funeral. A deep sadness settled over the house, and though I felt it and missed my father terribly, I had no idea what his death was going to mean to my life.

The following day Jack and I visited some other locations, then went to see an old friend who told stories about when we all used to hang out. Some of it I remembered, some I didn't. But what struck me most was seeing how this friend and his new wife lived. My God, if my mother hadn't gotten me out of town, I could have been them. For years I had hated her for making me leave, now I saw that she had rescued me from a similar fate. To hear them talk about us you would have thought Jack and I were Hollywood movie stars!

By this time I could not wait to get out of there. After visiting the cemetery where my dad was buried, we started out of town in a different direction than we had come, past the lakes I remembered and over the mountains to see some of Jack's relatives. They were the same mountains my dad had loved.

After visiting with his family, I told Jack that I wanted to go to Jackson. We used to go there for Fourth of July weekends after mom and John got married. After a heated debate – he was convinced that I was confusing it with Jackson Hole, Wyoming – we finally found Jackson, Montana. I didn't see the huge hotel I remembered. Some of it looked the same but it was much smaller. Amazing how everything on this whole trip was so much smaller. We ended up spending the night in one of the rooms. After a soak in the hot mineral pool, which was also much smaller than I remembered, we went back to our room, where the staff had started a big fire in the fireplace, and settled into sleep.

The next morning, we finally got out of Montana. It seemed we had been there much longer than a few days. My mind did not stop the whole way back to California, mostly about how I would deal with the guilt of hating my mother for so long. What's more, I couldn't even ask her the many questions the trip had brought up, because we were going through another period of estrangement and I didn't even know where she was living. I asked Bobbie, but she just told me to forget it. I couldn't really go to Billie, since she had left Montana right after graduation and probably wouldn't have any more information than I did.

On the drive back I relived our move to California in 1962. I remembered how I knew I would hate San Francisco from the moment we arrived. I knew it. *I was beginning to see what an excellent job I did at being miserable.*

- Do you know of decisions you made as a child that have affected your life?
- Are you still living those decisions?
- Where those decisions positive or negative?
- If they are negative, are you ready to change them?

I remembered how after getting there we went to my mother's cousin's place. These were the same relatives Billie had left with right after she graduated from high school. At least I'll see her, I told myself. But she had changed. She was working all day and had a boyfriend at night.

Soon we got an apartment of our own. It was a strange place to live because there weren't any bedrooms. An apartment with no bedrooms? They called it a studio. There was a bed that came out of the closet. This place was dark and awful... so I made me a bed on the floor under the clothes in the closet. That was my sanctuary. I met the girl down the hall, the same one who would eventually let me and Jack use her address to exchange letters.

There was one thing that remained unchanged from our life in Montana, and that was the constant fighting. One night I was the good child and John was the villain. The next night John was the good one and I was the monster. All we ever heard from Mom was, "If Minor Brown was alive, we would not be living like this." I wasn't sure what "this" was, but hearing it made me wonder what life would have been like if Dad hadn't died. Minor Brown, I thought, must have been the greatest man to walk the earth. I missed him so badly but never really knew what I was missing. I just knew that in Montana I was the only child in town without a father. At least here maybe no one would know.

Starting school was one of the most traumatic events of my life. It was in the Marina district, which I was told was the best part of town. That was why it was expensive and we couldn't afford bedrooms – enough of a reason for me to hate it. The school administrators didn't like the way I dressed and even called my mother to tell her. She told them that was all we had.

Back in Montana I knew everyone; here, no one would even talk to me. The school was half Asian, thirty-five percent black and just fifteen percent white. In our town back in Montana there had been one Asian family who owned the Chinese restaurant. When the restaurant was closed, we never saw them; it was as if they disappeared, like Santa Clause. There was one black family that we weren't supposed to talk to, but I did anyway. One of their sons was a friend of Jack's and mine, but we had to hide it. In time I would come to love the diversity of California; back then I just felt like a fish out of water.

For the first several months, all I did was study and play my clarinet, which I had been playing since the fourth grade. Now even that held no joy for me. Had I stayed in Montana I would have been in the high school band and having fun, just as my sister had done as a majorette. But not here, as there were no after-school activities. I can't describe how lonely I was and how much I hated this place and my mother for moving me here. My only refuge was that corner of the closet, where I went each night to do schoolwork. At least I was getting straight A's.

Soon we were able to move into a one-bedroom apartment down the street. Mom and John had a bedroom and we converted the dining room into a bedroom for me. It was between the living room and kitchen, but I didn't care. I was so happy to have my furniture again, which had been in storage since we left Montana.

After that things changed drastically, beginning with that party at the Presidio Army Base, which led to my meeting Mary. This was also when Bobbie and my niece and nephew came to stay, which was fun and for a time distracted my mother from what I was doing.

I thought about all this and more as Jack and I drove back to California. I thought again about what my life would have been like if my mother hadn't made us move to California. I'd probably still be living in that town; I probably would have ended up pregnant at fifteen or sixteen years old. At the same time, I thought about how I screwed up my life in San Francisco by hating everything. Now I had the frustration, guilt and all the what-ifs vying for attention in this busy head.

How could I ever forgive my mother, or myself, for that life I'd lived? At that moment I just wanted to find her and tell her thank you for moving me out of that town. Then reality quickly set in and I realized that finding her would end up the same way it always had – with fighting, miscommunication and finally, silence. In fact, years later, while talking about our mother, my sister Billie and I remarked how we didn't know where she lived. A woman overheard us and said, "Oh no, you can't find your mother?" Billie piped up and said "No, and we aren't looking either." The woman was speechless, and I am sure had her time to judge us.

With all the questions, visions and memories I had I couldn't wait to get to a class and find out what it all meant. The only thing I knew for sure was that I never wanted to go back to that town again. Perhaps I could just not think about any of this and it would all go away and never bother me again. Of course by then I had learned that just not thinking about something does not make it go away. I had learned it must be healed. Okay, then, another question: *How does one heal this open oozing sore?*

When I got home I continued following Mark around and taking any other classes I could find. Then Mark suddenly announced that he was leaving town and not coming back. Everyone who knew him was in shock, including me. It was one of the blackest days of my life. I knew that no one could help me like he always did.

All of my abandonment issues surfaced, and I was filled with anger, fear, loneliness, and every lousy other emotion I could have. On the bright side, the Healing Expo was coming to town. Ronney wanted to go to promote her magazine, and I went with her. Again, there were so many products and modalities being advertised there in the booths and on stages. I couldn't believe that with all the classes I had taken and reading I had done there was still so much I had never heard of.

At the Expo we came to a booth advertising a three-day event in a couple of weeks. If we signed up for it then we would get a huge discount. We went for it, and I started summoning my courage to break the news to Jack that I was going away for a weekend. As expected, it didn't go well. But I was going.

# Chapter 6

## Stop the Auto Accidents

*"We can't solve problems by using the same kind of thinking we used when we created them."*

**~Albert Einstein**

On Friday morning a few weeks later, I, Ronney and another friend set off for the event. My other friend was going through a nasty divorce and wanted help. We had no idea what we were in for.

There were fifty-three people in the group with quite a few helpers for the different processes they had us do. Some of these processes were done alone, others in different sized groups. Some involved writing, in others we talked; in some I just listened to others but in some way they all brought up issues within me.

By the first break we all looked at each other and said, "Wow! What do you think will happen next?" By midnight the first night there wasn't a dry eye in the house. Everyone had been touched deeply by all different issues, whether they knew they had them or not. They certainly knew now!

Saturday was more of the same, process after process for everyone. Some processes were done alone, some in separate groups. I found it amazing how the group processes worked to bring even more up inside of us. At one point one of the facilitators asked me, "Do you know why you want to die in a car accident?"

I guess I had mentioned the many accidents I had been involved in over the years, each one more serious than the last. I couldn't even give the exact number of accidents I had been in. Of course I told her I didn't want to die in a car accident. Her response was, "If you didn't, you wouldn't be having them."

She then asked me if I wanted to change that. Of course, I did! But I didn't know how or even that I could. After all that had transpired that weekend I wasn't sure I could even think clearly.

She took me over to a spot away from the others and asked to me to lay down on the floor. As she started talking to me, a scene began to unfold behind my eyelids, as if I were watching a movie. After my father's fatal accident, my uncle took me to the wrecking yard to see the car. Now in this "movie," I saw a little girl looking at the crushed car. I knew that little girl was me. I saw blood on the dashboard and elsewhere. There were even some pieces of my dad's shirt. While watching this, I was still lying on the floor peacefully. I described all the details to this lady. Finally, she asked, "What decision did that little girl make while standing there?"

My reply was, "The only way I can see my dad, be with my dad or have a daddy is to die like he did in a car accident."

Very calmly she asked, "Would you like to change that decision to an adult decision?" Sure, I would.

Then she asked what I would like to change the decision to.

"I do not want to die," I said, "I want and need to live to be with my daughter and granddaughter. Car accidents hurt me, they are expensive, and I am so tired of being in car accidents."

She then made me conscious of being in the room and told me what an excellent job I had done. I was in such disbelief of what just happened, and I didn't see how it could or would change anything. (As of nearly twenty-five years later I have never had another accident. I am thankful every time I get into a car.)

As amazing as these processes were, they were also very draining, and by Sunday we were relieved, thinking the most difficult part was over. The event was winding down and we would be going home in a few hours. After another break we walked into the spacious room to find that all the chairs had been moved. In the middle of the floor were different stacks of paper about three feet by three feet, along with colored crayons.

As they had done several times throughout the weekend, they broke us up into small groups then instructed each of us to draw a picture of what we wanted in our life. I immediately felt uncomfortable because I had no idea what I wanted. I started drawing anyway, though I didn't know what it was at the time. They next told us to take turns standing in front of our group and explaining our pictures with as much excitement as we could.

When it was my turn I looked down at my paper in surprise. How did these images even get there? I described an airplane flying to an island on the other side of the world, with people waving and waiting for me. There was a book I was going to write. There were two stick people holding hands representing a happy couple next to a two-story house. It made no sense, but I think I was excited because everyone else was.

All too soon, we closed out the event and said our goodbyes. I did not want to leave and lose the amazing peaceful feeling I had acquired during the weekend. Sure enough, when I got home, I saw that Jack had been drinking. I tried to explain all that happened during the weekend, but he got mad and just laughed at my picture.

"Gone for three days, spent that money and all you did was draw a stupid picture of traveling around the world with people waiting for you, writing a book and being a happy couple."

Totally deflated, I began thinking, *Yep, he is right. Who do I think I am? Where did that idea even come from? How could I have been so stupid to stand up in front of those people and tell them about this picture that was so absurd?*

The next day I took all my papers and stuck them in a closet. Thankfully, I had Ronney to keep me going. There were more and different classes to attend.

Life went on. Then one evening we walked into a restaurant and – bam! – there were my mother and John. By that time I hadn't seen her in a couple of years, and my whole body started shaking. At least I didn't have to be embarrassed in front of Jack because he knew how crazy the woman was. While trying to remain out of her sight, I called Bobbie and asked her what I should do. She told me to either leave or go to the other side of the restaurant and eat. She couldn't understand why I was so upset. Jack and I went to a corner where I was able to watch them leave. Then my emotions really kicked in. I had had my chance to see my mother and I chickened out. Now she was gone again.

## Chapter 7

### *There is Always More*

As the days faded into weeks and the weeks into months, some of the impact of what had happened in Montana and my classes subsided; I immersed myself in still more classes and other questions came up. Although my life may have appeared the same to others, within me everything had changed. For the first time in my life I had a focus. This focus was to feel better, achieve an understanding of my life and maintain the peace that I could now glimpse during and right after each class or process I did.

Since Mark's departure Ronney and I had become close friends and whenever I could I helped her with *Inner Words*. Since the magazine advertised different people and classes in town and throughout the country, this allowed me to become immersed in the metaphysical world. I still didn't understand half of what Ronney was talking about, so most of the time my mind was working overtime trying to put it all together. Plus, I still had Jack to keep peace with, Loni and Brittany to worry about, long hours to work in the salon, constant worries about money, and a house to keep together.

One of the classes I attended was led by Janice, a friend I had met years earlier while scuba diving with Pat. At the time I thought Janice was the strangest person I had ever met. She was always talking about spirits, angels, dolphins, channeling, and other weird things; she also drank carrot juice until she looked orange. Now that I was learning more about all those things, it was time to find out more of what she knew.

She had a very cute one-room office where she taught her classes. I loved to go there just for the peace it brought me. Her class was on channeling. I had heard her channel what she called the Dolphins and Orca Whales. Usually her channeling sessions were on global information and how to make the world and environment a better place. If you wanted her to get more personal information for you, she would, and it always seemed to make sense.

This is where I had learned to channel, specifically an angel called Marta. Though it seemed weird to me, I kept going because the information I got always made sense in some strange way. Months later during a channeling session, another entity came through who said she was Amel, a higher vibrational angel. She told me I had changed vibration and could now accept her. How that happened or when I didn't know, but I had to believe it. That gave me more go power to continue what I was doing.

During one of Janice's classes, Amel came through and told me that I'd had a past life in France. I'd died when I was about nine years old. She then told me that this time around I was supposed to live a long life, providing I made it past nine. That night while driving home I began to think of all the illnesses I'd had before the age of nine. I'd had my tonsils out when I was three or four; my appendix came out a few months later. I was told I had polio when I was about five and that was why my hips and back were so curved. I'd been in the hospital several other times, including during my sister's graduation and my own Confirmation, and almost every holiday I was sick with something. For the next few days I thought about all these childhood illnesses, but they did not explain all the illnesses and surgeries I had as I got older. Now I had to find out what those were about.

Back then, there were few people I talked to about this, for fear that they would put me down or tell me how stupid it was and to "be careful." After all, it had happened before, and not just from Jack. Even I still wasn't totally convinced that it was real. I must have mentioned it to one of my clients though, because one day her husband, who I barely knew, walked into the salon and handed me a book. It was called *Seth Speaks*. He told me he had underlined some parts for me to read. Okay then, thank you. That night when I read some of the underlined parts, I was shocked. The book's author, Jane Roberts, had channeled information from an entity called Seth, in sessions that spanned from the 1960s until Roberts' death in 1984. Just as surprising was the fact that my client's husband, a practicing Catholic, had read it. To me, this was a sign and the boost I needed right then to keep going.

About the same time, I was introduced to Sanaya Roman, another person who channeled information and wrote books about it. Man, what would I hear about next? Suddenly it seemed there were so many other people out there who channeled. Perhaps, then, this was an accurate way to find the information I was seeking?

In the meantime, I continued to take Janice's channeling classes, along with any others I could find. I also continued to walk a tightrope at home, doing whatever I could to appease Jack when he got angry about my time spent away from him.

During one of the classes, I was hit with a sudden asthma attack. I had developed allergies and asthma out of nowhere while in the process of divorcing one of my husbands. I had gone to a doctor, had all the tests done and had taken shots for months, but things never really got better. In fact, my allergies to coffee, perfume, mushrooms and mold had gotten increasingly worse.

That particular teacher had a way of using kinesiology, also known as "muscle testing," to diagnose such an issue. He asked me to hold my arm out, then he gently pressed down on it while asking me a series of questions. If my arm stayed stiff, then the answer was "yes," meaning it was true for me or my body. If my arm had no strength, then is was not true.

One day he used this method to find the exact time I had become allergic to mushrooms. I was cooking them for dinner when Gary, a neighbor from across the street, came in and we got into a fight over some situations that were going on with my then-husband, Pat. As the teacher asked questions or made various statements, the memories came flooding back. When I asked him about this and what it had to do with my allergy, he said, *"The body holds these memories until they are healed."* After that day some of my reaction to mushrooms became lighter. Then I worked with my allergy to coffee, perfume and mold. Although the reaction was still there it became tolerable.

I had developed the mold allergy while watering plants in an atrium that Pat had built for me at our house. In the end, I carried so much anger over having to leave my house because of his affairs that my body responded to the mold in the dirt, which became airborne when the plants were watered. The coffee allergy was due to getting up depressed every morning and drinking coffee when my body had had enough. I discovered that the perfume allergy developed because Pat liked it and we always bought it at duty free shops when we traveled. As much of the anger began going away during each process, so did my reactions to these products.

Some of these reactions still came up at various times when Jack and I weren't getting along. And these days things were always strained between us. We were just going through the motions of having a relationship.

I told myself that I had to stay with him because he knew so much and could help me. All the teachers would say, *"Jeri, there is always going to be someone in your life to help you with the issues at hand."* Somehow, I couldn't get a grasp on that. How could anyone but Jack help me, or know so much about me? Then the thought was followed by: ...*and at the same time know so little about me*... but I ignored it.

I kept going and managed to keep my life somewhat together. More classes helped me understand how the body holds information, most of which we are unaware of. I was also fascinated to watch others make their own discoveries about what their bodies were holding on to.

Every class, book, conversation or process I did would bring up more information that in turn brought up more questions. I tried keeping notes but soon they became so messy and disorganized that I stopped. I would think, *Oh this is so big, I will remember this one*. Then the next week something even bigger would come up and that earlier a-ha moment would be lost.

## Chapter 8

# Molestation and the Inner Child

Given Jack's attitude about my metaphysical studies, I was pleasantly surprised when he agreed to go with me to a class in St. Helena that Ronney had set up. Once again we would be using kinesiology to test thoughts, emotions and one's body. It was an excellent experience, and after a few hours, I was really beginning to understand how to access information inside the body.

When the facilitator got to me, my question was, "Why can't I have a satisfying sexual relationship with Jack?" I wanted to get to the bottom of the constant friction between us.

The facilitator first asked me generic questions and pulled on my arm to get a baseline for my body. He then went down a list of questions designed to address my personal issues, followed by questions about different people in my family who might be involved with those issues. When he mentioned the name of one of my uncles, my body responded, *True*. He instructed Ronney and me to continue the process in a different room. Ronney and I laughed as we went into the room and said, "Shoot, do we know how to do this?" We weren't sure, but since we always had so much fun together, we figured we'd give it a try.

A few moments later, neither of us were laughing. As Ronney sat me down and asked me questions, the memories began flooding back. In these memories, I was a little girl, lying on my back behind the garage and meat shed of the farm in Montana. My uncle was over me with his big penis rubbing my stomach and chest. It was dripping with something and he was trying to put it in my mouth. I was so scared, I couldn't even cry. I just wanted him gone. Soon it was over. Ronney brought me back to the current reality with a shocked look on her face. I looked back at her, shaking from head to foot. I had just relived being molested as a child.

We exited the room in a daze, not knowing what to say or what to do with this information. Parts of my life were still running through my head like a movie, and I wanted to be alone to work on putting these pieces together. Finally, on the way home, I explained to Jack what had gone on. We met Ronney for dinner and she and I talked, trying to involve Jack in the conversation. In many other classes women had talked about being molested and its effects on their lives. I did not know what this meant because I thought I had lived my life normally.

That night, as I lay down with my head still spinning with thoughts and emotions, Jack jumped out of bed and started screaming at me.

"Now you are going to be frigid! I knew you weren't a virgin when we started having sex, now I am going to have to go without sex at all, don't you get this?"

I burst into tears and went downstairs to curl up on the sofa with my knees under my chin to protect me. He ran up and down the stairs in anger, yelling like a madman. This went on until the sun came up.

How could this have happened? Thank God Jack had to work and I had a day off to myself. I spent it thinking and talking to people who might know something that could help me. That evening, I tried to make peace with Jack and reassure him that I was not frigid; however, even as I did this, I felt another part of me shutting down towards him, and myself. This was nothing new – as I was busy working on uncovering, and hopefully healing, my issues I had felt the growing need to protect the vulnerable parts of myself from others.

I didn't quite know how I was going to survive this, but I knew that somewhere there was another class where other survivors would understand and be able to help me. I found a group online called "Healing

Women" and learned they would soon be holding a convention in San Francisco.

In the meantime, I went to other classes that could help me with the anger. *That's when I remembered why that little girl I had seen at the stoplight that night was hiding in the closet. It was all connected to my uncle and what he had done to me. I also realized why I didn't go behind the garage on the farm when Jack and I went to Montana. That is where it happened first.*

Why hadn't I told anyone? Why didn't anyone help me? Was this why my uncle took me to see my dad's car after the accident? Did he molest me then, when my dad had just died? I then remembered a time in Chicago when my cousin (his son) did things to me in his bed. My aunt had walked in, looked, then backed out of the room and nothing was ever said. Had my uncle molested him also? Had he molested his sister? What kind of life did my aunt have? Is this one of the reasons I hated my mother – because she didn't save me? Why couldn't I tell her?

I also wondered whether this was another reason I did not connect with this God thing that people talked about. The night my dad was killed, this uncle, who was a Bible salesman, told me that my dad died because God wanted him. In one class I took, I realized that I didn't like God because He had taken away my dad. Why did this "God" that no one had ever seen or could explain to me need my dad more than me, a little girl? Even Santa Claus showed up once a year and brought me presents. This God took my father, and the person who sold Bibles molested me. Really? How am I supposed to believe in the meaning of those books he sold?

These realizations eased the guilt I had been carrying around about not believing in God. Some of my clients who referred to themselves my "nice Catholic ladies," had tried to get me to go to church so I wouldn't go to hell. Really? I think I just lived hell. Now I had to find my way out of it to a different life.

I remembered the many times my mother had used church as my punishment. I could hear her saying, "If you don't behave you are going to church." Yep, then she would take me and drop me off at church, coming back to get me when it was over. When I was a teenager I learned to use this to my advantage; I would do things to get into trouble, then when Mom dropped me off at church I would go in one door and out the back to meet Jack so we could have an hour together. I made "church" work for me.

And the awful memories kept on coming, unearthing more anger. I remembered how when Pat and I went to Atlanta to get married, the same uncle wouldn't let us sleep together until we were legally married. What a hypocrite! There was also the time we planned to take my aunt to Salt Lake City to see her brother. When Pat and I arrived in Atlanta to get her, my uncle started a big fight and she did not get to go. Did my uncle start this because he was afraid of me being alone with her? That I would tell her the truth? I would never have all the answers, but in my head things had finally started to make sense.

Do we ever really "heal" this? I thought back to what Mark had told that lady the first time I heard him speak: "I know how I deal with death; I don't know how you should deal with it." After all this time, I finally understood. I might find a way to deal with being molested, but surely not how anyone else would deal with it. I had seen in many classes that such things affect different people differently, and on so many levels.

One night, a facilitator from one of the classes came to our house to talk with me and Jack about what had happened during my childhood. He told us how he was molested at eleven years old and what he went through when he had to go to court.

Suddenly I had flashbacks about my brother-in-law. I looked up with astonishment and asked, "When you remember being molested, does it still bother you, even now?"

He couldn't believe my question. "Well of course it bothers me. Why?"

I started crying and saying, "Shit, shit, hell no. Not more!"

My teacher tried to comfort me, but I was afraid of setting off Jack again, so I did not tell him much. I just told him that I now remembered also being molested by my brother-in-law.

With what I had been though, I'd believed that only the things you don't remember should bother you, that they festered deep inside. And when it came to what my brother-in-law had done, all I had remembered was the guilt. Now I realized it didn't matter whether I remembered it or not, it had definitely affected me on every level of my being.

Over the next several days, new, awful memories came flooding back and with them more unanswered questions. What about my nieces and nephews? Had he molested them also? Was that why they all acted the way they did? Why there was so much dysfunction in their family? Had my sister known all along and never stopped it or protected me?

Oh, no one understands what a person who has been molested goes through. There are so many levels and ways that people deal with it. How could I ever face any of my relatives again? Was I the wrong one? Would anyone ever believe me? What would it do to the whole family if this ever came out?

In the days, weeks and months that followed, I recalled hearing about family and friends who had been molested and desperately wished I could revisit those conversations with them. That was not possible, however, I did begin talking with people in my current circle, including my clients at the salon. I was shocked by how many told me they too had been molested and never told anyone. Many of these women were older than me. As each one confided in me, I began to see how extensive the problem is in our population. I had no idea that I was only scratching the surface of how many men and women had been molested and all the ways it affected them. After this, whenever one of my clients said, "The world is going to hell these days," I would reply, "The world has always been going to hell, only no one talked about it."

As my clients began opening up to me, I learned how many divorces there had been, and how many parents had just walked out on their children, just as my grandmother had done to my mother. I even heard many stories dating back as far as the early 1900s, though people acted like these problems started in the 1960s. To this day, the one thing I regret is not recording all the stories I was told during my forty-five-plus years standing "behind the chair." Just the World War II stories would have filled a book. I am truly amazed how people make it through life.

Since beginning my spiritual studies I had done some work with my inner child, which I pictured as a little doll floating around in me to play with. It wasn't until now, when I started reading more and began putting my other healings and experiences together, that I realized how powerful the inner child truly is.

There are plethora of definitions on the inner child, but I will give you mine: the inner child comprises all aspects of us that run our adult life. It is behind many of our thoughts, our feelings and the reasons we make most of our life decisions. We may believe it is our adult mind, but usually that mind is being run by our little inner child.

Recall in the beginning of this book when I came out of the bathroom with my insides screaming, "Hold me, love me!" and my mouth yelling, "Leave me alone!" The "inside" was my inner child wanting to be held and loved. My mouth and head were the adult parts of me who had been hurt by this person (Jack) and others and just wanted them all to leave me alone.

During many of the classes I had attended and the healing I had done, my inner child showed up time and time again. I learned that in every relationship there are at least four people: each person's adult self and their inner child, acting out whatever she/he wants or needs at the time. Plus, at any given time there may also be internal battles going on within each of the individuals.

My inner child wants protection from the outside world. She wants me to love her. When I quiet myself and listen to her, the healings come.

My inner child did not want me to be her mother. She wanted me to hold her hand and walk *with her* through our healings. *She wanted out of that closet and for me to find out what happened to her.* She also wanted to grow up.

There were times the little girl would show up vulnerable and sweet; other times she would be hard-headed. There were times I was so confused as to who was who that I just cried. In doing so, I learned that this was what she needed, to cry and be okay with that. There were times when she wanted to set aside all the work we had to do and just play and be irresponsible. No matter how she showed up, my inner child became a major part of my life and healing.

Today, the inner child is an important part of my work with clients, especially during the shorter sessions and during Womb Work. I believe that as soon as the soul enters the fetus and brings the memories of past lives and all you have been, this tiny fetus begins putting it all together. I will cover more on the womb in the hypnotherapy section.

# Chapter 9

## Karma and Past Lives

While all of this was going on, I decided that after twelve years it was time to move to a new salon. I needed a fresh start. And because I needed extra money, I agreed to help clean the salon on the weekends.

Once, while cleaning with a friend I'd moved with, I had a flashback to when she and I were the owner's chambermaids in his castle in very early times. I told her about it and knew that I didn't have to do this in this life. I was new to past life investigations, so I asked some friends who agreed that this was a past life memory and that sometimes just recalling it would clear it from this life.

Shortly after this, we started cleaning on different weekends. One day, she accused me of not doing my cleaning because the back bathroom was a real mess. I tried to convince her that I had left it clean, but she wouldn't believe me. I was so upset that I quit. A few days later, she called to apologize when she found out that another employee had come in after hours and was sick in the bathroom and didn't clean up after himself. Did this happen because of the past life recognition, or was it just a coincidence? I choose to belief the past life recognition was the reason for all the occurrences. I learned that not all experiences leading up to a different ending always feel or look good. In this case, I decided I would not clean any longer, which didn't make her very happy.

During this period, I noticed that one of the other stylists was all over Jack whenever he walked into the salon. He loved the attention, but I didn't like it one bit. Finally, I asked a friend to do a past life regression on me to find out why this was happening. During that regression, I saw that the two of them were lovers and I was his little sister with a walking disability. She didn't like me because he took care of me. As we were walking across a creek, I slipped on a rock, fell and hit my head and died.

In the present day, this woman always wore long skirts or pants to work and constantly complained that she was hot. We told her to wear short pants or skirts. She would reply, "Oh no, if you saw my legs you would understand. They are ugly." Well, one day she walked in wearing shorts and we all gasped. Her legs were deformed. I thought, *Oh my, karma is a bitch*. She had laughed at my legs in that past life and now she had them! Two weeks later, she moved to another salon, and I have neither seen nor heard of her since.

## Chapter 10

# Magazines in Hawaii

In my free time I had continued to help Ronney with *Inner Words,* often as a salesperson. One day when she asked me to do this I flippantly replied, "If you want me to sell ads for you then it has to be in Hawaii." Hawaii is my place on earth and I went as often as possible.

She said, "Okay, let's do it!" and before I knew it she and I were on a plane to Hawaii with cases of magazines, laughing like crazy. This was before they started charging for baggage!

What the hell were we doing? Neither of us had any money, yet we managed to find places to stay on all four islands. Clearly, someone was watching over us.

I had been to Hawaii with Jack a few months earlier, which had not been a very happy time. During that trip, I had met a man in a metaphysical bookstore who told me to call him if I ever needed a place to stay. Yep, I did it. Ronney and I followed him to his house in a nice neighborhood in a rented Mustang convertible with the top down because all the cases of *Inner Words* wouldn't fit in a regular car. We were broke, but styling!

We walked into a hippie pad, complete with a ceremonial altar set up in the living room. He led us into a room with a massage table and an air mattress. I had to sleep on the floor because Ronney was afraid of cockroaches. We laughed ourselves to sleep that night.

The next morning, she woke me up with, "Shhhhhh, listen." There were monks out at the altar, chanting! We laid there laughing, then finally gathered ourselves together and walked out to chant with them. It was amazing. Then we started our first day of business, meeting people she had set up for us to sell ads to and distribute magazines each month. One woman lived in a beautiful home up on the hill, filled with oriental furniture. We were in awe of her items from all over the world. She sold essential oils from Egypt, and we arranged for her to come to Sacramento to sell them and give classes.

After a few days we moved on to Kauai, checked into a cheap motel and set off to meet our first client. She told us of a healing center where we could meet others who would be interested in *Inner Words*. I wondered how Ronney found all these people and set this up. This was before the internet is what it is today.

In the evening we walked to the beach, where I channeled. I channeled that Ronney and I had been sisters on that beach a long time ago. I saw us playing on the beach in front of our hut. There were many canoes on the beach, torches ready to be lit in the evenings, women working at their daily chores and men bringing in fishing nets. Could this be why I had looked so familiar to Ronney when we first met in this life?

The next day led to the surprise of Ronney's life. We arrived at the beautiful healing center with its dorm-type sleeping bunk beds, kitchen with organic food, massage/healing rooms, yoga room and big steam room with hot lava rocks in the middle and different places to lay or sit. The manager told us to go into the changing place, which had three walls but no ceiling or door.

Ronney asked, "What do we change into?"

The woman looked at her in surprised and answered, "Nothing."

I thought Ronney was going to die on the spot. It took a lot of convincing for her to concede and get undressed. From there, we went directly into the steam room for cover. When she sat down, she heard, "Is Ronney in here?" Again, she felt ready to die but had to respond, Yes, she was there. She wrapped up her first ad deal on Kauai in that steam room, and in the nude!

Our next stop was Maui. Ronney had found somewhere for us to stay, a very pretty home that was almost all outdoors. Even the floors in this home with paths to the bedrooms were breathtaking. The bathrooms were beautiful, with outdoor showers and tubs. At meals, we sat on big pillows on the floor before a low table and ate flowers along with our food. We managed to do a lot of business in a couple of days on Maui.

In Hilo, Ronney had arranged a stay at the beautiful home of an author and his wife. Although we had a little guest house, we spent much of our time in the main house as the owners were not there. The main house was U-shape, built above carports so we could see over the palm trees out to the ocean. At the end of each U were great glass rooms that served as their offices. As I sat at one of the desks, we did a little ceremony for me to become an author. Some part of me knew I was going to write a book. I had been told by a few psychics and channels that I had three books in me. It was hard to believe that, but I will go with it.

The next morning Ronney woke me up, yelling, "Oh my God, Jeri, get up! We're late!"

No time to shower! We bumped into each other while throwing on clothes, brushing teeth and hair, then finally ran out the door. I sped out the driveway and down the lane. We had almost reached the main road when Ronney burst into hysterical laughter. I was shocked to see her point at the clock on the dashboard, which read six o'clock. Ronney had forgotten to set her alarm clock to local time, and it was nine a.m. at home in California! I pulled to a stop and tried to catch my breath from laughing. We were glad that no one was at the house to see us skid out of the driveway with the dust billowing behind us. We had three hours to go back, take leisurely showers and get ready for our appointment in a cute little quilt shop on the southern tip of Hawaii.

We weren't quite ready for our second appointment with a lady that we met in a restaurant. She started by telling us that the gods of the island would be upset with us if we continued our quest to sell ads and inform the world what was here. Hawaii was sacred and should stay like that. But if we drank this holy water she had she could save us and maybe take us to a leader of their gods on the island. Just to get out of there, we drank the water out of her little bottles, then bid her adieu and told her we would contact her later. As we walked to our car, we looked at each other and began laughing, saying we sure hoped we didn't explode going down the road. What had we just done? Anything could have been in that water.

That night we went to walk the volcano. We drove to where the road ended at a huge pile of black lava. There we started walking, looking at the tree stumps, parts of boards and other items that had been carried along when the lava rolled down the mountain a few years earlier. We wondered what it had looked like before the lava scalded the landscape and turned it into miles of black. Soon it got dark and we didn't think we could find our way back. The land was black on black and now the sky was dark on black. We spotted a light coming toward us. Could it be the volcano mass killer coming to get us? No, it was a savior with a fishing pole who led us back. We had to laugh again when he explained that we would have had to walk hours to get to a point where we could see hot lava.

In another day we were off to Kona, my second favorite place on the islands. While we were driving, Ronney asked where we should eat.

I replied, "Oh, there is Wendy's."

Laughing again, she blurted out, "Oh my God, Jeri, this beautiful place, the ocean right there and you want to go to Wendy's?"

"Okay, okay, I got it - not Wendy's!"

We spent the rest of our trip at a little motel I took her to right on the cliffs. Our last two days were heavenly, with a few appointments amid gorgeous scenery and the sound of waves crashing all night.

We agreed that our two weeks in Hawaii had been a remarkable success: we had gone to four islands, had forty-five or so appointments, sold many ads, made contacts to distribute magazines, and arranged for a couple of clients to come to Sacramento and hold classes. We'd also had more laughs than we could remember.

Now it was time to go home to face the music!

## Chapter 11

# "Break a Leg," They Say

Ronney and I were on a high when we got back from Hawaii. That said, success had created a lot more work for us to do, including making arrangements to bring healers we'd met there over to Sacramento and making plans to send me back to sell more ads. I was also continuing to go to classes to learn as many modalities as I could and working many hours at the salon.

Several of my clients came in weekly to get their hair washed and set. One Wednesday morning, as I was taking rollers out of a weekly client's hair, I turned to walk back to my station when I tripped over her cane. Shocked, in pain, and of course embarrassed, I picked up the rollers, picked myself off the floor, and hobbled over to finish the job. My knee hurt and started to swell. One of my clients ran out to get me an ace bandage and, with ice, I was able to carry on. I was so busy I couldn't think about it much. Finally, in the afternoon, one of my friends who was also a client took one look at me and started giving orders. She told other stylists to take my clients, told someone to call Jack, and told me to get into her car. She was taking me to the hospital.

It was my worst nightmare when x-rays confirmed that I had broken my knee. I sat in total shock with a brace from my hip to my ankle. What was I going to do? I couldn't miss work – as it was I was barely hanging on financially. What would my clients do? Would they leave me if I took time off? And to top it off I had already paid for a three-day class in Las

Vegas that weekend. I had taken this class before and had so many amazing experiences that I was eager to repeat it. I wanted to see if I could jumpstart my life again.

I knew I couldn't work until I after I had seen the doctor the following Tuesday, when he would let me know what they were going to do with my knee. So Friday morning Jack and I boarded the plane for Las Vegas. They gave me seats where I could keep my leg up. When we checked into our class, they had doubts about letting me in for safety reasons, but I convinced them it would be okay.

Unfortunately, the pain was so excruciating that it kept me up at night and made it very hard to focus on the activities. I spent most of the weekend worrying about what was going to happen, and was devasted when on Tuesday I found out that I needed surgery to put screws in my knee.

At six a.m. the next morning I arrived at the surgery center crying, not because of my knee but because Jack was angry that I had to charge the thousand-dollar deductible. I was happy that Loni came to pick me up, which gave me a break from his anger, but for the next week I would be at his mercy until I could get out of bed on my own.

Surprisingly, it wasn't that bad. For a couple of weeks, Jack turned into a different person, kind and caring. While taking care of me, a different side of his personality came through.

In addition to the intense pain and worries about my future, I was on guard as to when he would change back to himself. I had read several books on psychological and holistic meanings for being sick; however, I learned this firsthand when I got my first kidney infection and attended a class on the topic given by a urologist. He said that kidney dis-ease was about losing one's self. That was after a divorce, and I had totally lost myself for a few years; that is, if back in those days I even knew where I was to begin with. Now, as I witnessed the change in Jack as he tended to my injury, I began wondering if that is why his first wife was always sick, so she could have this kind part of him.

There were many reasons that I came up with for breaking my knee. The most important one was that I had been told to slow down and had ignored it. The Universe has a way of hitting us over the head (or in my case, on the knee) when we don't listen.

One of the books I read had this to say about knee problems: *They (the sufferer) are having feelings that their beliefs in life about what they thought they could believe in and had to be true are being "blown out of the water." Their life course is changing dramatically, and they are having a great deal of difficulty accepting the direction it's taking. Right Knee: Their beliefs about things they really cherish are being betrayed. As a result, there are intense issues around the selection of the direction to acquire the resources for self-expression, social conformity and manifestation of their destiny. It feels like a matter of life sustenance to them.*

I couldn't stay in bed long because I had to tend to my clients. Some even came to the house and sat on the floor so I could work on them. I learned how to slide down the stairs holding my leg out straight in the brace. I found if Jack left his truck outside the garage door I could get out there, slide in the passenger door, pull the door closed with my crutches and sit sideways to drive. I was as free as I could be. I joined a gym down the street and started working out and swimming as best I could to speed up the healing process.

I also did every holistic modality that anyone told me about. I drank and ate things that were supposed to promote healing and had every service available. I even got help from one of the women Ronney and I had courted in Hawaii when she arrived in Sacramento with her essential oils.

One weekend I went to a Holistic Healing Fair in a wheelchair and told people who had booths that I would help them so they could have breaks. During my off times, I went from booth to booth and had every free service there was. I thought if a little was good then a lot would be great. After a few hours, my leg was swollen and painful and I was scared. My knee was in its brace, I hadn't been on the crutches at all and still the brace was so tight it hurt. I wheeled myself over to my wonderful chiropractor.

She took one look at my leg and said, "Please tell me you haven't let everyone here work on you."

Of course, I couldn't tell her that. She worked on me for a bit to calm the energy down. That was when I truly believed what I had been told before: *Slow down, you can't do it all at once!*

I also recalled how for years clients and some friends were always telling me I shouldn't ride my motorcycle, snow ski, scuba dive, travel alone or engage in other fun activities I enjoyed. They were always warning me I was going to get hurt. But not one of them ever said, "Oh, you shouldn't go to work or in the salon again because you got hurt." This was a real eye-opener with regard to how we view life, risk, obligations, and joy. This also showed me how fear can stop us from doing activities we believe are risky, when the truth is one can get injured anywhere, doing anything. When fear is going to stop you, ask if the fear is real and where it came from in your belief system. And always keep in mind that FEAR stands for *False Evidence Appearing Real.*

The weekend came to go to the Healing Women Conference for Survivors of Childhood Sexual Abuse. Jack took me because I was in a wheelchair. There were women from over fifty countries there. There were women who, like me, you would never know were survivors of childhood sexual abuse if you saw them on the street. Then there were women who carried stuffed animals with them and walked against walls for protection. I heard some of the worst stories and some heartwarming stories. We learned about how sexual abuse was dealt with in various cultures, including those in which it is acceptable and even desirable for young teenage girls to be given to adult men to get them ready for marriage.

Once again I was shocked to learn just how many molestation survivors there were out there. The most moving speech was from a woman who asked, "What do you want to do with your molestation issues? Yes, it happened, you lived through it and now what? Are you going to let it control you or are you going to take control of your life?" That was the moment I decided to choose the latter. Now I just had to find a way to make it happen.

It wasn't long before I was back in the salon with crutches and a brace from my hip to my ankle. I did the balancing act on one leg for months. This was the time when I had to quit doing discounts and working for free for my friends. Clients left, but new and better ones came. I was not sure how this was happening, but it did.

During an appointment with my doctor, he was amazed at my mobility and lack of pain. I gladly told him about all the holistic things I was doing. After I got home he called to say, "If you are going to continue doing all that stuff then I cannot be your doctor, be responsible for you or treat you."

"Okay, I will stop," I lied gleefully. This stuff was working for me, and there was no way I was going to give it up.

He had told me it would be a year before the screws came out. No, that wasn't going to happen either. In three months, I talked him into taking out the screws. I didn't like feeling them in there and knew they were no longer helping. Plus, if I waited until after the first of the year I would have to pay another insurance deductible and I couldn't afford that.

Three weeks after that surgery Jack took me to Cozumel, Mexico so he could do his warm water dive. I was diving again but the trip with him was another disaster.

I worked on rehabilitation, went back to work full time, worked with Ronney, took classes, looked after my granddaughter and maintained my life. I was back on my motorcycle in six months and snow skiing within eleven months.

## Chapter 12

# *My Babies*

"Jeri, are you happy?"

"No, I am not happy," I sniffled, my eyes darting this way and that to see if anyone was within earshot. All around me, stylists and their clients were engaged in their own conversations. "If I was happy I wouldn't be on the phone with you crying."

"When are you going to do something different then?"

I knew my friend was referring to that oft-quoted saying, *"The definition of insanity is doing the same thing over and over and expecting a different result."* I was aware of this, I believed it; now it was high time I started putting it into practice.

That night, when Jack started in on me after a few beers, I calmly looked up at him and said, "You have to leave."

He could tell that I meant it.

The next day, he quit his job. The next week, he pulled away with his U-Haul. We had not made a total break, though, and continued to speak on a regular basis.

When he left, I felt relieved and lost at the same time. Thinking that buying something new for the house would help, I walked through a few stores looking for that item that would bring a smile to my face and make everything alright. Except nothing did. *That's when I first realized that buying things doesn't make me happy.* I went home and began making my home bright without anything new.

Now that I was alone, I could do anything I wanted. Even the same classes felt different because I was free to learn and grow without having to worry about how Jack would feel or act. I no longer dreaded going home, and I felt a new sense of peace when I was there.

Then I realized that I was slowly but surely whittling away my newfound freedom by having to be available for Jack's phone calls. Clearly I had not completely healed the need to tether myself to him, even as I worked incredibly hard on my healing and growth.

As I searched for the answer, I once again recalled that day when I had shouted, "I hate my mother," then exploded at Jack over the license plate. I had thought Jack was going to leave, and it filled me with fear. Later, in one of my first classes with Mark, an investigation of this fear led to a major a-ha moment. I realized that although we had not been in touch for most of that time, Jack had been my savior for over thirty years. As a teen in Montana, I would run to him whenever I thought my mother was being mean to me. As an adult, when life was bad, I would look for him or contact him. Somewhere deep inside, I always believed he would swoop in and rescue me, but after living with him for a year and a half and learning all I had, that illusion had evaporated. Now I had nothing to hold on to, nothing or anyone to save me. I hit bottom. Have you heard the saying, "One has to hit bottom to begin their way up"? Now I was so thankful for that day of upset over the license plate and the realization that I didn't even know I had. That day is what helped put me on my journey.

*There is always something that we're holding onto, whether we realize it or not. Do you know what you hold onto?*

As I worked on integrating this information I had a different understanding of my clients and friends who clung to God. God is who they hold onto to be their savior.

Sometimes we have a sense of what we need to let go of but are unaware of how we are subconsciously blocking ourselves from doing so. I learned this lesson from a woman in one of my classes who kept saying, "I will try." The facilitator called her up and put a pencil on the floor, then asked her to try and pick it up. We laughed as she bent down to pick it up. The facilitator stopped her and said, "No, you are in the act of picking up the pencil." The woman stood up and looked at the pencil, and our laughing stopped as we tried to figure this out. The facilitator wouldn't let her bend down and pick it up. As she stood there looking at the pencil she knew that she wasn't going to get it done. Finally, the facilitator explained the purpose of the exercise, though he simply could have recited Yoda's famous quote from *The Empire Strikes Back:* "Do or do not. There is no try."

Since that class I've worked on eliminating "try" from my vocabulary. I find that simply catching myself saying this word helps me think about what I am doing or not doing.

In another eye-opening moment in a class, I realized how natural it felt when people yelled mean things at me. I felt nothing, no anger, no sadness, nothing. It was just normal. When I realized this, I recalled the many situations in life when I was mistreated by loved ones and just accepted it as "the way things are." I knew I had to change this but had no idea how or how long it would take before I would begin expecting kindness in my life.

As committed as I was to taking these classes, they could get expensive and I had to sometimes get creative so as not to break my budget. When a particular weekend class caught my eye, I signed up as a volunteer so I could attend for free. In truth, I wasn't sure what I would work on because I thought by now I had already worked on everything, yet still I was drawn to it. When the issue of death came up that first night, I didn't think much of it, and the following day it was all but forgotten as I was busy assisting the facilitator. When I woke the next morning, however, I clearly remembered my dream. I was at a cemetery with rolling hills and green grass. Hovering over a grave was Marty, my first ex-husband and the father of the twins. I was happy to see him as he smiled and watched over the grave. I knew it was the grave of our babies. I realized that in thirty years I had never been to the spot where they were buried.

On my way to class, I cried for my little girls. How did they feel knowing their mother had never been there? All that day we worked on this issue and I knew that I had to visit their grave. The class facilitator was very supportive in helping me find the strength to do so, but the truth was I didn't even know which cemetery they had been laid to rest.

I recalled that I'd once had a paper with the cemetery name and lot number of the grave, but I no longer knew where that paper was. The following week, I searched everywhere like a woman possessed until, finally, I unearthed it: a little white paper with all the information and directions to the cemetery in South San Francisco. I had to go.

The next Monday I was standing in the San Francisco Office of the County Clerk. I don't know how I found the strength to walk up to a window and ask for birth and death records for Katherine and Rhonda, but a few moments later I was holding the papers in my hand. They felt both icy and burning hot at the same time. I couldn't contain the tears and ran out of the building onto the sunny sidewalk. I dropped to the curb staring at those papers, reading and rereading as best I could through my tears. These were my babies, who had entered this world and left it in the space of three days. For a long time I just sat there, crying and shaking and oblivious to onlookers who stared at me as they passed by.

Finally I managed to pull myself together and follow the directions on the little white paper, and before I knew it I had reached the enormous iron gates that protected the cemetery like a fortress. Before going in, I had to visit the cemetery office, as the paper I had did not contain the number of the gravesite. The woman kindly listened to my story as I cried, then checked her system and found that ninety-eight dollars in dues had to be paid before I could get the information. It didn't seem like a lot after thirty years. I wrote out a check, not knowing if it was good, and she handed me the paper with the gravesite number.

As I tried to understand the directions she was giving me, a man appeared and asked, "Would you like me to go with you and show you the way?"

When I saw he was a priest, I fell into his arms crying. "Yes, please. They never had a funeral."

I jumped back in my car and followed his golf cart past the rows and rows of stones, then pulled to a stop behind him. As we slowly walked over the green grass I read headstones, most of which were for babies or toddlers. I thought, *Oh, how do parents do this?*, then it hit me that I was one of those parents.

He stopped at a blank section of green grass and said, "Here it is."

There was no headstone, nothing to let the world know who was there.

*Your mommy is finally here,* I thought as the priest slowly opened his Bible and began to read a funeral prayer. I cried and cried, telling the twins how sorry I was that in all these years I had never come to see them.

Afterward, I sat on the grass talking to them, crying and wondering if their dad was around watching us like he had been in my vision. It would be so wonderful if we could all be here, and I could make amends with him also. After a while, I noticed that the priest was gone, and I was getting cold. I must have been there for hours. I had to go, but the thought of leaving them again was agonizing.

On my way out, I saw a shop where they sold headstones and decided I must get one for my babies. I must have looked so sad as I wandered around the store. The cheapest nice one was five hundred dollars and, well, that wasn't going to work. I didn't have it. I thanked the clerk and told her I would design what I wanted and come back.

On my way home, I remembered a dolphin figure I had with a little baby on it. I knew that was what I wanted, but with two babies. Now I had the design, but where would the money come from?

Back at work, I talked to some of my clients about my weekend, as usual reserving my story for those who wouldn't think I was crazy or stupid or at least had never told me so. One of them was the woman whose cane I had fallen over when I broke my knee the year before. The next week, after she left, I found an envelope on my station with a check for five hundred dollars. She had gifted me the money for the headstone! I was so surprised and grateful, I almost passed out.

I quickly sketched out my design and a few weeks later I was on my way back to San Francisco to see my babies' new headstone. It was beautiful, exactly how I had imagined. Finally, after thirty years, my little girls had an identity. I knew where they were, and I believed with my whole heart that they knew I had been there. I also realized that working on my death issues over these last years had allowed me to be present to do this for us.

Though I've come to understand Mark's comment about dealing with death, I also believe that in sharing my story I can let others know they are not alone while grieving a loss. It was one of the reasons I was led to write this book.

Indeed, acknowledging and clearing my guilt over not visiting my girls had brought me a deep sense of peace, yet I knew in my heart that there was still much work to be done.

## Chapter 13

# Angels and Ghosts

I thought I had exhausted every aspect of my mother issues through all the classes I'd completed. And I had resigned myself that I would never have a mother to love or to love me.

Then one evening, my phone rang. It was my mother's stepbrother, and he was clearly intoxicated. I stood there holding the phone in surprise as he yelled that I was a lousy daughter, not even visiting my mother when she was sick. It was hard to get a word in edgewise to tell him I didn't know where she lived. Eventually he finished his drunken rant and gave me her address. I was shocked to find out that she and John lived across the street from where I worked. It felt creepy, like she had been watching me.

The next day, I worked up enough courage to go over there. We were both shocked – she that I was there, and I about how messy the place was. The people on *Hoarders* would have had nothing on her. I was also shocked to find that she was in a wheelchair, though I had no idea what was wrong with her. As usual she won't talk much about what had been going on with them but at least now I knew where she lived. I guess it was a relief. Now I had to do something, but what?

After that, I went over occasionally. Sometimes she would let me in, other times she wouldn't. When she moved to a different apartment, that place was a mess as well. Sometimes she came into the salon to get her hair done, which made me nervous as my mother was always unpredictable. I would be relieved when she acted sweet to my clients, only to learn later that she had called them and told them all kinds of lies about me.

In addition to all the classes I attended, I had gone to Al-anon meetings on and off for years. They had never helped me, except with my guilt over hating my mother. I finally found a connection in Adult Children of Alcoholics (ACA). When I mentioned to my mother that I had been to a meeting she became furious.

"Why are you going there? I'm not a drunk. Are you telling those people I am a drunk?"

After she calmed a little, I dried my tears and blurted out, "No, you aren't a drunk, but I come from a family of alcoholics."

"Who was an alcoholic?" she screamed.

I said, "Dad was an alcoholic."

"And how do you know that? You were only eight years old when he died."

"Yes, but I know he was drunk in that car. Show me one picture you have of him without a beer or a bottle of Jack Daniels in his hand. Then there was Uncle Walt, Uncle Bob, Uncle Lloyd, Grandpa Pete. You want me to name more?"

She sat there in shock. She had never thought of our life in that way. Never. It was normal to her and to many others back then. Even now there are families who live all their lives not acknowledging, just accepting. If they do realize what the problem is, they have no idea what to do or even that there is any help out there.

My mother had all the signs of what is called a "dry drunk." When someone lives in a family of alcoholics and is not a drinker, they can develop certain characteristics of mood disorders and dysfunctional behavior. Knowing that helped me better understand my mother.

Dealing with my molestation issues also helped me understood her more. After being abandoned by their mother, she and her two brothers were raised by various aunts and uncles. One uncle made my mother sit on his lap and do things she didn't want to do.

Then, at just thirty-one years old, she had lost her knight in shining armor and had to find a way to raise us girls. I kept this in mind, along with everything I had learned in my classes, as I tried to understand my mother and how she lived her life. She often told a story that took place about three weeks after my dad died. I came home from school to find her on the sofa crying, as usual. She said I smacked her on the shoulder and told her, "Get up and let's go to town and get a hamburger." We rarely went to restaurants even on special occasions, so this was a big deal, but we did go get that hamburger. She always said that was the day she decided to get going. And she did. She got a job in the office at the Anaconda Copper Co., and we soon moved off the farm and into town. My dad worked there before he died and that is where she met John.

In a class I discovered that was the day she turned her existence over to me. And I accepted the challenge. She was dependent on me. Of course, neither of us knew this. I also discovered that was why when I began getting older and wanting to pull away she really went crazy. She was not going to let me go. She was not going to have a boy or a man take me away. When I learned that, it was an awakening for me. She needed me so she could keep going. (I also learned that this type of dependency can start in the womb, if the baby chooses to take on whatever emotions they believe their mother needs help with.)

With each awakening it took me days, weeks, or even months to make sense of it. It was like fitting the proverbial square peg into the round hole.

In another class I discovered the reason why I felt she was often leaving and going into hiding. When I was sixteen and ran away from home, she hired private detectives to look for me. When one of her sisters disappeared with her seven sons, Mom hired detectives to look for her. I believe that she wanted us to care enough in return to go looking for her when she hid. Instead, we were just glad she wasn't around causing trouble with my sisters and me, our family and friends. When she was involved, there was always chaos and fighting.

At this point I could just tolerate being around her. I couldn't trust her, but I knew she needed help and so did John. Billie also tried to help her. She would clean up their place, only to become infuriated when it quickly reverted to a mess. It was dirty, disgusting and unsanitary.

My sister and I tried to get information from her – things like what was wrong with her, whether she and John had any money, and where her storage sheds were, but she refused to talk with us about anything. She had also John trained to not say anything.

It bothered me that she kept my dad's picture front and center on her television so when John watched television that was what he saw. He was the one who waited on her and put up with her, and yet had to constantly be reminded of her previous love. It had been forty years since Dad died, and she still had not gotten over it.

One day I went over there during my lunchbreak. She hadn't been out of bed in a few days; she also hadn't been eating because she feared that John was trying to poison her. I tore the sandwich I'd brought in two and handed her half. She gobbled it down like she was starving. I just sat there and cried as she ate my whole lunch, thanking me with each bite. I cried all the way back to work but walked into the salon with a happy face so no one would know.

John and my mom had been married on and off for more than three decades. She would divorce him and get alimony from him; then once the alimony ran out, she would remarry him and the whole cycle would begin again. How she accomplished this we will never know. It was just one of a dozen mysteries about this woman's life. How did she live? How did she pay for anything? How did she and John travel the world, just how? She never passed on any of her secrets. At one point, they went to the Vatican to have their divorces "fixed' so they could get married in the Catholic Cathedral in San Francisco. I missed that wedding because my sister was the favorite at that time. I only found out about it much later.

Now with each class I took my goal was to find a way to be at peace with myself if she died. In these classes it came up how I hated her for not protecting me when I was molested by her brother. I found inside me all the misinformation I had carried over my dad's death, including how I had blamed her for his being drunk the night of the accident. I had already tried to forgive her for moving me to California. Now I found I had to deal with more guilt over hating her.

So much was going on in my life that I don't know how I did everything. Jack had moved to Denver but we were maintaining a long distance and often turbulent relationship; Loni was pregnant with her second baby after trying for years and I was helping her financially and physically. This in addition to going to classes, working long hours, and keeping a motorcycle club going.

Before Jack left he had said, "You will never find anyone to ride your motorcycle with." I thought, *Oh, you watch me.* Shortly afterward, I made up a flyer about starting a club and brought it to a couple of motorcycle shops. I received plenty of calls, and when we set up a meeting over twenty people came. We arranged a ride for the next weekend and more than thirty riders showed up. When they asked, "Where we headed to?" I didn't know what to say. A couple of the men had arranged to meet another Honda Shadow Club at a town in the foothills where a former client had bought a pizza place. One of those guys said, "You want me to lead?" Oh my, yes! That fellow took over and put the riders in order and off we went.

At the pizza place we met the other group. They explained how they ran their group, and within minutes I was president of a new club. On the ride home I asked myself, "What just happened?" I had a motorcycle club and the best part was that they all knew how to run it.

Now in addition to my classes, kids, sick mother and work, I had a motorcycle club with rides to plan and meetings to put together. Okay, this will work. At least I had an empty house.

Jack and I were still frequently flying back and forth to see each other. One weekend, he picked me up at the airport in Denver and took me to a lake to meet up with some friends. Well, I went to sleep Friday evening and didn't wake up until Sunday afternoon. All so I could come home and continue the rat race.

Not long after that, my sister Billie called and told me to meet her at Mom's as soon as I could. I left work and found my sister standing in the middle of a huge mess. Someone had called the county and the social workers were there. If Mom didn't let us take over, they would. We started looking for a place that she and John could afford, as well as cleaning out that apartment and *eight* storage units filled with garbage. She had been paying big money for these units, so much so that hauling everything to the dump cost more than I could afford. After weeks of cleaning out garbage, we got them settled into a nice studio that included food and care and finally we could relax a bit.

One evening I got up enough nerve to return eighteen-hundred dollar worth of clothes with the tags still on. It was much easier than I expected. When the woman at the store asked me why I was returning them, I burst into tears.

"My mother is dying and won't be able to wear them."

Thank God that was one bill I didn't have to worry about.

*While going through all of this, I discovered in a class that there were definitely at least two people living in my mother's body. One wanted to be the sophisticated woman, driving her Lincoln, going to the opera in San Francisco in her mink coat, and taking world cruises and tours. The other was the sad lonely worthless woman with safety pins in her blouse working her butt off, the woman who didn't deserve to be that sophisticated well-dressed woman. This realization totally broke my heart. I had learned enough in classes and had watched enough of her mixed-up life that it began to make a little sense to me. Could this be part of why she was so out of control? Could this be part of why she was such a rageacholic, because of the internal battle she had always been going through?*

Not long afterward, we got a call in the middle of the night that she had fallen and was being taken to the hospital. My clients weren't happy to have their appointments cancelled, but it couldn't be helped. I spent most of the next day at the hospital. Mom had broken her hip and needed surgery. They had also taken brain scans and found that she had dementia. She might have had it most of her life. I also found out she was probably bipolar and had other mental conditions. I was relieved to finally learn the cause of her mental issues, but at the same time I wanted to scream at the doctor for telling me.

During surgery the next day Bobbie called to say that they would come for a little bit and then we could go do something fun.

In total disbelief, I said, "This isn't the time for fun. Mom is in surgery." She hung up on me.

My sister Billie was working and busy, so I forged on. Eventually my mother was moved to a rehabilitation hospital. It was nice but soon the insurance money ran out and she had to move again. One day Billie did come to the rehabilitation hospital, only to walk out with no explanation, never to return. She didn't return my calls either. Now I was on my own to deal with Mom and John.

I drove to the new hospital next to the medical van, where she sat in a wheelchair looking so very frail and lost. I cried all the way as she waved to me through the window like a little girl. I thought, *How can a woman who was such a tyrant all her life be reduced to this? How does this happen?*

John and I got her settled into her new room. I got them a television, made her an artificial bouquet of flowers for her nightstand, and tried to make her room as homey as I could.

The days became weeks, then months. We fell into a routine depending on what type of day Mom was having. John, or "Grandpa" as we called him, stayed with Mom all day, every day. Loni and the grandkids had referred to him that way because he was the only grandfather they had ever known; I now called him that as well because it was more personal than John and I couldn't bear to call him Dad. Mom had always fought us on this, but now she was too out of it to notice.

When I finished work, I would go to the hospital and Grandpa would go home. I would get home sometime after nine or ten, then I would call Jack and hear how unfair everything was to him. Some mornings on my way to work I would stop in and see how Mom had done during the night.

The nurses and I convinced Grandpa to join a lunch group for seniors so he could get out for an hour a day. Mom wouldn't let him read or do anything so basically he sat for endless hours next to her bed. I bought him the hardest math book I could find so he would have something to do during the day. He would hide the book under a paper or even a napkin so he could work those long math problems.

The nurses kept telling me that I also had to do something for me. So I flew to Denver a couple of times and continued to go to classes to make sure I cleared everything so if Mom died I would be ready with no regrets. I spent as much time as I could with Loni and her little family.

*One fall day, I decided to go for a ride with my motorcycle club. I had learned that if I spent the day worrying and sad it would be a wasted day. Even with a group, I could still be alone on my motorcycle with my thoughts and prayers. I spent many of those thoughts asking for help with everything that was going on. I enjoyed the day riding, just being and talking with myself as the wind wiped my worries away.*

*After everyone went their separate ways, I decided to stop by the hospital. The nurses were amazed at the transformation with me in my leathers, boots, helmet and gloves. They were used to seeing the dressed up, taking-care-of-business person. After some small talk about my ride they told me Mom had had a dreadful day. I went to the room, sent Grandpa home and told him I would stay for a while. As I settled into the room, I noticed the flowers I had made her were missing. No one seemed to know anything about it. Eventually I found them torn apart in her bottom drawer. The nurses admitted that she had torn them apart because she was mad.*

*When it was time to go home I walked out into the cool dark night air with tears running down my cheeks. I didn't know how I would be able to keep doing this. I got on my motorcycle and started out the driveway. When I reached the street, I was suddenly on the ground with my motorcycle on its side and my leg pinned under it. I managed to pull my leg out but didn't know how I could get the bike up. (I had dropped my bike a couple of times before and it always took two or three men to pick it up.) I stood there in the dark, feeling helpless. I couldn't leave the bike to go for help, and I couldn't budge it myself.*

*An old truck pulled up from around a bend in the road. A tall thin man got out, and without a word, picked up my motorcycle, handed me the handlebars, and started walking back to the truck. Then the truck just vanished! Time went fast and stood still at the same time. I have driven down that street hundreds of times since then and every time I look to see how the driver of the truck could have seen me in my black leathers in the dark, and my black bike on the ground, without driving past and needing to back up. There is no way. But the truck had come around the bend and stopped in front of me.*

*I sat on my bike shaking so hard that I was afraid to ride. I started riding slowly, trying to convince myself that what just happened hadn't happened. I couldn't do it. I knew something had happened. I knew I had fallen and I knew someone had picked up my bike. Other than that, the rest was unexplainable. I decided that when I got home if my chaps or jacket had scratches or dirt on it I would really believe that I had fallen. If I had fallen, then someone had to have picked up my bike. In the garage, I saw the proof on my right sleeve. Down my right leg there was more proof.*

*I have come to accept and acknowledge the angels in my life. They are always there for me. I believe the angel that night was my dad. I also believe he was around the hospital waiting for my mom and saw that I needed help.*

The days and weeks went by as we got ready for my daughter's new baby and the holidays. I loved my first granddaughter so much that I wasn't sure that I could feel the same about another, but the moment the baby was born I knew I could love her just as much. She had an issue with jaundice and needed extra attention. On Thanksgiving Day an incubator was brought into the house and I slept on the floor next to it for five nights.

Jack had flown in for the holiday weekend and was not happy with the circumstances, but I was staying with the baby and Loni, no ifs, ands or buts.

At Christmas, Brittany and I went to Colorado to see Jack and ski. Because she was with me it was a wonderful time. When we returned on New Year's Day, Loni and Grandpa met us at the airport. It wasn't good news – Mom was in Intensive Care. There had been some interference with her care while I was gone, and I was not happy. A week later she was moved back to the convalescent hospital.

The next two months were brutal. I would work all day, then go straight to the hospital and sleep there until about four or five in the morning when I rushed home to shower before heading back to work.

Often the nurses asked me about people that my mother spoke to all day. Yes, that was my uncle or aunt or her mother, but they were all dead. One night the nurse asked, "Did you run away from home when you were sixteen?" Yep, that was me. The nurse said Mom had been looking for me all day with private detectives. She talked about so many different things and I thought, *Why, why now?* So much was going on each night that I would just get lost in doing "the right thing."

I thought I knew everything that was going on with her. I was going to have no regrets when she died. I had a love for my mother that I never thought I could have. There were times when she looked at me and I knew, somehow, that she loved me.

The time came to call the priest to give her last rites. I stayed all that day, a Monday, waiting for her last breath. In my thoughts, I asked her to please wait until Saturday to die. I told her I had a very busy week and needed the money to pay for her funeral. At this point that was all I could think of: how will I pay for this?

Tuesday, I was off to work with my heavy heart. Wednesday and Thursday rolled by. Thursday evening, she was so bad I called my Friday clients and told them I couldn't leave and would let them know. I stayed all day Friday at the hospital. On Friday afternoon, I called a couple clients and met them at the salon and worked for a few hours. Then I went back to the hospital to spend the night.

About four a.m. on Saturday, I had an awakening. I realized that I was keeping her alive for me. What was I putting her through? I told the nurses to take her off everything and give her something to keep her peaceful. They needed a doctor's order to do that.

I went home to shower and then to get Grandpa. When I got back later that morning, I tested her heart rate and blood pressure as I usually did, but I couldn't find a pulse. I asked a nurse to check. The nurse left the room and I called a friend. When the nurse returned a few minutes later, she told me my mother had died. I told my friend why I had to hang up and was in shock when a few minutes later her husband ran in the door. I was very grateful that he took over. But as they rolled the bed out the door, I blurted out, "I haven't told her everything." He kindly told me to go find her and say what I needed to say. She could still hear me, he said.

I ran to the front desk, asking where her body was and was pointed to a door. Inside the door I was stunned to see that her bed was in front of a beauty salon wash bowl. Despite my pain, I chuckled to myself. How appropriate that the woman who for thirty years had owned salons and worked as a stylist (though admittedly not a great one) was resting in the beauty salon! As I looked at her body, trying to come up with the right words, I saw movement in the air above her bed. As I focused on the movement, I saw her with my dad. She was wearing a dress that I remembered well from the farm days and the two of them were holding hands, dancing, swinging back and forth. They looked so happy to be together.

I cried, wishing I could feel that happiness instead of the sadness I was feeling. Mom and Dad told me they were busy and to come back later. Mom also told me she had waited until Saturday like I had asked. *I didn't realize that she had heard every word I said under my breath that Monday about my busy week. And she had waited! That poor woman, everything she had gone through that week was because of my request.*

With no way to wrap my head or heart around this, I wandered back to her room. My friend's husband had packed up everything and put it in Grandpa's car. He also called my sisters for me. Bobbie said not to call again as she would mourn the way she wanted to because all hope was gone now. He asked her what hope that was, and she told him, "to ever have the kind of mother I wanted." Billie told him to let her know when the arrangements were made.

Loni and I went with Grandpa to the mortuary to set things up. They were so good to us knowing we had little money. Grandpa chose an open casket and the pink dress Mom had worn to Loni's wedding, and the least expensive urn we could find (a priest had told him cremation was allowed). We worked all day Sunday getting artificial flowers ready.

The morning of the service, Loni and I set everything up beautifully, then I did Mom's hair and makeup so she looked her best to say goodbye. Then, to my surprise, people started coming in to pay their respects. I'd thought no one would be there except us. I was amazed at the flowers that were sent and the number of people there. My sister Billie and her family came. The service was lovely. Jack flew in to help.

Afterward, I did not want to leave her. My girlfriend called me to come outside, where I saw the most beautiful double rainbow. I knew it was meant for me, to tell me I had done an excellent job. I wanted to go back in and be by the casket, but they had already moved it out. Everyone told me to be happy and leave with the rainbow.

In the days that followed, I thought a lot about the ending of her life. She had stayed until Saturday while my dad waited to welcome her. How does that all happen? How did she hear me? How did I see that and hear it all? So much was just unexplainable.

I forced myself to buck up and went back to work the next day and the days after that. Two months later while in the grocery store I saw a sign for Mother's Day cards. I started looking through the cards when it hit me: I did not have a mom any longer. I could not buy her a Mother's Day card. All the years that I didn't want to buy one because they never said what I wanted them to say, and now I couldn't get her one at all. I cried so hard that I left my basket of groceries behind and walked out of the store.

I decided not to wait until summer to bury her ashes in Montana and told Grandpa to get ready. A couple weeks later he and I set out in a snowstorm over the Sierra Mountains. It took sixteen hours but we finally reached our destination.

Grandpa had it all set up: a service at the Catholic church and then to the cemetery where my dad was. Walking up to the gravesite, I saw my mother's copper urn sitting in line with the Anaconda Copper Company smokestack in the distance. How perfect! This company was not only the lifeblood of the town, but the place where my parents and Grandpa had worked at one time or another. At that moment, I had gratitude and happiness that I was the one who got to take her back to my dad and their roots.

The next morning, I felt the town closing in on me and was once again struck by my good fortune at having left it when I did. I was thankful that Mom had taken me out of there when she did. Now, after another sixteen-hour drive I would be free to begin a different life.

I was back to work, taking care of Grandpa, Loni and the kids, the motorcycle club, keeping peace with Jack and working on some way to financially make it. I was also dealing with an unimaginable lawsuit over medical bills from when I broke my knee.

I found an ad for a dating site and decided to check it out. A picture of a man on a boat who said he wanted someone to water ski and go to dinner with appealed to me. I wrote, and soon was water skiing and having dinners with him. This was fun and helped the summer pass by.

Yet bigger adventures soon beckoned, in the form of a friend who needed help with a ghost in her house. Yep, a ghost.

This friend was visiting from the East Coast when she told me about hearing screaming in the middle of the night in their bedroom. When she or her husband got out of bed the screaming stopped as "something" went through their wall. Their two dogs didn't hear it. I knew right away that it was a ghost, but she wasn't convinced. Only when another friend of mine had the same response did she take it seriously. She was so taken aback that I thought she would pass out.

The other friend channeled, seeking more information. She found that there had been a young girl hanged in their barn who needed to be released. A couple weeks later, my friend called from her home in shock. She and her husband had been cleaning out the loft in the barn, and they found a rope tied on the rafter. She was certain that it had been a noose.

I calmed her down by promising that I would come out and see what I could do. I went to classes and the bookstore for more insight about ghosts, then headed east. I was excited about using my newfound knowledge to find the ghost. I also planned to surprise my businessman friend who had remained in the background for years.

In fact, my first stop was at his office. I still felt all the butterflies when I saw him. All the feelings resurfaced as he grabbed and kissed me. I could hardly pull myself away from him to leave.

During the week, though I was busy sightseeing with my friend and researching the history of her property, I found the time to speak with him on the phone. He always had reasons why he couldn't break away to meet. Then I had an a-ha moment: he must be married. Shit, not another one. I quickly shook off my disappointment. I had a ghost to contend with.

I channeled and got the information that this young girl had been caught with a man. In those days, that was totally unacceptable. Her father had hanged her from the rafter in the barn. Her soul had hung around because it did not know where to go.

That night my friend and I, along with her two big dogs, went out by the trees behind the barn. I took all the paraphernalia I'd read about in the books and we performed the ritual, burning sage, holding hands and releasing this soul. We told her she could finally go on. All of a sudden, my friend's Doberman jumped up and barked while looking at the top of the trees. We knew the soul was gone. My friend and her husband never heard the screaming in their bedroom again.

My mission completed, I journeyed back to the airport by way of my businessman's office. To my surprise, as he tried to hold me, I pulled away and said, "No more. I am not going to put myself through this again." Afterward, I sat in the airport waiting for my flight and wondered where that had come from. How could I just release all those years of yearning, all the butterflies I felt when he called? It was as if, by magic, all those feelings had suddenly been transformed.

So many parts of me were different that sometimes I didn't even recognize myself. All I knew was that when I arrived home to get busy with life, I felt a peace that I hadn't realized I was capable of.

## Chapter 14

## Magic of Peru

Over the Christmas holidays, Brittany and I went skiing in Colorado again. We had a wonderful time, but I came back to face something unpleasant: an appointment with a bankruptcy attorney. For years my financial situation had been unsustainable, and now, with no more credit cards to use, I had to bite the bullet. I felt every emotion: guilt, sadness, fear, shame and relief. I knew that I could never allow myself to be in debt again. In addition to making my own lifestyle changes, that meant I had to stop helping everyone else – they would just have to manage on their own. As I went through this painful process, I thought about what I would have to give up. Mostly, I wondered whether I would ever be able to travel again.

I had a new client with whom I really enjoyed talking. She told me she was going to Florida to visit her son and would be back at the same time I returned from Super Bowl weekend in Denver. Jack had bought me another ticket so I could get away and relax. (Others may have assumed I was living the good life on that trip, but when I returned all I had were bad memories of a terrible weekend of drinking and fighting.)

When this client came in for her next appointment, I was looking forward to hearing about her wonderful week in Florida. She certainly had had a better time than I did! But before she even said hello, she handed me an envelope and said, "I have never seen my son do this, but he said he thought you needed these."

I opened the envelope to find vouchers for two airline tickets anywhere in the world. My mouth dropped while my mind raced in so many directions that I didn't know what to do or say. Why me? Why airline tickets? How did they know how much I loved to travel and how sad I was at the thought of not being able to do so? How did I say thank you for this? Why? Why? Why? Could this be the Spirits' answer to me for all my guilt and feelings about the bankruptcy, telling me that I wasn't a bad person?

All that day my mind worked overtime. Where should I go? Hawaii? Atlanta, to see the cousin I had just found again after many years? Should I take Grandpa and Brittany? Should I even tell Jack? I could go anywhere in the world! But wait, I had no money or credit cards and was barely making it now. How could I do this? My mind was in a whirl the next few days.

One idea came to my mind: I had wanted to go to Peru since meeting a woman five years earlier and hearing about her amazing experiences there. I also remembered a person in Ronney's office telling me she saw me on Machu Picchu with two priests. I wasn't even sure what Machu Picchu was, but these thoughts continued to swirl in my brain for a few days.

Okay, Peru it would be, but who to go with? While thinking about it and during meditation, I kept hearing, "Go alone." That seemed like crazy thinking, because how could I go to Peru alone. I kept hearing, *Go in a month that starts with M*. It was February now, so May would work!

One night a friend asked me if I wanted to do a fire walk on March 20, the spring equinox. I agreed, and we made some plans. Afterward, I realized that March starts with an M, and that's the autumn equinox in Peru. I felt that I couldn't get it together so quickly, especially with no money. When I thought about it, my body trembled, and I didn't know why – was it fear?

The next day Ronney called to ask what I was doing on the equinox next month because there were events planned all over. I answered, "How would you like to spend it on Machu Picchu with me?" She was aware of my financial situation, so she was shocked to hear my question. I told her what had happened and convinced her we could do it cheaply. She thought about it but decided she couldn't go. I would have to keep her posted.

I needed answers that no one on earth could give me, so I would have to go to those souls who dwelled somewhere beyond it. I arranged to get together with two friends I channeled with. I had been getting the information that someone new wanted to channel through me and sure enough, when I started to speak I knew this wasn't Amel, my usual angel.

"Who is this?"

"St. Michael, I am here to help Jeri with her trip to Peru."

This entity told us that I would be protected, and this would be life-changing for me. Everything was being taken care of, but there would be tears during the trip.

Okay, I may cry but I will be protected. Not too bad.

I spent a few frantic days researching, working, taking the grandkids to school and babysitters, looking after Grandpa, and of course listening to Jack on the phone every night telling me how crazy I was. My plan was in full motion when I suddenly remembered that I was helping to organize a St. Patrick's Day dinner for one of my clients, and twenty-eight people had already signed up. Oh no, I can't be away that weekend. I'll have to travel another weekend, but that would mean missing the equinox! Then the lady I was organizing the dinner for called. They had lost the restaurant and so the dinner would have to be cancelled. She apologized, but it was the best news I could have gotten. I could still travel for the equinox! I knew this was magical.

More telephone calls, emails, and decisions were made. Martha, my travel agent friend, hit the roof when I told her my plans.

"You can't go there alone!" she said, "There are terrorists, they rip people off, it's the Third World..." and on and on.

I said, "Man, I'm glad I told you something good."

"I know you are being sarcastic, but someone has to tell you how bad it is there."

After that, I was brought low and questioned whether I was doing the right thing.

Many more people shot me down. Their fear, judgements and ignorance were overwhelming, so I decided that *silence is golden* and stopped talking about my plans. My daughter was also not in favor of my trip, but she was so busy with a new house and baby she didn't have time to spend with me. I tried to avoid talking about it with Jack. *God, I just want someone in my life that can support me in my ventures and adventures. Someone with whom I can share my fears, desires and dreams, who won't sabotage them, but help with them.*

The day before my flight, the airline I was to take from Lima to Cusco went on strike. I emailed Julio, the travel agent in Cusco who had booked my hotel and tours. He replied that they would be back to work by the time I got there and not to worry.

Okay then...

The day I was to leave, work was very busy and I felt nauseous. My friend came by and reminded me what we had learned through channeling: *The solar plexus will be reaching out to feel what is ahead for me. The solar plexus, our third chakra, is the core of our personality, our identity and our ego. It is the center of willpower. The gift of this chakra is sensing our personal power, being confident, responsible and reliable. It is the center of our self-esteem, our willpower, and our self-discipline as well as the warmth in our personality. The energy of this chakra allows us to transform inertia into action and movement, it allows us to meet challenges and move forward in life. The third chakra is very powerful and means I have the power to choose.*

That explained why I felt nausea in my solar plexus. Onward we go.

I had a stopover in Atlanta, during which I planned to visit the cousin whose wedding Pat and I had attended a lifetime ago. As mentioned earlier, we had recently reestablished contact after several years, this after I found her contact info amongst my mother's possessions. When I found out that she was now in an alcohol rehab center, I decided it was good timing. I would be there to offer her support, if only for a little while. This girl had been adopted as a baby (her father was the same uncle who had molested me starting when I was three, and I had to wonder what he had done to her besides pass on the alcoholism). Later, her brother shot himself and my aunt and uncle were both dead. She was divorced twice with two children, and I heard, had a boyfriend.

My last two clients cancelled, which meant I could leave work early – more help from the Spirit! It was time to get ready, say goodbye to Loni and the girls, and then Grandpa could take me to the airport. There I found out how these tickets worked: they were standby passes and I would only know right before takeoff if I had a seat. I did get on and flew to Atlanta.

My cousin's boyfriend picked me up and told me she was being released from the hospital. When we arrived there, she walked out of the double doors, hugging and kissing me and apologizing that I had to find her like that. After stopping for breakfast, we went to her house where I showered and had a nap. When I opened my eyes, she was sitting there just watching and waiting for me to wake up. We talked for a while and I even did a couple of processes that I had learned, hoping they would help her.

We talked about how little our parents had left us, other than stacks of bills, then moved on to other family stories. I didn't think she could handle my memories of her parents, so I just let her talk. Turned out her memories weren't so good either, but I was somehow comforted to have gotten more information. We visited with her children then left for the airport.

This time, I settled into First Class without a care in the world, experiencing a peacefulness that I had not felt for a long time or maybe ever. *Here I am with no money or credit cards to my name and sitting in First Class, how did this work?* After eating, drinking and visualizing getting used to the better things in life, including travel like this, I drifted off to sleep. I woke to hot towels and a wonderful hot breakfast, and soon I could see Lima out the window. I was really here.

I went through customs like I knew what I was doing, then walked through the doors into a big bustling airport. I had thought Lima would have a little broken down, third-world airport. Wrong. There were hundreds of people, all of them yelling, but since they were yelling in Spanish I had no idea what the matter was.

As I stood there amidst the chaos, someone stopped me to tell me my shirt was up in the back and my money belt was in plain sight. Oops, that was stupid. I then spotted two policemen with their rifles on their shoulder and I confidently went over and asked them where my airline counter was.

They looked at each other and then at me and said, "Española, please." I thought yes, that would be nice, but instead I said, "English."

One of them snapped his fingers at two women walking by. They came over to us and asked me, "Yes, what do you need?"

When I told them which airline I was looking for they informed me that it had gone out of business but they would help. I thanked the policemen while one woman took my bag and said to follow her through this big airport with lines of people all yelling and trying to get somewhere with no airplanes. I wasn't even thinking, I just took it all in.

The women took me to sit in a corner with a line of chairs. While I waited for them, I began to worry about the situation I found myself in. Shit, what did I do? Then a family caught my eye. I could see the love between them; they had tattered clothes, but they were traveling. I reached into my suitcase and took out a couple of crayons, tore a couple of pages out of the coloring books and a couple of small toys I had taken to give to the children in Cusco. They were clearly overwhelmed with the gesture and thanked me profusely, and as I watched these two little children, so happy with so little, I experienced deep gratitude for what I have.

Soon the ladies were back asking for money for my ticket. I handed it to them and they walked away. Oops, I had just given them some of my precious cash. Soon they were back with a handwritten ticket. One answered her cell phone and passed it to me, saying, "It is for you."

Yeah, right, for me. I almost started laughing.

Reluctantly I took the phone and said hello. The voice on the other end said, "This is Julio in Cusco. You are in good hands, do what she says, and I will be at the airport to pick you up. I know what flight you are going to be on. See you in a couple hours. Have a nice flight."

When I handed the phone back, she took my suitcase again and I just followed. We walked through lines of yelling people up to a doorway where she handed my ticket in. I was to go down the hall and turn left where there would be a waiting area for my plane. I thanked the two women then watched them disappear into the crowd.

How did all of this just happen? Hundreds of people were yelling and waiting, and I am getting on a plane. That was just unbelievable. The phone call... how?

Walking out of the little airport at Cusco I was greeted by a nice-looking man holding a sign with "Miss Jeri" written on it. He introduced himself as Julio, then took my suitcase and led me to his car. As he put my suitcase in the trunk and me in the back seat, I saw that another man was driving. Suddenly I became nervous. I realized that there was not one other person in the world who knew where I was or who I was with. They could do anything to me and no one would ever find me. Fear hit me, and I thought of my daughter and my grandkids.

*What the hell am I doing? What if everyone who warned me of danger was right?*

Julio started telling me the history of Cusco. I didn't want to let fear take over and thought of a way to manage it. I asked if I could send an email to my daughter to let her know I had arrived. He told me they would stop at their office and I could send it from there. Maybe Julio felt my fear, for he told me his boss would wait outside while we went in. After he turned on the computer, which was even slower than mine at home, he told me he too would wait outside. Hanging on the walls were plaques and licenses so I could see that it was a business, which made me felt better. I emailed Loni and then headed back out to the car. My peace was back, and I stared out the window in amazement as we drove through the center of this big city, then pulled up to a lovely, quaint hotel.

Once inside, I was given coco leaf tea to prevent altitude sickness, then Julio and I made plans to meet for dinner to discuss my schedule and I was shown to my room.

Bright and early the next day I was on a bus tour around Cusco and the surrounding countryside. Suddenly the bus pulled over on the side of the road and a man got on the bus saying, "Miss Jeri, Miss Jeri, here is your emails." They were from my daughter, saying she was glad I was safe, and that she missed me already but hoped I had a good time. And did I ever! I could go on forever about everything I saw, experienced and loved.

The second day was a walking tour around the city center. As we entered the cathedral, which hundreds of years earlier had been an Inca palace, I got an eerie feeling. One minute I was standing there listening to the guide recount the history of the place and the next I nearly dropped to my knees as I visualized the Spanish army rush through the huge doors, grab a princess, and drag her outside to rape her in public. Somehow, I knew that princess was me and the man who had me was my brother-in-law in this life who had molested me starting when I was the age of nine.

I was so shaken I could barely walk but knew I had to keep up with the group. This was the first time I could remember having a past life recall totally unsolicited. I couldn't wait to get back to my room for the night so I could think about this.

The next day I left on another bus for a tour through the Sacred Valley of Peru and ended up at a retreat center I had found. I stayed there for a couple of wonderful nights and explored the little town. There were few lights, and at night the sky was amazing, just like in Montana when I was a child. What a shame thousands of people live and die without ever knowing the incredible number of stars that are in the heavens.

Then I was off to Ollantaytambo, a beautiful town on the Urubamba River, where I would catch the train to Machu Picchu. Up the mountain the train steadily climbed, and once we arrived a guide was there to lead us into the gates of the mountain. I cannot explain the power of that mountain and the feelings that ran down my spine as I entered. After the walking tour they led us back out to the restaurant for lunch. We could go back down the mountain on the bus to Aguas Calientes when we wanted to.

As I stood outside by the souvenir shop I realized I did not want to leave. Huge clouds formed and it began to pour. Everyone ran for the buses, but I didn't move. It was like my feet were glued to the ground. As the last bus left I thought, "That was stupid." But the clouds parted, the sun came out and it was beautiful again.

I walked back into the gates to Machu Picchu and noticed there were only about five people on the mountain. I gazed over the beauty, trying to remember as much as I could of the history and feel what I could while quietly listening to the roar of the Urubamba River three thousand feet below. I walked over to one of the little huts and sat down, then pulled out some paper and began writing. To my surprise it was a list of everything I wanted in a relationship. It was so profound I even made a copy of it before burning the original in a ritual I had learned. *Where did the foresight come from to bring paper, pen, candle and sage?* I didn't know, yet I had it all with me. I did every modality I could think of, then ended with "and so be it."

Finally, I tore myself away from the mountain and went to find my hotel. It was clean but had no hot water. I went out to the hot springs and talked to other travelers. On the way back, I had pizza and played with the children on the streets, giving them crayons and paper to color on. Back in my room, I was trying to get comfortable in the bed when there was a knock at the door to tell me I had a telephone call. Oh, not another call, out of nowhere. It was Julio again, checking on me and letting me know he would pick me up at the train the next afternoon.

The train ride back down the mountain was everything I had heard it was: leisurely and awe-inspiring. The mountain was beautiful and green, and we passed little villages with children playing and watching the train.

Mostly, it was incredible to watch this train navigate the turns on the very steep parts of the mountain.

Back in Cusco, I went to dinner with Julio again, this time to recap my journey. The next morning I would bid farewell to this amazing place. I could fill yet another book with everything I saw, learned, heard, felt and experienced.

I then asked Julio to call the ladies who had helped me at the airport when I came in. The number he had for them was not a working number and there was no way to find them. He did not know who they were. *In utter disbelief, I wondered, were they angels that came to help me? The experience resembled other angel encounters I had experienced, and that was enough for me. I didn't question it further, just went into deep gratitude for them being there.*

This time the Lima airport was calmer, the lines and yelling people gone. I took a cab to the hotel Julio had recommended. It was nice but plain. I would only have a few hours there before my flight in the morning. I was planning to leave a day early so I could stop in Denver on my way home. I was going to make peace with Jack.

The next morning, I discovered that my flight was full and I couldn't get on. When I tried to return to the hotel, my cab driver wouldn't take me there. He wanted to show me better, safer ones. That scared me, so I told him I didn't have enough money for the extra drive. Hesitantly, he took me back. As he carried my bag into the office, people began jumping behind the counter, yelling, "Get down, take cover!"

The taxi driver pushed me behind the counter and pulled me down. We heard shots in the street. I had never heard that many shots all at once. When the noise stopped, and it was quiet for a while, people started crawling over to the windows to look out. Okay, all clear.

The taxi driver looked at me and said, "Good luck with your stay here, I told you it wasn't safe."

I don't think he even waited to be paid.

I checked back in and called Jack to say that I would be there the next day if I could get out. Then, alone in my room I started worrying. What if I couldn't get a flight? What would I do? I didn't have enough money to buy a ticket home, nor enough to stay.

The next morning, I left for the airport, this time with a night's prayers behind me. The ticket counter was packed. The flight was full, and I had to wait and see. How could the angels let me down now? My heart sank further with each name called for standby. Finally, I heard my name, and my body began to shake with relief as tears ran down my face. *Oh, these are the tears they told us about when we channeled. They were tears of joy. Thank you, thank you.* I wiped the tears off my face as I settled into my First-Class seat. Back to the United States!

I was able to stop in Denver for one night and then home sweet home. It still felt sweet even with all the troubles.

Back in everyday life, I got to see people's reactions to hearing that my trip was lovely. They saw the pictures of me with other people, so they knew I wasn't lonely there either.

Best of all, I still had one more ticket, at least one more opportunity to travel first class.

## Chapter 15

# A Love Meeting with Lessons

*"If you limit your choices only to what seems possible or reasonable you disconnect yourself from what you truly want and all that is left is compromise."*

**~Robert Fritz**

One Sunday in May when I turned on my computer, the Digital City Personals page popped up again. (This was the site where I'd met the man I waterskied with and had dinners the summer before. He had disappeared as fast as he had appeared during that fall.) I decided to look at some of the pictures and read some of the bios of the guys who signed up. As I clicked through the pictures I saw one guy sitting up straight with a suit on, nothing like my usual "type." The text said, "If you would like to learn more about this kind spirit, email me." *Okay, wise guy, I will.*

I wrote to him saying, "Okay, tell me," then went off to bed.

On Monday there was an email from him. Well, more like a short story! I immediately put him on my buddy list so I would know when he was online. I was just curious. He signed on, and when I finished reading, I sent him an instant message. We chatted briefly but as we both had things to get done, we planned to meet back online later that night. I got that exciting feeling that accompanies the possibility of a new friend while I did my evening chores and tried to get back to the computer without appearing too anxious.

He was there, waiting to start instant messaging again. I learned his name was Marty, the same name as my first husband and the father of my twins. I also found out that we only lived two freeway offramps apart. We talked about our likes and dislikes, things we enjoyed doing, all the preliminary information you exchange when you first meet someone. Before our goodnights, he asked me if I had a picture of myself online. All I had was the picture of me on the website for the motorcycle club, so I told him he could look there.

Tuesday night after work started the same way. Instant messages about our day and our lives and a discussion about the picture of me by my motorcycle, which was very different from the "motorcycle mama" he had imagined. I typed faster than he did, so soon he gave me his number and I called him. As he tells the story, "Here is this fast-typing, motorcycle-riding person who goes to nudist resorts, calling with a very soft *hello* on the telephone. He asked himself, "Is this really the same person?" To hear him tell the story is pretty funny.

We talked way past my bedtime, so I gave him my work number and told him he could call me there. By two the next afternoon he had called and asked me to dinner. I said yes, but he'd have to wait until seven when I got off work. He said that was fine, then we began the where-do-you-want-to-go dance everyone goes through. I was busy and didn't have a lot of time to discuss it. All I knew was I wanted something good that was between my place and his. So, out of my mouth popped IHOP.

"You mean the International House of Pancakes with the blue roof?" he asked.

Yep, that was it.

There was silence on the other end for a moment, then he said quietly, "Are you sure?"

Yep, I was sure, pancakes and peanut butter with milk sounded very good. Okay, then IHOP at about seven-thirty. With the flutters in my stomach and questions running through my head I went back to work.

It wasn't long before the telephone rang again and he was asking me if I was *sure* I wanted to go to IHOP, because he would take me anywhere I wanted to go. I finally convinced him that I indeed desired IHOP.

When I once again returned to work, I told one of my long-time clients all about this internet meeting and that I was going to meet him in person. After a few jokes, her closing words were, "Does he have a router? If you don't like him pass him on, someone else will."

I was already starting to like him, albeit cautiously. When we spoke on the phone I had been very up front and hoped he was too. I asked him if he was open to going to a nudist resort. He told me he was, that he was born naked and been that way all his life when he takes his clothes off. I told him about being a sexual abuse survivor and that I would not date anyone who had not read Grant Cameron's book, *What About Me? A Guide for Men Helping Female Partners Deal with Childhood Sexual Abuse.* He told me to bring it and he would read it. We talked about past relationships, present feelings about relationships plus what we were willing to ask for and how we felt. I talked about my daughter and granddaughters and that my stepdad was living with me. He told me about his six (yes, six!) children, one of whom was only six years old. I had vowed to never date anyone with children under eighteen.

Before I knew it, it was time to start heading over to IHOP. I drove there like I knew what I was doing. Looking back on it now, I have no idea what helped me do this. Where was I going to tell Jack I was? Then I turned into the parking lot and saw this cute guy standing at the back of his car just waiting for me. Hmmm, not bad. Very polite, he walked over to my car door and introduced himself as I got out. But as we made small talk and walked into the restaurant I couldn't help but notice how short he was compared to Jack.

We sat down and started talking, and I soon found myself getting into the spiritual side of my personality. I then asked Marty if he would take a test. He gave me a curious look, but agreed. The test is about finding out what you want most out of life. I had just done it at a party with one of my teachers the previous Sunday. Happily, his answer was "Love" and mine had been "Trust." We agreed love and trust in a relationship was a pretty good place to start.

When I ordered my pancakes and peanut butter, the look on his face was priceless. How picky can one person be? Oh, well, I didn't care; this is me and this is what I like. With eating and talking, the evening went by fast and I was amazed at how comfortable I felt. When we got to the car he gave me a soft kiss on the cheek. Hmmm, I liked that feeling and hadn't felt it for some time. As I floated home, thinking and not thinking, I knew in the back of my mind that I had to deal with Jack. I had been missing for a whole couple of hours, plus he would say I was keeping him up too late. Then again, if he wanted to rag on me he could stay up all night. He had done it many times before.

That night, after I dealt with the necessities of life and Jack, I ended up on the telephone with Marty again. He made an appointment for me to cut his hair the next day and said he would take me to lunch. Luckily, this was a slow week so I had time to go. I didn't tell anyone at work, but when he walked in with a little bag in his hands I could feel all eyes on us. He handed me the bag and, oh, how precious, an aromatherapy candle and the stand for it. That was a wow from him, as was how good looking he was.

As I shampooed his hair and started cutting, I realized I was quite nervous. I had learned that his first wife was also a hairdresser, and suddenly felt my shop was somehow inadequate. I also knew of some of the places he had lived, and they were expensive places. I could tell from the way he was dressed that he was not used to lower-class salons. At that time, I felt like I just couldn't live up to this man. Somehow I made it through the haircut, thinking that it had turned out well only because he had beautiful hair.

Then it was time for lunch. I felt weak in the knees as I turned to tell Vicki, the salon's owner and a friend of mine, that I was going out, because everyone was watching and when he dumped me I would have to explain it to them. I gave him the book on sexual abuse survivors and he told me he would read it. When we got to his car I realized that it wasn't an expensive car and maybe I was good enough, plus we were away from all those eyes. We went to a sandwich shop and though he was not a smoker, we sat outside so I could have a cigarette after we ate.

As we walked back to his car he put his arm around me. Then, as we stepped off the curb, he kissed me. Wow. He opened and closed my door for me, then walked around, got in, turned and looked me in the eyes, and kissed me again, again and again. Oh my God, I was in heaven; the feelings that were running through me were unbelievable.

When I got back to work, everyone was dying to ask questions. I didn't care, I had my wows and they could say anything they wanted.

That night when we talked on the phone Marty told me he had read part of the book. I told him there would be no sex until he read it all. He laughed and told me to hang up so he could go read. We laughed and kept talking for quite a while. What had happened at lunch and how we felt were the big topics.

I had to deal with my alone thoughts the next night because he had an appointment after work and would be late. My doubts started, but at least I could deal with Jack and not have to be afraid Marty would call. It was late when he finally signed online. Our conversation was short, but we made tentative plans for Friday night. He would come over and look at my computer, which I had been having a problem with, and I would color his hair.

Can a day be long and speed by at the same time? Trust me, it can. On the way home on Friday, I picked up a pizza. Loni wanted in on this, so she asked if we would bring my pizza over and eat with them. While I was on the phone with her, Marty drove up. Suddenly I felt that wow again. I walked over to the car window, leaned in and kissed him without even thinking about it. I told him the new plans and we got Grandpa and went to Loni's. That night went well but I knew Loni didn't like whatever she was feeling.

After dinner we came back to my house to do his hair and work on my computer. Upstairs, with hair color in hand, I asked him to take his shirt off so it wouldn't get stained. He did, and that's when the fun started. As he sat before my computer with the color in his hair, we relaxed, laughed, talked, and I rediscovered feelings I hadn't felt in a long time. Then it was time to lean him over the bathtub to wash the color out. The kissing started as I dried his hair, and by eleven o'clock we were joking about being in our fifties and waiting for my stepdad to go to bed so we could continue.

When Grandpa went to bed so did we. I had never had feelings like this. I had never made love so gentle, kind and yet with so much emotion. It was the most amazing feeling I had ever experienced.

The next day I had a motorcycle ride, and though my heart wasn't in it, I knew it would serve me well. The biggest reason I ride is to be alone with myself, think and let the answers flow through me. That day what went through my mind was all that had happened the previous night – every word, feeling and touch were with me. It was all I could do to make it through the day so I could go home, call him and make sure he still felt like he did when he walked out of my house in the middle of the night.

Yes, he still felt that way and was waiting for me to come over as soon as I was ready. And boy was I ready; I wanted to see if this was all real. I wanted to experience that feeling again if I could. Walking into his apartment was an experience in itself. It was the neatest, cleanest man's place I had ever been in. Everything had a place and it was there. He showed me through it and apologized that it wasn't more. But we had talked about his last divorce and giving everything to his ex-wife or selling what they couldn't keep. His closet made me want to laugh. All his shirts ironed and hanging, his dress slacks all hung by the cuff with the shoes to match under them. I thought, this man will never be allowed into my closet. Then onto the more serious stuff. Yep, after a couple of beers, some chips and talking for a few hours we found out the feeling was still there. Wow, was it there. Where could this all go? Was he for real? Could I now feel safe with a man?

On Sunday I had a big charity ride to put together so off I went. Couldn't wait to get home and change so I could go to his house again and make sure things were still the same. Yes, they were.

Each night that week was the same, except on Thursday night, as we were lying there after making love, I heard Marty say something to himself. When I asked him what he had said, he replied, "Oh, nothing." What I thought I had heard was something like, "Why people can't just let other people live their lives?" My instant thought was, *Is he bisexual? My next thought was, Scratch that. No way could this man be bisexual. I must be making something out of nothing.*

Friday night I had a pedicure and thought I was getting ready for the weekend. I knew he had his daughter, but I didn't know that meant not seeing me. He came over on Saturday but was very distant. After the two of them left I was totally confused and down on myself for falling for all of this. It was Memorial Weekend and I was spending it alone. The one saving grace was that it was a full moon.

After getting a very confusing email from him I decided to go to the labyrinth. (A labyrinth has a circular path running clockwise to the center from the entrance. You will use the same path to walk out as you did to walk in. They are calming, as they slow you down while you wind your way through the path, usually in some type of meditation.) I was hoping there wouldn't be many people, because I just needed to be alone. I got my wish; no one else was there and I lay in the center of the labyrinth all alone for about an hour, just looking up at the moon and talking to myself. It was peaceful. I was peaceful. That was surprising, considering all that was going on inside me with Jack and now Marty.

Marty and I didn't speak all weekend, but we did exchange several emails that I found very confusing. By Monday I had had enough.

*I don't know what's up,* I wrote him, *but it's not my job to judge. Tell me so I can understand.*

He told me he was going out of town for the evening but would write later. Sure enough, I got an email that said, "I need to talk to you."

I thought, *Okay, talk to me.*

We agreed that he would come over on Tuesday. When he arrived a friend was there working on my computer, and Marty seemed anxious as he waited for us to be alone. Finally, my friend left and we moved to the bedroom to talk.

By this time the air between us was heavy with anticipation. I curled up on the bed stacked with pillows, and he nervously sat down on the side. With a very solemn look on his face and his eyes glassy with tears, he said, "There is something I need to tell you about me before we can go on with this relationship."

Even as my stomach turned, I thought, *What could be so bad?*

"Okay, what is it?"

He just looked at me and said, "I am a crossdresser."

Remembering my thought the other night, I asked, "Are you bisexual?"

"No, most cross-dressers are heterosexual."

I took a breath. "Sooo, what is a crossdresser then?"

He started to explain but I don't really remember what he said or how much of it I understood. All that mattered in that moment was the realization that the rotten things I had been thinking about myself all weekend weren't true. He wasn't dumping me, he didn't hate me, he didn't think I was beneath him; in fact, it wasn't me at all. *Like everything I had been learning for the past seven years, the way people react to you isn't about you; it is about the feelings inside them.*

I told him that before I made any decisions I wanted to see how this played out in his life. We set a date for Friday night for him to dress for me. I told him I wanted to see the whole thing, from start to finish. My God, growing up in San Francisco with all the gay people and having gay friends, how did I not know about crossdressers?

The night ended with him staying for hours, making love and just holding me. He was so soft and gentle, and the feelings inside me were unlike anything I had ever felt before. The main feeling was safety; in fact, I think that was the first time I'd ever really felt safe with a man. I was also experiencing an incredible sense of peace. *Had I healed my molestation issues? Was it his softness that allowed me to feel safe?*

The following day we called each other several times, I guess just making sure that the other was still there. He asked me to come over that night. He wanted to start educating me about crossdressers. Okay, fine, I can do that. He wanted to make sure I had enough information to decide for my life.

That night I went over to his house with the usual six-pack of Corona and bag of lime chips. When he opened the door our eyes met with the same look of awe we'd had before his big reveal. We couldn't get into each other's arms fast enough. Pop the beer and open the chips and just unwind and relax. Only tonight was the start of the rest of our lives together. This was truth time, time for each of us to go to the bottom of our lives and tell it like it was, or at least how we perceived it.

Marty started telling me how and why his other relationships had broken up. His first marriage had lasted for twenty years; the next one lasted for twelve. That one ended when his wife came home unexpectedly one afternoon and caught him dressed. After a couple months of counseling she just couldn't deal with all the what-ifs. His last relationship had ended over money; he didn't have enough to keep up with her lifestyle, plus she didn't like his dressing or that he had a small daughter that took up every other weekend. Marty gave me the abbreviated version of each story. All we had was a few hours and there was a lot to cover.

Then he took me to his computer and started showing me different websites on cross-dressers. I looked, listened and thought I got it. There was so much information and the old, slow internet connection took quite a while to load all the pages. It gave us time to talk. He told me that before getting online and finding these websites he'd thought he was the only one in the world who felt like this. The evening ended in bed, and I was once again in disbelief of how beautiful making love could be.

Thursday night, with Corona and chips in hand, we watched a movie called *All About a Woman*. In the film, a wife goes away with the children on a holiday and comes home early and finds women's clothes all over the apartment. Of course, she thinks her husband is having an affair, and without letting him explain, she divorces him. He moves into a flat and continues dressing, and then the landlady finds out. However, this woman doesn't desert him. They fall in love and experience many of the problems crossdressing couples face. It is a beautiful love story, and shows what dressers go through, the fears of being found out, why they lie about it, why they hide it, and many other things that I did not know I was going to eventually live.

Then it was Friday, only hours to go until my life would take a big turn, and I didn't even know it. I was only thinking of myself. It came from inside myself, my feelings about my body, my shame of it. Those issues from being molested. I had been a nudist for years and I was only now realizing how ashamed of my body I was. *Molestation survivors have a different reality of their body. Well, today was when I finally got everything they had been trying to tell me for months, years.*

I had to conquer this tonight, I decided. Little did I know how much Marty went through every time he dressed. I had no idea the stress he was under all day. All I had on my mind was my own stress. How was I going to tell him? How was I going to do it? The day went by quickly, too quickly. For the first time I didn't want the day to end.

As usual, I stopped at the liquor store but tonight I picked up a twelve-pack, rather than the usual six. As Marty opened the door and the eyes met, along with the smile and kisses hello we could feel the tenseness. We popped open our beers and walked to the bedroom.

As I turned the corner, I couldn't believe what I saw. His room, always so neat and precise, had turned into a messier version of Loni's room as a teenager. There were blouses, skirts, shoes, nylons and undergarments all over the place, and he had the most makeup I had ever seen outside a cosmetics department. I was so shocked and intrigued that for a bit I forgot my fear and what I was going to do. He started telling me what all this stuff was for, then began applying his base makeup. I just stood and watched, with no idea that all the talking was to cover up his fear and all the other emotions that go on inside a crossdresser as they dress. I watched some of the makeup go on, then whatever it is that makes them look like they had a facelift. I thought, shit, I want some of that.

After more makeup, he started putting on hip pads, nylons, and breast forms. That's when I asked how much all this cost. My God, if I could afford those I would have them too. Then my fear began to creep back in. His watchful eye saw this and right away he said, "What's wrong? Do you want me to stop? Are you alright with this? I will stop if you want."

He was so concerned that I was okay with what he was doing. Like me, he had no idea of the stress I had been under these last few days. I convinced him it wasn't him, but me. He walked over to me, put his arms around me and quickly pulled back.

As I looked up at him, he asked, "Is it okay if I touch you?"

"Of course, why wouldn't it be?"

Looking down, he said, "Well, I'm dressed."

I put my arms around him. "So?"

I thought he was going to cry, but I didn't have time to deal with his feelings because mine were screaming.

I started telling him some of what had been going on with me. How sexual abuse survivors are about their bodies – either very open or very closed. I told him that while he was dressing I was going to undress. That his fear was about dressing the way he wanted, and my fear was about being undressed, naked and exposed in a relationship.

He laughed and said, "But you are a nudist, aren't you?"

I tried to explain how, number one, that was before I had dealt with the molestation issues. That was before Jack did all the things he did the night I found out about being molested. The torture of having him screaming at me while I was huddled on the couch. That the nudist resort had a story of its own and was different from what I was doing now. Getting naked to have sex was different than right now. Everything was different than right now. I was going to be naked, walking around or sitting, whatever we were going to be doing, just naked. That would be the ultimate judgment time. That was the most fearful thing I had to face.

By now I just wanted to run out crying and never come back. But I couldn't show him that part of me. That would be too ridiculous. Oh, why had I told him? Now I couldn't back out.

There was sincerity and caring in his eyes but not understanding of what I was saying. I wasn't sure I even understood what I was saying.

To break the tension, I guess, he very nonchalantly said, "Well I guess you better take something off because I am ready to put my skirt on."

Obediently I took off my blouse as he put his first skirt on. He then changed out of that one and put on another, then another until he ran out of skirts and had to pick one. Then it was time for blouses – the same thing, try them all on. Nothing really looked good enough for him. I didn't really notice what a hard time he was having because I was so engrossed with my own pain. Likewise, he didn't notice my problems because of his.

*This is how most of life is, we believe others are noticing everything we are doing. Most people are so engrossed in their own problems they don't even notice ours. If they do notice, usually it is forgotten quickly, as they go back to their lives.*

Then somehow, he was totally dressed, in high heels, wig, makeup, skirt, blouse, and jewelry. It was truly amazing. What was even more amazing, though, was that I was standing there naked. How did that happen? We stood there for a moment just staring at each other, then he took me by the hand and led me out to the living room, saying how hot it was in the bedroom.

"You have a beautiful body," he said as he sat me down on the sofa, "and you have nothing to be ashamed about." Then he flashed me a smile and said, "You don't know what I would give to have your body."

I smiled back and said thank you, then told him how amazing he looked. And I meant it. Yes, it had taken him almost two hours to do it, but the results were amazing nonetheless. I mean, he was actually *stunning*.

Soon the compliments going back and forth turned to tears. For a while we just talked and had our beer and chips, neither of us able to believe the safety, vulnerability, softness, kindness we felt. Holding hands, rubbing legs and little kisses led him to start to undress as well, then we were back in the bedroom and there was no turning back. At one point I opened my eyes and saw the wig and blue eye shadow and, yes, it was a shock. Then that feeling of peace came over me and I knew I could do this. I knew what was under the wig and eye shadow and I wanted it.

*This was another experience when I consciously acknowledged how we make life decisions in a split second. In a split second our life can change forever.*

This began my journey of being with a crossdresser, though at the time I didn't know it was going to be a journey. We had a great weekend together, though it brought up feelings and questions inside me that I couldn't even begin to understand. Where to go for these answers? I decided I would go to my gay friends. I told myself they would understand.

That's when I learned that some gay people are just as prejudiced against crossdressers as straight people are. This was an eye-opener. How can people who are judged so harshly turn around and do the same to others? I believe that this is how people make themselves feel better. *Mark was right when he told me there will always be someone in your life to help you learn lessons. This was huge. Mark was also right when he said, "When things upset you, it is because you have those same issues within you."*

Right again, Mark.

Like everyone, I had my own prejudices and always believed they were justified, but now I realized, what right did I have to judge anyone? *Again, the lesson comes to me. I didn't know what made me do things, so how could I possibly know why someone else does what they do?* The more I thought and talked about Marty, the stronger my feeling of protection for him grew.

That said, most of my gay friends were understanding. Some questions they could answer, others they didn't even understand. They had been asking some of these questions of themselves their whole lives.

A much larger lesson was about to begin, however. What straight people did I trust enough to talk to about this? Who are my real friends? Trust! That is what I wanted most when I took the test I gave Marty on our first date. If trust is what sparks the spark in me then where is the real lesson? How trustworthy am I? Now I was back to judgement. Shoot, this is one of those vicious circles I live in.

The responses were certainly interesting whenever I found someone I thought I could trust with my new secret. It was a secret that I shared with the millions of crossdressers in the world. Yes, millions. At the end, *Just Like A Woman* revealed a statistic: one in nineteen men cross-dress in some form. At any given time you may be sitting next to one of them. Once, while Marty and I were talking about it, I quipped, "I'll bet that Dave from down South who I went waterskiing with is a crossdresser." Suddenly, such a notion seemed possible. Dave shaved his body, though he said it was because he was a jogger.

I was amazed by how many people, upon hearing my secret, revealed that they too had a crossdresser in their life. In this way it was similar to when I had told people about the sexual abuse I had endured. On the other hand, there were some who were much more judgmental about the crossdressing, and my acceptance of it. The lesson here was how many of my friends I couldn't tell or trust and why. It was a true weeding out process, though it wasn't long before the need to tell others faded away and our "secret" just became part of our lives.

Every evening Marty and I would spend hours just talking. He was excited just to have someone to open up to. As our love, acceptance, and trust grew, I realized I was the only person in the world who knew the real Marty, and he knew the real me as well. We could tell each other things that neither had ever been able to tell anyone else. We could laugh, cry and make love without any judgements. And yet, we were both afraid that one day it would end, and we clung to each other with almost a passion that bordered on desperation.

This was so different from how Jack and I had talked about our lives. My own stories seemed to somehow change from all doom and gloom to more of "this is what happened." I could even appreciate some of my stories. The big pain was no longer there, and it made me see, perhaps for the first time, how much I had grown.

Even with all of this going on, I was still having my nightly fights on the phone with Jack. One night on my way home, we were in another heated discussion when he said, "If I find out you are seeing someone

## A Love Meeting with Lessons

else, I will never talk to you again." Then he hung up. I never called him back and he never called me either. After decades of pining for him, after all the ups and downs and attempts to hold things together, our relationship ended in the blink of an eye. It was surreal, yet not painful in the least. Finally, life became peaceful, if at a chaotic pace.

One day, Marty expressed his fear that his crossdressing would eventually break us up. I said, "I'm not afraid of your dressing breaking us up, it's the other stuff."

Very surprised, he asked, "What other stuff?"

I shocked myself by saying, "Oh, money, seven children, thirteen grandchildren, jobs, our past, our differences, just to name a few."

Honestly, I don't think he got that. He just couldn't see where any of this would matter as long as I accepted his dressing. I didn't understand why crossdressing would be the deciding factor of whether our life worked or not. It took many nights of talking about what it might mean to us, and even then neither of us knew how much we had to learn.

One night, he found out that most of his children knew about his crossdressing. He was relieved, but also felt all the other emotions of fear, guilt and anger at how they had found out. But there was too much going on to dwell on it for long.

Our life was one excitement after another while at the same time, like most new couples, we just wanted to spend as much time as possible wrapped in each other's arms. But we were now entering the big time. We were going to a crossdressers meeting. Yes, they had clubs and meetings.

That Saturday night we were both very anxious. By the time I got to his place, he was pretty much dressed. I took one look at him and thought again that he was so much better than me, had better clothes, looked better and, shoot, what was he doing with me? All my self-esteem issues were raging. I always felt self-conscious when we went out and he was in "Guy Mode."

Yes, that was part of their vocabulary: Girl Mode, Guy Mode; I was now a GG (Genuine Girl). I told myself I would deal with my esteem issues some other time. Tonight, we were going out.

I drove because of my fear of him being stopped, as had happened to the guy in the movie. When we got to the restaurant he was a wreck and I couldn't believe how someone could want to do this so badly and still be so scared. And besides, we were going to a place where there were others. Finally, we went in and were seated for dinner. They were so nice to "her." It was just so normal, like being out with a girlfriend. There was a closeness created through that dinner that neither of us recognized at the time. As I looked up and down this table of about twenty women, I couldn't tell whether some of them were the wives or men. When I quietly asked him who was whom, he confirmed that they were all men. I was the only GG there! Most of them were all dressed up and probably looked better than me. After dinner we were going to go upstairs to dance, but it wasn't open yet. First, we would have drinks at the bar.

As we walked across the floor, Marty asked, "Jeri, what do you want to drink?"

I told him, then sat down at a table. There was a certain awkwardness as he got the drinks, because now "he" wasn't the man on the date. "He" was another girl out for the evening. If I was out with a girlfriend I wouldn't go sit down and tell her my order and take it for granted that she would pay. But those thoughts were pushed aside quickly.

As I sat down, some ladies from dinner walked up and one asked, "Do you ride a motorcycle?"

My heart sank. Who from the motorcycle club comes here? At the same time my thought was, *Well, if they are dressed like this they won't tell anyone either.*

I searched the face to see if I saw some familiar feature, something recognizable.

"Have you been waterskiing lately?" she asked, then, "Have you been down South lately?"

By then Marty had brought our drinks to the table and sat down. After listening to the conversation for a few moments he said, "It's Dave." He had pieced together that this was the Dave with whom I had gone waterskiing and to dinner the summer before. I was still looking at the face, trying to recognize something.

She says, "Yes, it's Dave, better known here as Linda."

Oh, my God. My thoughts and feelings were not deciphered until later, but first, I realized that it wasn't my fault I had never heard from him again. He had simply been hiding his secret.

I heard Marty say in his deep male voice, "Sorry, bud, you are too late. She's mine now."

Stunned into silence, I leaned over and hugged him, catching his wig on my glasses and almost pulling it off.

Dave went on to say that he had come close to confiding in me a few times, as he figured as a hairdresser I would be more open-minded than most, but in the end fear had won out. He also said he had thought about me many times and just couldn't contact me. How sorry he was now that he hadn't! I assured him that I understood.

Then Marty and I shared with him the abbreviated version of how we had met and the way Marty had revealed his secret to me.

Dave waited until we went upstairs to dance, then finally asked me if he could email me. I told him that would be fine because Marty and I had a very open relationship and we didn't control whom the other talked to. He did write and apologized again for not reaching out earlier. He also made it clear that he would never infringe on my current relationship but if there was a chance for us in the future he was more than open to it.

I learned a couple of things through my interaction with Dave. First, I learned that Dave's earlier disappearance, which had triggered my self-esteem issues and abandonment issues, was not about me at all, but about his own fears. Second, though my relationship with Marty was most important and nothing or anyone would come between it, I realized I still needed to look at and work on other feelings that rose inside me around trust, commitment, openness, love, money, and fidelity, to name a few.

The concept of faithfulness in particular loomed large, as it had been an issue throughout my romantic life. I had cheated and been cheated on, and now I needed to take a deeper look at those relationships. When I did, I came to a knowing that somewhere along my path whatever had driven me to be unfaithful had evaporated, and that I could never be unfaithful to Marty, ever. I also realized that I could never know what had made others be unfaithful to me.

I recalled again Pat's words to me when I found out about his affairs: "Jeri, this has nothing to do with me not loving you or wanting to hurt you, it has to do with my insecurities."

Boy, I hadn't believed that one! Now I did, though, which was proof that a deep healing had in fact taken place, apparently without my realizing it!

Finally, I also began to see how much these men have to sacrifice just to be who they are, Crossdressing was, and still is, misunderstood and shunned by the larger society, which drives people to live secret lives. This made me think about other kinds of biases as well. Discrimination against any human being hurts all human beings. Who or what gives anyone the right to choose what is wrong or right for another?

*This was my first introduction to the fact that when one gains their rights, another (or perhaps many people) will lose their right to their belief.*

I began to see why Marty got emotional when he saw homeless people, disabled people or anyone less fortunate than him. He deeply felt the pain of anyone who was different or who was ostracized by others, especially people who could not hide their supposed "flaws" the way he did. He knew this pain well, as he had also been wounded by several people with whom he had been close but turned on him as soon as they found out about his dressing.

He also took great issue with the double standard for men and women with regard to dress. This was when he told me about the book he wanted to write, called *Who Said?* Who said women can wear either men's or women's clothes, but men can only wear men's clothes? Who said women are the only ones who look better wearing makeup or are supposed to enjoy having facials, manicures and pedicures; getting their hair done; or wearing vibrant colors? Look around any men's department, he'd say, and you'll see the only choices are black, brown, gray, blue and darker shades of green. How would women feel if that were their only choices? Things were getting better, but there was still a long way to go.

Hearing his perspective led me to contemplate the things we all do in order to fit in and be accepted. Yes, for crossdressers, the line is very clear, for others not so much. The pressure to conform to societal norms can be as subtle as it is intense, and we often don't realize how much we are compromising ourselves until it shows up as depression, a feeling of being trapped, and even physical issues.

One night as we walked into the house from a weekend class, the phone rang. In the class, Marty had written and worked on being closer to his children. The call told him that it had all been taken care of, completely out of his control. How life changes so quickly! It was a big lesson that we only think we are in control of our lives. *Another big lesson is how working on issues inside us creates change on the outside.* Working on issues in classes or just going truly within changes the energy between people and experiences. Not only for the good, but when we have bad thoughts about someone or something they get it energetically. They may not know how or where it is coming from but there will be some type of change.

In the coming weeks and months I attended more dinners with Marty's crossdressing club – in fact, I was the only wife or girlfriend who ever went which in their eyes made me just about the greatest person on earth. Each time, I got to know a bit more about their experiences. I learned how young these men were when they noticed they were different (sometimes as young as three or four!) and started living their lives undercover. I also learned how much they beat up on themselves for their differences. It made me even more protective of Marty and more determined to support him while he dressed; however, I had no idea of the impact this would have on my life or how much I had yet to learn.

Each day I would watch Marty unfold his life and his feelings. From the beginning I explained to him that he could not hide such a big part of himself without hiding a huge amount of himself in every other area of his life. That would be like trying to keep the smoke in the smoking section. It just could not happen. When one part of you is suppressed to that extent other parts of you have to be distorted.

One of these "distortions" is the tendency of these people to become overachievers. It's no accident that many crossdressers are judges, attorneys, teachers, architects, and corporate executives. Then there are those who go into the military or law enforcement because they're looking for ways to prove their manhood to the world, all while keeping their secret carefully under wraps.

While I was getting a crash course on crossdressing, both Marty and I were trying to figure out how to blend our very busy lives. As mentioned earlier, Marty had six kids – the youngest of which was only six years old – and twelve grandchildren! I felt like I was spending a great deal of time just trying to learn all their names and who belonged to whom. One day we all met at one of his sons' apartment to have lunch and swim. As Marty and I walked over to the common area pool, my mouth hung open in surprise. With spouses and kids, they numbered about twenty-five or thirty! I had said I was *never* going to date anyone with kids under eighteen. Was this one of God's bad jokes?

Determined to get to the bottom of this manifestation mystery, I went back over the list I'd made on Machu Picchu. What I had asked for was "someone who understands children, so they will understand my relationship with my daughter." Well, certainly having six kids would help one understand kids! But what about his six-year-old? Grown children were one thing, but she needed actual parenting.

I kept asking what I should do, and one day the voices answered, *Let her have her father.*

Okay, that would be easy. On the weekends he had her I would do my own thing. It would be like I had every other weekend "off." We also learned that when she and Marty had Friday night together after he picked her up the weekend went well. If on the other hand we tried to make it a threesome on Friday, the rest of the weekend did not go as smoothly. She needed her dad time. Okay, got it. Her weekend meant the whole weekend. Whenever my feelings of resentment or insecurity crept in I would just repeat to myself, "Let her have her father."

My daughter Loni was not happy about my seeing Marty, and hadn't been from the first night she met him. This was very worrisome to me, as Loni and her kids were the most important people in my life. After a rocky period, my relationship with Loni had been much better since Jack moved back to Denver. I had helped them buy a house a few blocks from me and we spent a great deal of time together. I wasn't willing to jeopardize that.

Realizing I had to do something to get her on board, I set up a family meeting at their house. Loni's fiancée started by looking at Marty and saying, "Marty, we just weren't ready for you. It has always been Jeri and us."

I got mad, Loni started crying and Marty became the mediator. I think we were all shocked when Loni suddenly fell into Marty's arms, crying, "Don't take my mom."

He gently explained to her that he wouldn't and couldn't ever take me away; he was here to enhance our lives the best he could. I was incredibly moved by his words, and figured the matter had been solved. My daughter has always been and will always be first in my heart and somehow, she had to know this.

As the weeks passed, we were still going between two households and working at putting together our lives. By the end of the summer he got out of his lease and decided to move in with Grandpa and me. He had plans to attend a wedding in Massachusetts so he moved his things in before he left.

The last day of his trip he kept calling and reconfirming that I loved him and wanted to be with him. I thought this was strange, but I was too excited that he was coming home to waste much time thinking about it. When I picked him up at the airport he was acting a little different but again I was excited. At home we got all ready for bed and then it happened. He pulled out a little box, got down on one knee by the bed and asked me to marry him... Surprise!

Of course, I would! Now we had our own wedding to plan while Loni was getting married in about three weeks. Talk about busy! For Loni's wedding present, we redecorated her kitchen in a weekend. We put our two households together, we took care of Grandpa, I got to know Marty's family and was still trying to understand this crossdressing part of our lives. We were riding motorcycles and going to a nudist resort. Everything was perfect, but those months were pretty much a blur.

Loni and her fiancée had done all the planning, and one of the things they decided was that her father and I would walk her down the aisle. I hadn't seen Gary in years, then suddenly there we were, standing in the back waiting to go down the aisle. He asked me where I got the breasts I had now, then told me what he would like to do with them and many other disgusting things he wanted to do with me. I was horrified and froze in disbelief. Thank God it was time to walk. He walked me halfway down the aisle and left me by a chair that I sank into while he went back to get Loni.

I saw his ex-wife Rita, her sister and her children sitting in the aisle in front of me. As I looked at them I went away mentally, thinking, What just happened? Why now after all these years? But this was a familiar activity for him.

Suddenly I realized Rita was talking to me. "Jeri, Jeri stand up."

Shaking, I stood up as Gary and Loni walked up to me. I took Loni's arm and we walked down the aisle. I didn't want to leave her, I wanted to protect her from him and I wanted her to hold me. Soon Marty was telling me to sit down.

The rest of the day was spent pretending I was fine, that's what survivors do – they never tell anyone.

With that behind me, my thoughts returned to my own wedding. Before we moved ahead with our marriage plans, I asked Marty to attend another of my weekend classes with me. He did not understand, and asked what I thought I saw in him that made me ask him to go. I told him a lot of anger, which he also didn't understand because he is the most easygoing person I had ever met. Indeed, he already possessed a lot of the knowledge that it takes many individuals years to acquire. It was one of the things I loved most about him. Ever since I'd started going to these classes, women had insisted that whomever they met would have to be involved with spirituality; however, I never really thought like that because, as the saying goes, "Being in a garage doesn't make you a car." In fact, I had seen quite a few men in these classes that I didn't think got it at all. Marty did get it, but that didn't mean he didn't have his own stuff to work on.

During that class he found out many things about himself, including where some of the anger came from. The experience brought us closer together. It was also when I decided I never wanted to be the recipient of that anger.

We set our wedding date for New Year's Day, 2000 to signify the beginning of a new millennium, century, decade, month, week and *us*. The wedding was amazing and magical, not only for us but for our more than two hundred guests. We managed to do it all very inexpensively: Marty cooked all the food, and friends chipped in with decorations, cake and even the DJ.

The day after the wedding we went to Reno for a four-day honeymoon. I told him that all I wanted was to go to dinner the first night as Mr. and Mrs. Roraback; after that I didn't care how much he dressed. At the time I had no idea what that meant to him. He could "dress" for three straight days.

When the hotel learned it was our honeymoon, they gave us a suite instead of a regular room – there was even a hot tub! When we walked into the room we could not believe the amenities: the biggest bed I had ever seen, huge television, sofa and table in one room, and the bathroom and dressing room around the corner.

We went to dinner that night as husband and wife, then it was party time. We did facials on each other, we did hair and makeup, and even dressed in different outfits he'd brought. This was truly a new adventure for both of us. I was so in awe of all of it that I didn't realize that he too was having a life-changing experience.

We also came face-to-face with a grave disappointment. When he was dressed we were no longer "husband and wife" in public, but two girlfriends out on the town. One night we went to the show at the casino, and as we walked past the slot machines and card tables, I turned around to kiss him but quickly stopped because I didn't want to draw attention to two women kissing. It was a sobering moment for both of us.

Much of our time, though, was spent in our suite enjoying life as a newlyweds. Making love for me was amplified to new heights on the second night when the voice in my head said, *It's okay, he is your husband.*

Suddenly I was flooded with mixed emotions. Part of me wanted to continue enjoying the moment, but the bigger part of me wanted to stop and go into myself to examine that statement. How could him being my husband make lovemaking better than it had been the last few months? Does one have to be married in order to make lovemaking okay? What about all the other partners I'd had? Did I really not enjoy them? What about the husbands and boyfriends I felt I "had" to make love to keep the peace? Was that sexual abuse? What had it done to me and my body? What did it mean when Marty and I made love while he had women's clothes on? What does it mean if I can make love to him as a man or a woman? And the big one: how come every time I think I'm okay, something comes that presents me with more questions than answers?

*Again, just like Mark told me, "There will always be someone in your life to help teach you your lessons."*

When we returned home, I decided to give up being president of my motorcycle club. I just didn't have the time now, with my new marriage, new large family, and work responsibilities. Plus, Marty wasn't really comfortable with the men in the club – he said they were too macho – and even when we rode with the club we kept to ourselves so he wouldn't have to interact with them. Eventually, we rode less and less.

We also began the task of painting, wallpapering and redecorating the upstairs. It was ours now and we were wiping out the energy and memories of past relationships that had been spent there. Decorating

## A Love Meeting with Lessons

our room led us to the hall, the other bathroom and two bedrooms. The upstairs became totally different.

Every time I walked downstairs I would say to myself, "Man, I wish we had the money to redo the downstairs too."

One day at work the lady who had given me airline tickets handed me an envelope with one more ticket in it. She said, "Some of my best memories of my husband were from our travels, so go make memories."

This solved my dilemma of what I would do with the one ticket I had left over from Peru. We could go somewhere together. The question was where? How? Marty, who was in printing, had been out of work for a few months and money was very tight.

I called him and asked, "If you could go anywhere in the world and money was no object where would it be?"

Immediately he answered, "Italy."

Okay, Italy it is. I had never really thought of Europe before because I was always a beach and ocean person, but now I began to get excited about sharing this new adventure with him. I told him about the ticket and we began looking into Italy.

At first, it was hard for Marty to forgo making reservations for each night. He had never been out of the country or traveled for recreation. With much persuasion I finally convinced him it would be cheaper and that we would be free to go where we wanted, when we wanted. I also told him about some of my past trips when I had flown by the seat of my pants and everything turned out great.

My only request was that I see the Swiss Alps. He wanted to go to Ferentino to see the town where his grandparents had lived, then on to Rome, Venice and wherever else we were inspired to go. Days of planning turned out to be in vain. Marty handed me a calendar and said, "Show me how we can do all of this and see the Alps in twelve or fourteen days."

I figured and figured only to finally say with disappointment, "Okay, then we will skip the Alps."

We didn't know how we were going to pay for everything, but we gathered up as much money as we could and set off.

On the way, we stopped in Atlanta to visit my cousin again. After spending the night and next day with her we got to the airport to find the flight was overbooked by forty-four people. The waiting area was full of nuns in habits, and we immediately realized that God was going to get them to Rome before us.

I looked across the aisle to see an empty area with a plane leaving for Stuttgart, Germany.

I asked Marty, "Do you know where Stuttgart is?"

No, he didn't, but he replied, "Bet it is closer to Italy than Atlanta."

I ran over and changed our ticket, and we boarded the plane to Germany. It was only after we were airborne that we saw a map of the location of Stuttgart. We were in First Class heaven, on a transatlantic flight with amazing food and service. The cabin crew even gave us a bottle of champagne to take with us on our second honeymoon.

After landing and collecting our luggage we found a room for the night and set off to explore Stuttgart. What a beautiful city to be in love in! We found we could take a train the next day to Milan. The energy of my prayers had worked! The train took us from Stuttgart to Milan up one side of the Alps and down the other. As we boarded the train it was snowing – the biggest, most beautiful flakes I had ever seen. We spent hours looking at the most majestic scenery I had ever seen, then ate the delicious food I had taken from the hotel buffet that morning. This was no ordinary continental breakfast, but a feast fit for a king. After we had finished eating, I filled another big plate with two big croissant sandwiches, hard boiled eggs, yogurt, cookies, muffins, fruit and anything else that looked good. Marty was mortified as I slipped them into my bag.

"What are they going to do?" I said, "Throw me out? I'm ready to leave anyhow."

Plus, on our way to the train, we stopped at the best chocolate store in the world. We had food for the entire day.

As we pulled into Milan I felt very uneasy but didn't know why. I trusted my intuition and told Marty, "I don't like it here and I'm not staying in this town."

Marty raised an eyebrow at me. "What? Then where are we going?"

I answered, "To Verona." One of my clients had told me about it and it was somewhere down one of those railroad tracks.

"Fine," he said, "you go exchange money, I'll get the tickets and we'll meet back here."

The Verona train station wasn't in the middle of the town, so we took a taxi to a hotel I found in our guidebook. We found that many hotels were sold out because it was Carnival week. I had to reassure Marty that I had never slept on the street before and wouldn't now. We eventually got a lead that paid off: a beautiful hotel that had just been renovated and hadn't had time to get booked up. Our room was so beautiful that I took pictures of the marble bathroom. As a bonus, it was much cheaper than anything we found in the book. We dined in a restaurant that had been a seven-hundred-year-old convent, then walked along the river in the moonlight. The next day we explored the quaint town and saw the Romeo and Juliet garden. Those days were magical to both of us.

Next, we were off to Venice. On the train we saw a newspaper headline saying something about two million people but we couldn't read the rest because it was in Italian. The book said when you walk out of the train station you will get your first glimpse of the Grand Canal. As we tried to walk out of the train station, we definitely could not see the Grand Canal because it was shoulder to shoulder people. We could not believe our eyes. Then the bits of information began making sense. Carnival. Oh, two million people. Somehow, it seemed like even more than that.

We shuffled along the passageways dragging our luggage, trying to work our way to San Marco Square. My eyes and mouth were wide open, watching all the costumes and people. We learned that every hotel within one hundred fifty miles was sold out and even one that far away was going to be about *four hundred fifty* US dollars! All the restaurants and business in town closed by two p.m. so I had to beg for one piece of what they called pizza for Marty, who was quickly losing his patience. Finally, he told me he was leaving and going back to Verona, that this was totally crazy. I wanted to stay and watch the party that night and soon found myself following him and begging him to stay. This was challenging, because in Italy they all have black hair so to pick him out of the crowd was not easy. To make matters worse the sun was setting and it was starting to get cold.

"Please don't make us go!" I kept pleading.

We pushed our way over the last bridge over the Grand Canal to find that the police had closed off the train station for crowd control and were diverting everyone around and down the next passageway. About three buildings down I stepped out of the crowd under some scaffolding to look back to what I could see of Venice.

Just then, a man came out of the hotel and asked me if I needed a room. What? A room? For how much? One hundred dollars if we paid cash.

I started yelling, "Marty, Marty, come back!" while telling the man, "Yes, yes!"

Again, it was a newly renovated hotel and a beautiful room. While I was in the bathroom, I heard the pop of the champagne we had been given on the plane. Marty handed me a glass, lifted his own, and said, "I don't know how you do it, but I am sticking with you."

After a couple of amazing days in Venice we boarded the train for Florence, which had a different type of beauty. On our second day there, a couple of Australians advised us to visit the Pitti Palace instead of going to Pisa, so that's what we did. We went through the palace and then out to the terrace and in the gardens.

As we walked up the hill on the side of the palace Marty grabbed my arm and asked, "Did you hear that?"

Yes, I heard it, galloping horses but there were no horses anywhere. We realized that it was from a past life many years before when we were young lovers galloping away on our horses. I was amazed at this first real experience of a past life together and felt an even deeper closeness. Even though Marty had no belief in or experiences of past lives, he knew in that moment that it was real.

Another day, we saw the statue of David and the beautiful art depicting different parts of the Bible. Marty explained the different interpretations of the Bible according to Christians, Jehovah's Witnesses and Orthodox. I learned more about the Bible that day than I ever had before.

Then we went to Rome, where we definitely did *not* have the most beautiful room. We saw the Trevi Fountain (which, to my disappointment was in the middle of the city; I had always believed it was in a beautiful park) and toured Vatican City.

One day, we had just gotten cash at an ATM when Marty was attacked by a woman with a baby and three little children. The little girls ran away quickly but they had taken Marty's money right out of his front pocket!

"How could you teach your little girls to steal?" he screamed at the woman.

He was so scary I was afraid we would be arrested. For the second time I decided I never wanted to be on the receiving end of his anger.

We continued walking and ended up at the Spanish Steps, where I was again disappointed. In all the pictures, the stairs were covered with potted plants and beauty. In person I saw none of that, just people in our faces trying to sell things.

We went back to our room to rest only to find the toilet overflowing. What a day! We lay on the bed and Marty gave me a choice: "Do you want to go to Ferentino to see my dead relatives or go to Massachusetts and see my live relatives?"

It was a no-brainer, we had seen enough of Italy. "Let's get out of here!"

Somehow, we had found the time to do everything on our wish list, including the Alps, and meet his family.

*Amazing how the energy works when one just goes with the flow.*

The next morning, we flew to New York, rented a car and drove to Massachusetts, where I met his perfect family with the perfect houses.

When we arrived home we settled into the busy routine of work, kids, riding bikes, and the ongoing discovery of all the sides of cross-dressing. On the days Marty "dressed" we would take off for the day before Grandpa got up, then Marty would sneak in after he was in bed.

On Memorial Day weekend we came home to find the living room ceiling hanging down with water dripping. Within days the insurance company had the walls torn out and the pipes fixed, or so they thought. Water was now dripping through the new fan and recessed lighting Marty had put in while the ceiling was out. Two and a half months later they jackhammered the floor to fix the pipes. Finally, the walls and ceiling were back, we had new paint, wallpaper and clean carpets. *The moral of this story is to be careful what I ask for, or at least to be more specific about it.* This was not the way I had intended for the downstairs to be updated.

We had a great summer and accomplished a lot. Marty was finally working and I was in the middle of writing my first book. But there was another adventure about to start.

I was excited when Marty joined me for another three-day class. At the end, the facilitator asked, "Jeri, when are you going to do something with all of the knowledge that you have learned the last seven years?"

My response: "Monday."

"Good!" she said, "and what are you going to do?"

"Go to hypnotherapy school."

"Great! Call me when you sign up."

The class was to be in about a month. Marty told me we would figure out how to pay for it as we went along. Of course, it all started falling into place. One of my clients announced that she had just signed up for hypnotherapy school – the same school and the same classes. We could share driving and rooms.

Within the next week, one of my longtime clients left me an envelope and told me to open it when I got home. What a wonderful shock! There was a check for three hundred dollars and an amazing solitaire diamond ring with a heart of diamonds around it that moved when your hand did. My happiness was short-lived as I remembered the day about twenty-five years earlier when I had first admired this ring. She had told me, "When I die I will leave it to you." Her gifting me the ring must mean that she was dying! I called her right away, and she told me she had cancer and wanted to keep her promise. She wouldn't leave me anything in her will; instead she was going to pay three hundred dollars a week to get her hair done until my school was paid for. Oh, how wonderful she was!

I was determined to study hard and do well in my course. As it turned out, school was so amazing that I couldn't wait for the next weekend to do more. And, as Marty had his daughter Karen every other weekend, I didn't feel like I was neglecting him.

Marty offered to help me with whatever he could. I had always been in charge of managing the money and making sure the household bills were paid, and I told him I could continue to do it.

He said, "You need time to study. I can pay the bills, so you don't have to."

My first thought was not to trust, but he was persuasive. Soon he was writing out the checks and keeping track just like I did. I watched, I checked, and I finally had to believe that we still had electricity, water and a place to live. I began to feel pretty good having someone who could take care of things and still love me.

Each weekend at school we did sessions on each other. Each session was eye-opening even after all the years I had worked on my issues. Using hypnotherapy, I found out so much more about myself than I had in the last seven years of classes. At the same time, I recognized that doing those classes and healing had helped open the doors for this.

In one of my sessions, I went back to when I was a small girl having my appendix out. I was on the operating table with Dr. Long standing over me and the nurses, who were nuns, trying to put the mask over my face. I was wiggling around, trying to get away from them and crying. Dr. Long was saying, "Don't let her do that, she can't get away, hold her down." I had then made the decision that *I can never get away, I can never do what I want and will always be held down.* I realized now that I had to change that decision. *The truth was, I could have what I wanted, I could get away, and no one was holding me down but me*. I began understanding how much I had held myself back throughout my life.

We did another session where I discovered why I never disliked being in the hospital. In fact, I kind of liked it, which of course people thought was crazy. I realized that at eight or nine years old, right after my dad had been killed, I was hospitalized. The nuns were going to move me out of my private room. I had them call my mother and she told them not to move me. *That day I concluded that the only time my mother was nice to me or stood up for me was when I was in the hospital. I was always looking for her to be nice to me. And later in life, it was the one place I could allow myself to totally let my guard down and let go. Someone would wait on me and I could sleep.* I knew I needed to find out how to relax without being in the hospital. My mother was dead, so getting affection from her was no longer an option. I was free to release this from my life.

It wasn't long before I concluded that hypnotherapy was my fate. I also realized that every other type of class I had taken, every process I had learned, incorporated aspects of hypnotherapy. One must be able to go into the subconscious and superconscious to get to the true healing. I completed my course and looked forward to working with others and helping them.

I was also looking forward to having my weekends free to spend time with my husband and enjoy life. Friday evening I came home from work to find Marty's daughter sitting on his lap. I had forgotten he had Karen for the weekend. I stopped in my tracks, then ran upstairs crying.

Marty followed me to the bedroom, took me in his arms and kept asking me what was wrong. All I could tell him was, "I don't know." And I didn't. What in the world had set me off like this? Why was I crying so hard? I had been feeling so good after completing my course.

Then Marty stepped back, put his hand over my heart and asked, "Why is your heart crying?"

I fell into his arms and sobbed, "Because she has the father I always wanted and never had."

Once the truth came out, we were able to talk about what I had missed and how he could help fill the gap. After a bit I felt better and told him to go back to Karen. He and I had a lifetime to work on this. I was aware and very grateful that working on some of my issues in school had allowed me to reach the right time for this healing.

I stayed upstairs to be with myself and look back on what I'd missed not having a dad. Although my stepdad loved me, it wasn't the same. Grandpa was always nice to me unless Mom was around and he was afraid to; he had also idolized Loni since the day she was born, though Mom kept them separated when she got jealous. He had lost a little girl during his first marriage years ago, so we were his kids, and we had grown even closer since he moved in with me.

No one can ever replace an absent parent, whether one losses them through death, divorce or just not being present. This short time by myself saved me, saved our marriage and helped me resolve issues with a stepdaughter more times than I can count. *Now I knew what the voice had meant when it told me to "Let her have her father."*

If there was one class I wanted to teach it was helping people who did not have a parent or parents. I also wanted to help couples blend children from different marriages, which can be a deal-breaker.

As mentioned earlier, there are at least four people in any relationship – you, the other person and both of your Inner Childs. Aspects of your parents are the also present, especially when that relationship is a marriage.

- Do you know who is talking with you and helping make your decisions?
- Do you know what your Inner Child wants?
- Does your partner know what their Inner Child wants?
- Are you aware of the role your parents or anyone else is playing in your relationship?

Our first year of marriage went by in a flash and we were looking forward to our first anniversary. On December 12, 2000, I was busy at work and planning for Christmas on a tight schedule. I had run out of the beauty shop to quickly get some lunch because Marty was too busy to bring me something. My phone rang as I was pulling out of a fast food drive-through. It was Marty asking me to give him a ride.

"I just totaled the car," he said.

I have been in totaled cars and was never in good enough condition to call for a ride back to work. As I drove to meet him, every accident I had ever been in ran through my mind. I worried about how badly Marty was hurt, what we were going to do with only one car, how much this was going to cost... and *could I have caused this by wishing we could get a new car?*

As I turned the last corner I could see the front of our car under a semi-truck, which it had hit head-on. Wide-eyed, my gaze shifted from the car to my love, who was standing there, dressed in black slacks and a black leather jacket. I flashed back to the movie we had seen the previous night about death, with everyone dressed in black. But he was alive and fine! I was relieved I ran up to him, wrapped my arms around him, and burst into tears.

Eventually, the logical part of me took over and I started finding out information and cleaning out the car. Soon the car was towed away, and we went to drop Marty back at work, but they already knew about the accident and had delegated his work to others. I sent him to the hospital and the chiropractor, then returned to the salon to finish my appointments. By the time I got home that night he was determined to go back to work the next morning. He even handled the insurance, which was another great relief. I had gone through it too many times with my own accidents and dreaded having to do it again.

I had always wanted to go to the Auto Mall and look at all the cars, and now we had the perfect excuse. On Christmas Eve day, instead of the usual last-minute shopping at the mall, we headed over there. We knew what cars we didn't want (although that isn't usually how to create what you want); we also talked about money, the year of the car, and the options we wanted. It was great to have someone to talk to and not fight – Merry Christmas, indeed! There was just one thing we didn't agree on: he wanted a brand-new car and I wanted one a year or two old so it would be cheaper. This was a departure from my usual self, as I was not known for frugality.

"Not more than fifteen thousand," I said, "That way it will be paid off in three years."

We left there with a pretty good idea of what we wanted, but as of yet no deal had been made. That night, I was gazing off into space when Marty asked "Where ya at?"

"I was just thinking about the Auto Mall and kind of in disbelief that we didn't find the car. I know that it is just sitting somewhere waiting for us because that is what they have told me."

"Who told you?"

"My angels that I channeled. They said, 'It is just waiting for you.'"

"Hmmmm," he said. "Honey, it just isn't time, we don't even have the money from the insurance company yet. It will happen, be patient."

The day after Christmas, as I drove to work, I thanked the Universe for a great Christmas, along with all the other things I thanked them for each day. Then I had had it. I wanted a great first anniversary and New Year's weekend and for me that meant having a new car to go away in.

While stopped at a light I closed my eyes and said, "Okay, angels, spirits and guides, I want this car and I want it now. I want the price, financing, year and the options I want, now, so show me what to do or where to go. Thank you."

When I opened my eyes again there in front of me was a new Chevrolet. My first thought was *No, we told you we didn't want a Chevy*. Then I noticed the license plate holder where the driver had bought the car: Daugherty Chevrolet.

When the light turned green and we started moving again, I asked, "Oh, is that where we are supposed to go to find the car?"

*Yes, go there. It is waiting for you.*

At the time I thought this was very profound, but between my hurry to get to work and my worries over not having the "perfect" first anniversary, I quickly forgot all about it.

At about five-thirty my love unexpectedly walked in the front door of the beauty shop and asked if I would get something to eat with him. I almost said no, as I was busy and then had to take Brittany to my cousin's in-laws, as she was going skiing with them the next day.

"Okay," I told him, "I'll go eat but it has to be quick."

Over dinner, Marty asked me if he had to go to my cousin's. No, I said; then I could stay as long as I wanted and he could go do his thing. With a sigh of relief, he told me that he wanted to go to a few dealerships and look at cars. The insurance company had called him during the day and made arrangements for him to pick up the check the next day at lunch.

That's when I remembered seeing the Chevy that morning and hearing that the car would be waiting for us.

When I told Marty, he said, "But I thought we didn't want a Chevy. "

We didn't but I couldn't ignore what I had seen and heard.

He gave me that look and said, "Okay, Jer, if I have time after I go to the Buick, Pontiac and wherever else I'll stop by Daugherty."

At ten p.m., after a wonderful visit with my cousins, I called Marty to tell him I was on my way home. He chuckled and said to hurry, because he had a story to tell me.

When I walked in I found him sitting at the computer, comparing prices. He turned around with this huge smile and said, "Come over here and hug me."

He started telling me that after going to the Buick and Pontiac dealerships he had decided to by Daugherty Chevrolet. After not seeing anything he was getting into his car and sort of feeling like a failure because he hadn't found what I was so sure was there. The salesman, in a last-ditch effort to make a sale, said, "I don't know how you feel about Mercurys, but we just bought that dealership and while they were doing the inventory they found three brand-new 1999 Mercury Mystics on the back lot."

Off they went to see these brand-new 1999 Mercurys. We even had our choice of colors.

Immediately, a rush of feelings rose up in me: disbelief, happiness, pride, and the ultimate *I told ya so*.

"Well, did you buy one?" I asked him.

"No, I wouldn't do that without you, you know that."

The next day Marty picked up the check from the insurance company and went to the dealership to start the paperwork. I would meet him there when I finished work.

I walked into the dealership to smiles and hellos from the salesmen. I listened for a bit and then went outside to look at the cars and have a cigarette. When I came back in they were about to sign. I looked at the papers on the table and asked, "Is that the price?"

The main closer at the table said with a smile, "Yes."

Out of my mouth came, "That's too much." Even Marty's mouth dropped. I looked the man straight in the eyes and said, "I'm not paying that much."

He started justifying the price, explaining all the options it had. I told him I didn't even want the leather seats. Back and forth we went. Finally, he looked to Marty for help. Marty just said, "If she says no, it's no." The salesman kept trying to convince me, but nothing he said helped.

Eventually he said, "How much will you pay?"

"Fifteen thousand out the door," I replied.

The figuring went on for a bit until he said, "I will have to make a phone call and see if they will lower it that much. I am doubtful."

By now it was pushing nine p.m., but there was nowhere I had to be. He left the room to call whoever, and returned a few minutes later with a surprised look on his face. The deal had been approved! All that was left was for them to wipe the sweat off their foreheads and for Marty to sign the new papers. The salesman wanted to know if there was anything else I wanted.

"Are you finished yet?" Marty asked. I wasn't; I ended up with cups, calendars and pens. I almost got us jackets!

When the paperwork was finalized, Marty drove off in his brand new 1999 automobile, a year old but never driven, for fifteen thousand dollars, and with financing that would be lowered even more later. We had gotten more extras than we had asked for or even knew we needed or wanted. Everything was perfect.

When we got home, Marty laughed and told me that when I had gone outside to look at the cars, the closer had told him how quiet his wife was. Marty didn't ask him later if he still thought so.

We drove down the coast to Santa Cruz for our first anniversary and New Years' weekend, so in love and having a wonderful time in our new car.

## Chapter 16

# The Magic of Greece

*Imagine that intention is not something you do, but rather a force that exists in the Universe as an invisible field of Energy.*

As our second year together began I was so happy that I didn't believe life could get much better. One evening we took Richard to dinner to thank him for giving me the airline tickets for our wonderful trips. At the dinner table he gave us an envelope with two more tickets. He told us I was the first one to ever thank him for these gifts!

I had always wanted to go to Greece and now with the new tickets from Richard, it was time. We started researching our journey and decided that the end of September or first part of October would be perfect, as that was the end of the high tourist season and prices would drop accordingly. We soon had the tickets in our hands and the excitement was building.

In the meantime, we were looking forward to a very busy summer – with few exceptions, every weekend from April to October was planned. I was finishing my hypnotherapy certification and was excited about starting my own practice. There was so much to do that it left little time to really think about the trip except an occasional check on the internet to find out facts and dream.

From the start, the main teacher's goal was to get me to quit smoking. He had tried many times in class sessions and it never worked. Before I finished school, he suggested we do a private session. We scheduled it for a Saturday night, then had to postpone when I got sick. In the meantime, I went to a friend's house and we did a little session on me. I was told, *The pain is your stuck power.* I then asked for more power to complete my dreams. *Why,* they said, *would we give you more power? You haven't used what we gave you already.*

Well, that was an eye-opener!

I remembered that my mom had gone many times to psychics and anyone she could find to tell her how to be happy. But she never did what they told her to do.

Oh man, I am just like my mother!

*Take a minute to think about your life. Do you use all you have within you to be happy and to have what you dream of? Very few of us use all of our potential. We can come up with more reasons not to do what we want than reasons and ways to get what we want. Now, write down a dream you have. Make two lists, one with the reasons you use to not get what you want, the other list with all the reasons you believe you are doing what it takes to get your dream into reality. Which list is longer?*

The next weekend, the teacher was determined to get this session done. I was sick again, but he went ahead with it anyway. That session went nowhere. Back to my girlfriend's I went. I was so sick that I made the two-hour drive back to Sacramento and could only remember a couple of minutes of it. My back was killing me, and at midnight I went to another friend's house, hoping she could ease the pain. As she put her hands on my back, she said, "This isn't your back, it is your gall bladder, and I am calling Marty." I remember hearing sirens and knowing they were coming for me. I heard Marty's car pulling up as the EMTs were getting ready to transport me to the hospital.

Yes, it was my gall bladder and it needed to come out. I spent the next few days rushing to move my schedule around and getting things ready, and stressed out because Marty had a hernia surgery in a couple of weeks.

A few days after my surgery two friends came over to help with my healing in any way they could. As we did a healing ceremony I heard, *Do not mourn the loss of a body part but rejoice in the rejuvenation of your life.*

Okay, I shall rejoice in my life and carry on through these next few months until our vacation.

After finishing school with all my requirements and becoming a Certified Alchemical Hypnotherapist, my next step was to take advanced classes and assist in other classes. I loved every minute of it.

In one of the advanced classes, on Inner Archetypes, the teacher decided to try another smoking cessation session on me, as an example for the other students. Again, nothing happened. He sent me back to my seat and started with someone else.

As I was sitting there watching, my body began to shake. I started sweating and crying. The teacher looked at me and asked, "What is going on?" In that minute I had an incredible epiphany about the hold smoking had over me.

Back in 1981, I'd had surgery on my nose so I could breathe properly while SCUBA diving. Before that operation I had been hypnotized to stop smoking. As I was coming out of anesthesia, my then-husband was telling me that President Reagan had been shot, along with White House Press Secretary James Brady and Secret Service Agent Tim McCarthy. Four months later, we'd had a big auto accident on Interstate 80 and I was revived while lying on the hot pavement. A couple of weeks later my nephew was threatening to commit suicide because he had been in an auto accident that day and one of his friends had been hurt. My takeaway: *I had put together a story that if I quit smoking everyone would die.*

After that realization, I also looked at that car accident on Interstate 80 more deeply. I remembered that as the car was skidding down the freeway on its side, I had a vision of my dad surrounded by the brightest light I had ever seen, with his arms out for me to come to him. As I was about to run to him a vision of Loni stepped in front of me. "No," she said, "you can't take my mom." I knew I couldn't go because I had to stay for my daughter.

Was that one of those Near-Death Experiences I had read about? Was that what it was like to choose not to go? I needed to know more about this.

I still had so much to learn, but as the summer drew to a close, my primary focus was on our upcoming trip to Greece. My friends I channeled with came to visit and after a snack and some small talk, it was time to get serious. We started our visions for each other. Of course, I wanted to know about Greece and what was in store for me there. They had done this before I went to Peru and much of it had come true.

The other pressing topic was the kind of business I should work on creating. Information on both was coming through each of them as we took turns channeling. The color of the inside of the business should be peach instead of my original pink, one of them said. She went on to tell me how much better peach goes with skin tone, how much softer and peaceful the color is. The business should be closer to my home instead of in the part of town where I now worked. Then they went on to Greece. The other friend saw a big crystal coming out of the sea as an activation for me.

Our excitement grew as our trip plans progressed. Then came September 11, 2001, the day that would change me and the rest of the world forever. I watched in disbelief as the second plane flew into the South Tower. Thousands of thoughts all at once and no thoughts at all. I knew I had to get ready for work and go out into the world as usual, yet there was no usual any longer. Finally, in my car on the way to work the most important thought was, how can anyone hate so much? What is there in life, in anyone's life, that is important enough to justify killing thousands of unknown people? How can sisters choose to not talk to each other because of their differences? In the whole scheme of things, what can be so important? These questions and others would continue to consume my thoughts for days, but as was so often the case, the answers continued to elude me.

The next night, a Wednesday, I had planned to be with my friends from hypnotherapy school, to do a session on my feelings toward Marty's former wife. Because this was a concern for both Marty and me, we decided that he would be present for the session. I wanted to know why I felt so controlled by her and why Marty was always saying "the right time will come" with regard to various things concerning the ex and their little daughter.

Most of the session was on a past life the three of us had shared. My memory started with us in Venice, Italy. I was crouched down in the bottom of a gondola covered with a blanket. His ex-wife, who thought she was a princess, walked up to the gondola and found me and put me in jail. She thought I had taken her baby, but I hadn't. Marty, who was standing next to her, was her guard, but when he wound up protecting me from her she put him in jail as well. He and I were together there, and happy, which of course only made her angrier.

As the story continued, my friend Michelle, said "Jeri, bottom line, how can you get out of jail? How do you release the power of someone who only thinks she is a princess?"

My response was, "Live in sovereignty." It was a word I did not know the true meaning of.

I heard Marty explaining the meaning of sovereignty to Michelle. I then heard them turning the pages of a dictionary. *Thank God he's here*, I thought.

Michelle then turned back to me. "How do you live in sovereignty in this life?" she asked.

"Live in my power," I replied, *"The power we think anyone has over us is only in our minds."*

We brought that thought into this life with us. There is no power. There is no jail.

"Are you ready to do that in this life?" Michelle asked.

"Yes, I will live in my own power."

After wrapping up that part of the session, she asked, "What is going on with your right hand? Why is it waving?"

I smiled and said, "It's waving goodbye."

"Goodbye to who?"

"To you, to everyone."

"Why, where are you going?"

"I'm going to Greece," I said, "We are going to have a wonderful trip." I couldn't remember much more about that part except I knew I was going to have a wonderful time.

A few days later, Marty received an email saying that the airline had cancelled our tickets to Greece. Oh, how could this be? How could a trip that was supposed to be a divinely organized journey be cancelled? Now what? Was my life cancelled also? Where was I to go? To be? What happens to the rest of my life? God, no. I am too excited and too ready for a vacation. The plans and dreams had kept me going during my recovery from surgery – and now I can't go. No, no way.

Then I started to feel anger. *Don't take a trip away from me. Not when I have given up so much, after I had saved money and gone without other things to be able to lay on a beach in the sun with my love. No way.* Next, I felt worry, then self-pity, then anger again. Finally, I started thinking rationally, sort of. I had to find out what was going to happen to my life if this divine journey didn't happen.

I decided to ask Robert, a psychic my friends had been recommending. I had to wait until the following Monday for the appointment, and it felt like an eternity. Finally, the day arrived. After brief introductions, he said to start talking about the weather or something that had no meaning to this reading. I tried but couldn't.

"I can't do this; the weather has been about the same for weeks. What's to say about seventy-five to eighty degrees and sunny?"

"Okay," he said, "Ask me a question and we will see how it goes."

Me: I have had a couple of readings on a trip to Greece that just got cancelled because of 9-11 and all the chaos with the airlines. These readings all said this was to be a divine setup and was to be wonderful for me. So now what? Where am I supposed to be? Where should I go?

Robert: Go to Greece. To a rocky coastal location. NYC to Greece – dark circle – south coast – you are drawn there – a pivotal place.

Me: You don't understand. I don't have any tickets now.

Robert: I don't care how you get there but there are certain times when certain people need to be at certain places on the planet and this is your time to be in Greece.

Silence.

Robert: Find a way. Take another path. Don't be distracted by global events.

Another silence.

Robert: Who are you meeting there?

Me: No one.

Robert: Yes, there is someone waiting for you. Reaching the location in Greece there is a new connection of light. A new type of awareness, a vista of awareness.

Another silence.

Robert: Something about this time for you to be there.

Silence.

Me: Is this a person or spirit?

Robert: Person, little, short, with dark hair.

Me: Great, how am I supposed to find this person in all of Greece?

Robert: I know you know enough that when things are to happen they do. Just sit, think about Greece, meditate, hold your palms up and allow this person to bring you to them. Close eyes, focus reaching, contacting with earth to help draw you there.

He told me to call other airlines, try other things.

I thought, *Right, he doesn't get this ticket thing at all. Three million people in Athens and this person is going to find me. Sure...*

Robert: Don't second guess the process of going. Don't think about it, listen to your heart. Have faith. Close your eyes and open the doors. Open yourself up. Going to Peru opened your heart and going to Greece will open your head. On your journey I see your husband following you. I see you being very quiet. He will be fine with that.

As we went on, I asked him about the first book that I had been working on for so long but hadn't finished. It was always on my mind but I couldn't make myself sit down and write.

Robert: The book is too diffused for you. There is no goal. Bring down the focus. You have no attention span.

Silence.

Robert: You must take it step by step, page by page. You are not the kind that can lock yourself in a room for days and come out with a book.

I told him that my husband calls me the "The Queen of We Can Fit It In." I can be focused on something, then something else will come up and off we go doing that, and then it's back to the original focus.

Robert: Take advantage of that. Not many people can do that. That is one of your successes. You have the ability to change what you are doing and go back without missing a beat. That is a talent or skill. Go with it but learn to control it. Work with it.

After the reading had gone on for some time, I asked, "Is there any other message I need to hear?"

Robert: Meditate. Now. Go to a higher vibration, a higher frequency. To absorb more, higher information, quiet the conscious mind. Go inside. Recognize your own completeness. You are very well entrenched.

Another silence.

Robert: There are negative, low vibrational people around you. Don't accept these people or their energy. Meditate. Go to your greater awareness. There is a complete package inside of you.

There really isn't any more. Go be with that.

As we hung up and I looked over the notes I had taken, my excitement ran rampant. Man, how am I supposed to do this?

Okay, I'll call my love. He'll know. I gave Marty a summary of the reading, and when I got to the part about opening my head, he giggled and said, "Baby, we are going. We will buy tickets."

That sent shock waves through our little savings account.

He said, "Look at it logically. We already have a few hundred tied up in this, so we will put a couple hundred more and go with it."

That was Monday. On Wednesday I called Marty as I left work so he could leave from home and meet me at the airport. We continued the conversation as we each drove along different freeways, going over what we were doing and whether it was right or not. We talked about the reading. As I pulled off the freeway onto Airport Boulevard, I asked him where he was.

"Look out your left window," he replied.

Sure enough, there he was, our bumpers aligned exactly. He had come over the overpass at the same time as I came off the freeway. What were the chances of that, coming from twenty miles away in opposite directions? We snickered and drove to the parking lot.

As we hugged, I said, "Do you think that there is divine timing somewhere here?"

He kissed me again. "Isn't there always?"

We walked with arms around each other into the airport.

The clerk at the desk saw us coming in and Marty slid the tickets toward him and said, "That's okay, we are here to turn these in and buy other tickets. We still want to go."

Without missing a beat, the clerk slid them back and replied, "No, you aren't going to buy tickets. The embargo will be lifted and you will be able to go."

There were three other clerks standing about, and they all agreed that no one was flying now and the embargo would be lifted. Business had to go on.

We did change our travel plans, however; we extended our stay in Greece instead of going to Massachusetts as we had planned. We talked for a long while and as we left, walking with our arms around each other again, passing through the doors, looking at each other, almost simultaneously we said, "If it is meant to be, we will go next Thursday."

Well, the embargo was lifted and our tickets were a go. We were going to Greece in six days! I started a list of all that had to be done before we left. The days flew by so fast it seemed more like minutes. When we arrived at the airport at four-thirty in the morning there were television stations there interviewing travelers about how they felt about flying. Marty was one of them. Of course he said that flying didn't bother him.

We checked in without delay and were soon changing planes in Salt Lake City, then it was off to New York City. It was sad to see so many of the airport stores closed and so few people walking around. A very somber feeling was everywhere. There were only a few people flying. We sat in Business Elite again, so peaceful, so much room, such a wonderful experience. Part of me didn't even want to land in Greece, I was so happy to read, lay my head on Marty's shoulder, talk, eat, and drink. It was the start of two weeks of just us together. Everything was paying off. We were happy, content, peaceful, knowing that all was working out for another divine plan in action. Just going with the flow.

I began the elven-hour flight by thanking the Universe for all that I had. I focused on enjoying First Class and getting used to being treated very well in life: on being comfortable with *being* first class again and having a good life and all that goes with it.

*I know that thanking the Universe for what it has delivered is more important than always asking for more. I know that working the process is the most important. If we don't do the physical work they tell us to do, they can't give us more. The steps must be taken. I work on remembering to thank the Universe, my angels and guides throughout the day, all days.*

After eating, sleeping and more eating we arrived in Athens. On the descent I went to the other side of the plane to see all I could see. Inside the new terminal, getting the luggage was as usual very interesting and exciting. On our way out, we saw the line of customer service travel counters and decided to make this our first stop. We made our choice of hotel and got reservations at one that a client of mine had recommended. At the last minute we decided to get air tickets from Mykonos back to Athens for our return. The agent told us what bus to take into Athens and how to get to our hotel and out the door we went.

We found the bus, but I stopped, my feet refusing to move.

Marty asked, "Aren't you getting on?" He wasn't surprised when I told him no, I didn't want to ride the bus. He gave me a look and went to sit on a bench. He was so cute sitting there that I had to take his picture.

After about ten minutes he stood up and motioned for me to come with him. Okay, we were going to take a cab. We walked to the first one, he looked at the cab and then at me and said, "Not this one." He walked to the second one and again said, "Nope, not this one."

By now the cab drivers were all looking at us. He started talking to the driver of the third cab, and decided, yes, this was the one. We got in and started down the new freeway. We found out that the driver had lived in Massachusetts. He told us all about Athens and what kind of tours he could do for us since we only had one full day there. By the time we got to our hotel we were full of information for the rest of the day and had arranged for him to pick us up in the morning to take us around.

We had a wonderful day in Athens on our own, resting and making love, then we went out on the town, shopping, looking around, having dinner and seeing the city at night.

The next morning Spiros picked us up early and took us to see everything: The Acropolis, many museums, statues, churches, changing of the guards, the new subway system built for the Olympics, and different districts in Athens. He then took us up the coast to the Temple of Poseidon and for lunch at a cute little beach restaurant. We stopped at the healing Lake Vouliagmeni, just outside of Athens. It was perfect, a little cool but so wonderful. It was the first time Marty had been in water where he could see the fish. We felt like we had seen it all.

As we hugged and kissed in the cool lake we heard Spiros calling us to tell us he had called Santorini and had a wonderful place for us to stay and would make the reservations for us. Of course, that would be great. He went to make them, and we went back to being in love. We just couldn't get enough of each other.

That night we went out for another great dinner and walked around more. We wanted to take it all in. The whole thing was so perfect.

Early in the morning we set off to Santorini on a sea jet, peaceful, relaxing and so beautiful. The boat was almost empty, which was sad for the economy, but I was thankful to have the peace and just be with Marty.

As I was thinking and staring out the windows I decided to write down my thoughts. I really believe that there is something bigger than ourselves. Getting me here and having everything so perfect showed me again that I am not running the show.

I asked within, "What is the fear that people have on canceling flights and trips because of what happened on September 11th? They see car accidents, sickness, murders and everything else every day and still get into autos, still do unhealthy things, eat unhealthy foods, take drugs and go outside. So where is the fear of flying? Then there is the big question that I asked a few of my clients last week as they were trying to reason with me not to go: If you believe in God and that He is the creator and it is His choice when you leave this planet, do you think He can't find you if you aren't on an airplane or in a foreign country?"

*Fear limits so many things in our lives. Just notice the emotion that comes up next time you are making any decision. Fear is always there. If we had let global fear keep us home, we would have missed this whole experience of Greece so far, plus the life experiences that are to come.*

While traveling we only encountered very kind people and never any anti-Americanism.

I paused to look out the windows and be in the moment to appreciate where I was and how I had dreamed of being on the Mediterranean (well, I know now that I was on the Aegean Sea), seeing movie stars on their big yachts and dreaming of someday.

I hoped that the trip took longer than four or five hours so I could keep enjoying everything about the day. The next thing I wrote was, *Our mission is to show others how two ordinary people can make it. Show beliefs of abundance and acceptance of each other. Do I accept the challenge? Yes. Show me.*

*Stay with something long enough and do not walk away from the challenge because of the adversity it brings. Be with me. Do you accept that challenge, desire and success? Yes.*

We had to be ready to get off the boat as soon as it docked, as they unload and leave again very quickly. Watching the port coming closer,

I couldn't wait to start exploring. Wasn't sure what we were going to explore but there was a reason I was there, right? Right!

On the dock, we were amazed by all the people. Where had they been hiding on the boat? We wondered what the place would be like in high season and tried to keep our luggage from falling into the bumps on the street. I was as usual looking around and walking into people.

There was about a hundred feet of flat ground and then the mountain went straight up. Across the front of the mountain was a switchback road to the top. I wanted to look in all the little shops, but Marty kept me straight, saying that we would come back. Soon I found the man holding the sign with our name. I may have been looking and stumbling around but I could still read.

Out the cab window we saw the dock dropping below us as we climbed higher, how beautiful! We hugged, held hands and looked; this was the start of the real romantic part of our journey. Surprise, the top of the mountain was not flat! On Santorini you never go downhill, or at least not for long. When you walk, everything is upstairs or uphill. The biggest part of the town of Thira is built hanging onto the side of the mountain—it's amazing how they did it. The cab stopped on what I thought was the top of the mountain, but no, a man took our luggage and told us to follow him… uphill. Shortly there were stairs down to the hotel gate and more stairs down to the lobby. A woman greeted us and explained as much as she could in a few minutes. We asked her about everything around the island and she would set things up for us. Out every window was the Aegean Sea, which I still thought was the Mediterranean, with part of the volcano dead center. I kept repeating, "My God, how pretty." Down more stairs, she opened the door to our room and then the door to the balcony. Oh, it was so beautiful—the water, the sun, the volcano, everything. She was nice, but I wanted her to leave so we could be alone to enjoy it, love each other and take it all in.

I just wanted to sit on the balcony, breathe in the sea air and hold Marty. The view was breathtaking. We had to pull ourselves away from each other to go look around town and get our bearings. Words cannot explain the feelings, thoughts and sights we experienced as we wound through the narrow paths among the shops and restaurants.

The next day we rented a Jeep and went all around the island. We also went to a museum. As we walked in Marty took my arm and started quickly toward a picture made from little tiles that looked like two boys fighting each other. I looked at him and noticed he was tearing up. I asked him what was wrong, and he said, "That was us." Oh, another past life reflection from him on a vacation. We stood and hugged each other.

That night we went on an incredible boat ride to watch the sunset. Santorini had to be one of the most romantic places on earth, I thought. No wonder it was a big honeymoon destination.

Our last day on Santorini, Marty and I were lying in bed when I decided to do a past life regression to see how we were connected there. I was shocked when he said he saw us swimming as mermaids in Atlantis times. I knew we had been together before, but *Atlantis*? Was this really where Atlantis was? I had read it somewhere, but really?

I had to ask him why he couldn't swim now since he could in that previous life. He shrugged his shoulders and said, "No need."

No need? Really? If you could swim, I thought, then you could scuba dive with me. I guess that wasn't a need in this life either.

After the session, he became emotional and said it was the most peaceful beautiful place he'd ever experienced. We took time out of our last afternoon there to make love with the beautiful scene out the window of the crater and the sea.

The next morning, we headed to Mykonos. I wasn't sure why Mykonos had a different feeling. Even though it was very windy when we got off the boat, it felt peaceful. We had such a relaxing time on the boat ride and stopping on Paros for a couple of hours to see more of Greece. We knew that we would be where we needed to be.

We checked into another perfect hotel, halfway up the hill where we could look back on the port and the harbor. What a sight with the windmills against the sea. Just another beautiful site in Greece. Total perfection was becoming the standard.

As Marty was taking care of check-in, I looked around the lobby and onto the scenery outside: the pool, deck, white buildings and again, the blue green sea. I then noticed a flyer for a massage. There was a steam room, spa and a massage, and my body knew that is what it wanted. I told Marty, and he agreed. In the meantime, we enjoyed the evening in town. We were surprised that the town was so quiet in the evening, but we ate and walked around before trekking back to the eighty-three stairs inside the hotel compound to our room.

The next morning, after I'd booked an appointment with the massage woman, we rented a jeep and explored the beaches and sites of Mykonos. For dinner, we would go into town. Mykonos is known as the gay island or the San Francisco of Greece, so we looked for places where Dianna (Marty's female name) could go out. We discovered that restaurants in Mykonos don't even open for dinner until nine; the bars open later than that and stay open until the morning hours. We learned that summers are so warm that everyone sleeps in late, goes to the beach or pool until three or four in the afternoon, takes naps until about eight in the evening and then gets ready to party all night. Then it starts all over again. It sounded great to us.

Morning came fast, as we had to get up early for our massages. Breakfast was on the deck above the pool, looking over the town and out to the sea. We watched the boats come in, unload and leave within minutes. There were always cruise ships in the port to fantasize about.

For our massage, we walked to the windmill and turned right up the hill. It was supposed to be the second house on the left. Nope, not there, so I asked the people who lived there where it was. After a phone call they told us to just walk to the windmill and the massage lady would pick us up. In a few minutes a little red car appeared, and Marty said, "That is her." Indeed, it was. She was young and kind and called Marina.

Her office was nice, modern and new, which somehow surprised me. She showed us into the steam room and explained what to do. Marty and I sat in the steam room, realizing that something was going on and we didn't know what it was. In the meantime, we steamed and scrubbed before going in the spa. We discussed whether this was what we wanted to build at home: a total beauty and health salon. I noticed that it was painted peach. With everything in Greece white and blue, the peach really stood out. I remembered the reading that my friends had done where my workplace was peach color – it all fit. We talked for about twenty minutes about how it could work while we relaxed in this wonderful place; we just connected with all of it. Then Marina came to get one of us for the massage. I went first.

After drying off, I followed Marina into the massage room and sunk onto the table. As she started to massage my body, she asked, "What do you do for a living?"

I told her I was a hairdresser, to keep it short. I don't like to talk during a massage.

Then she asked, "Have you ever had a massage before?"

I told her yes, that I was also a hypnotherapist and I had a couple friends who were massage therapists. We often exchanged services. She didn't respond right away, and I thought, *Now on to the massage*. But then she said, "You do hypnotherapy? I want a session with you before you leave the island."

I said, to my surprise, "Okay, we can do that."

While I was digesting that, she said, "Do you believe in mediums?"

"Yes, some."

She stopped massaging and started telling me she had gone to a medium about six years earlier. That lady had told her about the business she now has, that there would be steam connected to it, though at the time she didn't understand what this meant. She also told her about an immovable rock. While her place was being built one day she was sitting on a rock that couldn't be moved and she was crying. They had to find a way to build around the rock and it would cost a lot more.

By now I had turned to look at her.

She said, "And she told me there would be an American woman coming to me that would help me." She was saying, "You are her, I know you are her, you are here to help me."

I was still reeling when Marty walked into the room for his session. "Honey," I said, "wait until you hear this one."

After we'd told him, he said nonchalantly, "Well, that Robert guy told you someone was waiting for you, and there she is. You found her."

Astonished, Marina asked, "Someone told you about me?"

"Yep, about two weeks ago." Marty and I then gave her a condensed version of my reading from Robert.

Somewhere during this conversation, I just drifted off to somewhere. I couldn't tell you what was said or happened until I became aware that I was outside having a cigarette looking at the beautiful scenery. I knew I needed to lie down so I went back into the spa room. When they woke me up I knew I had been somewhere in the dream state but couldn't tell you where or what happened. I just knew something was going on within me, with strange feelings.

We made an appointment for the next afternoon to do a session at our hotel room. While talking for a bit she told us to go to the island of Delos the next morning, it was an archeological site and would be very interesting. As we walked back to the hotel, Marty and I talked about what had happened. We both knew it had happened, but it is one of those things that one just can't put together.

Back at the hotel we had a snack and lay by the pool until it was time to dress and go to town for dinner and some night life. The whole time, our thoughts kept coming back to the events of that morning, and occasionally, one of us would remark on them. The remark always ended with, "Can you believe it?"

Another day of our Greek fantasy passed, and the next morning we ran for the boat to Delos. Our boat looked pretty good until we realized that the big boat that we were getting on was just to walk across to get onto the little boat behind it. We chuckled about that as we found a place to sit on the small boat and hold each other. After two and a half years we still loved to hold each other and make love all the time.

It was a beautiful morning as we sailed across the water. Delos was different, with the ruins that rumbled out and up the hills. It felt somehow familiar and we walked toward a big building, which was a museum, snack bar and gift shop. We were fascinated by how they could dig up half an island and come up with enough ruins to put together statues, bowls, vases, animals and even buildings then fill in the missing spaces. We walked around in awe.

After a snack we went out to see the sites and take pictures. We walked up to a short metal fence surrounding a hole, knowing it was a grave, and Marty said, "That was yours." I didn't feel good about that and was suddenly ready to leave the island. Marty wanted to walk up the hill to take some pictures. I just wanted to be the first one on the boat, so that is what I did.

We got the first boat back. Looking over the side into the water with Marty's arms around me, I suddenly said, "Let go." He was surprised but dropped his arms, so I could go sit on the nearest bench. A voice said to me very clearly, *Write this down.* I grabbed a notepad and started writing. When I was finished writing, I said to Marty, "Listen to this." I had written:

*Our mission is to show how to love self then each other. Through past lives into this life the ones ready will come and show and tell others to come the information contained inside Amel and Marta* (two angels I channel). *They will show the way.*

*Has been with me since before time. A long wait they say for me to open to higher information. They are bursting with excitement to spread their word. If I will write what they say all will succeed. Correct to start with my life now and grow details that are important will be described. They sent me Richard* (the guy that gives me the airline tickets) *and he is open to all info also.*

*Swim in the sea for more info tomorrow.*

*Help tonight is valuable info. Write it down. Marty there too. Marina best friend before. She will bring us back to Mykonos Trust her. The end for now.*

Neither of us knew quite what to say so we just looked over the side of the boat into the blue green sea. My insides began to tremble, and I showed Marty how my hands were shaking so much I couldn't hold them still. He just held me as the boat came into port.

We walked through town back up to the hotel and the eighty-three stairs to our room. There was a message from Marina. She asked if she could bring someone with a video camera. That was fine, I didn't care. We then tried to rest by the pool, but part of me could not relax. Soon it was time get ready for Marina and her session.

When she arrived, after quick introductions she lay on the bed and was ready. I didn't need to explain much. After a short induction she was in the depths of a session. After a very few questions, she started giving me more information than I think I was ready for. She went into past lives that she and I had, and others that included Marty as well; she also talked about lives she had shared with her friend with the video camera. There was so much that my mouth hung open and I glanced at Marty occasionally. She told us of future events we would share: a lake in Switzerland, traveling together, our healing hands together, a book we would be reading together, a baby that was to be born that I would be there for. It was amazing. She told us that we were totally connected and had a lot to learn from each other. Two hours went by like five minutes. She told us that this was the end for now, but more information would be given to us as we learned more.

When I brought her out of the session we were dazed and in disbelief. There wasn't a lot to say about what had happened. All that remained was to wait and see if and how it all played out.

As Marina hugged us goodbye, she told us that she had more people for us to meet and tomorrow she would pick us up at one-thirty for a baptism with her family.

Marty shrugged his shoulders and said, "Tomorrow isn't the day at the beach to rest either, is it?"

The next day, I wore the only dress I had brought, and now realized why I had packed it. As we got out of the car, her little girl, twenty months old, walked up to Marty and put her arms up for him to pick her up. Marina and her husband were amazed that she felt so comfortable with him so quickly. She stayed in his arms through the entire baptism.

After the baptismal ceremony there was a buffet for the guests. As I walked to my table, several women wanted to talk to me about sessions. I told them I would see them when I returned to Greece as tomorrow we were leaving for home. Marty later told me he was thinking, *Why is she telling them she will be back? She can't come back, we don't have any more tickets and we can't afford another trip.*

Later, Marina took us to her home and to the beach nearby. The water was cool, and the beach was rocky. As I was trying to get in Marina kept saying, "Come on, you are strong. You are strong." When I got in we swam and stood in the water talking. I ended up swimming in the sea, just like the writing had told me to do. I didn't realize at the time that "you are strong" was the answer I was to receive.

When she took us back to our hotel we exchanged email addresses and promised to keep in touch.

At the time, we had no idea how amazing this whole experience was.

The next day at the Athens airport waiting for our flight, I suddenly looked up at Marty and said, "Africa is calling me."

He replied, "Oh, I really don't want to go Africa."

I said, "Oh, okay."

He realized what that meant and asked, "You wouldn't go without me, would you?"

"Sure I would," I said. I went back to reading and soon we boarded our flight.

## Chapter 17

# Shampoo, Indians, and Life Between Lives

When we arrived home from Greece, there were exciting emails every day between Marina and me. She was hungry for knowledge and wanted to know everything I knew. This gave me more go power to learn more.

We were busy at home with work, kids, grandkids, caring for Grandpa, making time to get out so Marty could dress, motorcycling, skiing, going to advanced classes for hypnotherapy and writing my first book. We were looking for editors, designers and publishers.

In all the busyness, I managed to find a new facilitator of classes, and the author of some books I had been reading. Marty and I went to San Diego for her weekend class. In her opening talk she spoke about being accountable for your life. I raised my hand and told her my realization that I had never been taught to be accountable for my life. In fact, the only thing I could remember my mother really teaching me was to leave the damn boys alone so I wouldn't get pregnant. As I said this I realized that I didn't hate my mother any longer, which caught me off guard and took a while to sort out.

Later, during a group interaction, a tall man put his arms around me to hug me. My body froze, and I started crying uncontrollably. Suddenly, I knew why I avoided tall men in my relationships and was so scared of them. Damn, I was having flashbacks of my uncle who molested me.

He was tall and big. As fear ran through my body it answered so many questions of my life.

*It is always amazing to me how many unknown questions can be answered in one process.*

Was this another reason I felt safe with Marty? I had months ahead of me to sort this all out and work on forgiving myself for decisions I had made, based on this additional information.

During this weekend, Marty signed up to become a Life Coach with this organization. Now we would be even busier with him going to school and traveling back for additional classes.

Before long, Marina and I were planning my next trip to Greece. She suggested I meet her in London, do a couple sessions and then go on to Greece with her to do more sessions there. As excited as I was, I wondered, how could I leave Marty for two weeks? With the exception of his trip to Massachusetts before he proposed, we had never been apart.

A couple weeks before I was to leave a girlfriend who had grown up in Liverpool talked to me about England. I don't know why I asked her about Manchester. She told me she often took the train from Manchester to London or Liverpool. That sounded interesting, but I was only going to London.

I was excited and apprehensive about the trip and how I was going to live up to what these people expected of me. Marina had many people who wanted sessions. When I got to Atlanta I found that my luggage was going to London but I was not. I had been bumped off the flight. The airlines found me the next flight to…Manchester! Okay, I'll do it, but now I had about six hours to allow my head to go crazy.

I became so stressed about the trip that I called Marty, crying, "I'm not going! I am coming home, I miss you. Call Marina and tell her I can't make it." One would have thought I had never travelled before.

After listening to me in distress he said, "Jeri, you are going on that plane to Manchester, get on the train and go to London. Marina is waiting. I will call her and tell her you are on your way. Call me when you get to Manchester. I love you. Goodbye."

He hung up and I had to buck up and go get that plane.

How good can a first class plane ride to Manchester be? Really, Jeri!

When I got there, I called Marty to let him know I was in one piece then bought a ticket to London. I had a couple of hours on the train to wonder whether I would even recognize Marina, but as the train pulled to a stop, I saw the woman with the long black hair and realized I would have known her anywhere. She was there with her brother and after a brief greeting off we went. We stepped into a tunnel in the station and I knew instantly that I had been there before in a past life. Walking quickly to keep up with them, I tried to recognize the feeling and get information as to when and what had happened to me in there. Everything was going fast, and I was trying to catch as many sights as I could plus I was tired, so I didn't get more information.

I spent a few days tracking down my luggage, seeing London for the first time, and doing a few sessions, then off we went to Mykonos. I had told Marina I need two hours for a session, and she set a full schedule, with the first session beginning at eight a.m. and the last session ending at eight p.m. One of the first evenings she had also set up a talk for me to do. A couple of the other nights there would be a group class down at the port.

When I unpacked, I found that a bottle of shampoo had spilled over ninety percent of my clothes. Marina took them away to wash, and then next day I went to retrieve them, only to find that they were hanging on the line and it was raining. My first introduction to Greek living: Marina did not have a dryer. Okay, I was back to the only clean outfit I had.

We held my first talk about my life and how hypnotherapy had changed it. I was excited, scared and ready for whatever life had to offer me. I talked, they listened, and Marina and her sister took pictures. This was before cellphone cameras, so I would have to wait until I got home to develop the film.

The rest of the week was a blur. I had individual sessions from morning until night, then a group session. A couple of times someone who couldn't wait followed us home and I started another session at midnight. After only a couple of hours sleep, I was up again. It was exhausting and exhilarating at the same time.

Marina and I worked out a system so she could translate for me in sessions. Just to watch her amazement would have been enough for me, but then to watch the results from the sessions was a huge bonus. Together we were miracle workers.

After two weeks of this, it was time to go home and try to take in all that happened. When I got the pictures back, I stood there, mouth open, my mind trying to process what my eyes were seeing.

*There I was, standing in front of a group of people giving a talk in a pink outfit, holding a manila folder. Exactly what I had seen that first session, when Mark ask me to imagine the essence of my life.*

Nearly ten years had passed since I had seen that image. Wow, did that mean I now have an essence for my life? Could this mean that everything Marina said in her first session was true? Could everything else I had seen or been told be true—that this is my destiny?

I still had a glimmer of a doubt, but the daily emails between me and Marina continued.

This gave me more motivation to learn more, do more and be more. We were still busy maintaining life and keeping our ducks in a row. After six months I went back to Greece to see Marina and do many more sessions.

This time she met me in Athens and said we were going to Delphi. Not knowing what or where that was, my first thought was, *Oh no, I'm not going to be working or making money.* But we set off for Delphi with one of her friends.

Soon I was sitting under the columns at the Sanctuary of Apollo in Delphi. It was breathtaking. Marina and her friend went to climb the ruins, but I wanted to sit and take it all in.

I took out a paper and starting writing what I heard:

*You must let go of control of not only the mind but also the body for all to move forward.*

*My Books*

*Let go of how I think it should look.*

Then suddenly, I saw an anthill of like flying ants. I asked why I hadn't seen them there before because I had been sitting there for at least fifteen minutes. I asked why I needed to see them now.

*I was told that is what the world looks like. I am not in that group. I was chosen to fly above the chaos, but I am choosing to hang on to the chaos, which is holding me back.*

It was okay for me to live differently.

*You must just open up and accept the miracles of it all.*

*Life and Body*

*Eat the better food.*

*Stretch the body and it will stretch the whole experience of life. Always stretch.*

*This trip not about the money, not about how many I can do, but about me/us. Take that home — it won't be about the money or how hard I can work. It is about opening up to miracles.*

*Let them be delivered.*

*That is what will allow for more travel and acceptance on those travels.*

*Go home — fix home for peace light, bring, peach and olive green.*

*Enjoy home, you won't be there long.*

*Get rid of what you wouldn't want to move. Only keep what you're connected to.*

*Spend time writing. Writing will stretch and release more to move ahead.*

*Love self and love will spread, and you will get the recognition you desire that will create more energy to spread more.*

*Self-recognition is most important to grow.*

*Me not worry, focus on accomplishments and that will allow miracles to flow.*

When they returned, I put that in my purse to read it again later. At dinner, they told me we would go back to the ruins after dark.

I said, "They will be closed."

Marina told me it would be okay, we will climb the fence and be there for the full moon. I thought, *Oh my God if I get thrown in jail they will never let me out.* I had to call Marty to tell him that if he didn't hear from me I was in jail in Delphi. They laughed at me and off we went to climb the fence. We did it and it was another amazing experience, with no jail time.

After a couple of great days exploring a different part of Greece we went back on Mykonos so I could work. Marina and I had established a great relationship by now and it was time to help her learn how to channel. Now we could get more information from unseen sources. We worked hard, played, talked and planned for her to visit me in the States.

When I returned home, Marina sent me an email telling me she had channeled that there was an Indian in New Mexico or Arizona that I had to find so I could take her to him when she came. I tried to explain to her how big these two states were, that we could not just go onto a reservation and meet an Indian. She didn't buy my logic at all.

"You found me in Greece," she said, "You can find an Indian in America."

Okay, my challenge was in front of me.

I started channeling to see what I could find out. I told Marty that for our anniversary over New Year's we needed to go to Arizona so I could find this Indian. We had been talking about moving and we could look there.

As we left town, I felt my body relax from the stress I had been under the last six weeks. My car had been broken into and my appointment book stolen, so over the holiday season I wasn't sure of my schedule. I also had daughter issues, Grandpa was getting older and needed more attention, the holidays were stressful, I was working on my first book finding editors, designers and everything else needed. I was also working on putting the hypnotherapy business together and traveling to Greece for work and Marina.

*This was while everyone around me thought I was living the high life traveling.*

Our first stop in Arizona was Bullhead City, a cute small town not far from the Colorado River. We looked at a few very nice houses. Not long before, someone had talked about moving there, and I had started with all the negatives that it probably had. Now that I was actually there, I had to ask myself, *How and why can I continue to make decisions and judgements based on absolutely no information?*

Then we were off to Flagstaff for New Year's Eve and our anniversary the next day. We didn't want a hot party night; we found a nice room and went to dinner. The next morning we set off to find the Indian, only to realize everything was closed for New Year's Day. We changed plans and drove to Sedona to see a friend and ended up spending the night there. The next day we explored more of Arizona, ending up on Highway 40 again, about fifty miles west of Flagstaff.

As we sat along the freeway, I said I wanted to go back to Flagstaff, spend the night and find the Indian the next day. Marty thought I was crazy. There was a blizzard predicted for that night. I reassured him that we both knew how to drive in snow. We went to Flagstaff to find another hotel. I kept seeing the place of Cameron, the Gateway to the Grand Canyon, in a magazine. I thought, *That's it, that is where we need to go.*

When we woke to four inches of snow, Marty was not on board with going north to Cameron, but I persuaded him. The snow got heavier along the way, but we continued over the pass. Down the other side, it was clear with not a snowflake in sight. I was relieved and happy that we made it.

We drove into Cameron and all we saw was two gas stations.

"Okay, where now?" Marty asked.

"Stop here for gas and I will go to the bathroom."

The restroom was a little old building behind the gas station. A little lady was there loading her pickup. I greeted her on my way in. It was an old building, but nice, with showers and everything a traveler would need.

As I was going to the restroom, someone came in and I said hello again, but it was not that little lady but a young-Indian looking girl. We exchanged information about the weather up on the hill. She was upset because she said she needed to be back from Flagstaff by seven p.m.

I asked her if she could answer a couple questions for me. I told her I was looking for an Indian. She smiled and asked what kind of Indian. I told her my story and she said, "You are looking for a medicine man. That is easy, that is my grandpa."

She told me that her brother had been in an accident a couple days ago. While he was in Intensive Care, their grandfather stayed with him, and in two days the young man walked out recovered. They were going to do a Thanking of the Gods ceremony at seven.

She gave me directions to his place, and we wished each other well.

I almost ran back to the car. As I opened the door, Marty said, "You found one, didn't you?"

"Yep, I did. Let's go!"

We followed her directions until we found the place. As Marty put the car in park, he said, "You go, I'll stay here." Several men stood around looking at us.

I knocked on the door and heard, "Come in."

I opened the door to see an older gentleman standing there, surprised to see me. I asked him if he was the medicine man. "Yes," he replied with a nod of his head. I asked him if he would work with me.

He called someone on his little flip phone, speaking in his language so I didn't understand. In a minute the door opened to a younger man and woman and an older woman. The younger woman asked me many questions. I answered them all, then told them about meeting the medicine man's granddaughter.

The woman translated all of this to the medicine man. They spoke for a moment, then she said he would work on me, but it would cost money. I told her that was fine and asked if my husband could come in.

I went to the car to get money and told Marty to come in.

He asked, "What for?"

I told him I didn't know but I wanted him to watch so he could tell Marina what he saw.

Then all six of us were sitting crowded up in the living room of an old, ten-foot-wide trailer with a wood-burning fireplace blazing away. The medicine man opened a box that looked like the fishing tackle box my dad used to have and took out his paraphernalia. He sprinkled something over me, blew his whistles, had his feathers and rattles going, singing and tapping my body.

Suddenly, he pulled up my sweater and started sucking on my side! For a split second, the sucking felt like a bite or rip. Then I heard him coughing and gagging, getting rid of what he had sucked out of my back.

The woman said, "Something happened to her as a little girl that went through her body like a bolt of lightning." Then through translation, she asked Marty, "How old was she when her father died?"

I sat there in shock as Marty said he thought I was about eight years old. How did the medicine man know that my father died?

This went on for a while, then he pulled out my sweater and sucked on my neck. After the final whistles and sprinkling of something on me, he handed me a shot glass of water mixed with something and said, "Drink this."

I lifted the glass to my mouth and asked myself, "Shit, what if this kills me?" But I swallowed it down anyway and heard a voice inside say, *I believe.*

They then told me to pour the remnants in the glass into my hand and rub it on my lower back.

They translated more questions and Marty answered yes to all of them, on how things had been with my back and leg. I told her that I had had surgery on my back to take out a lump, but the feeling had never totally gone away. He told her that if I hadn't come there eventually it would have paralyzed my right leg. (That is what doctors had told me about twenty years earlier, which was why they did the surgery.)

When I opened my eyes, I saw Marty's face with his mouth open, it was priceless. The medicine man said through translation: "Rest and do not eat any salt for twenty-four hours or you will get sick."

We got back into the quiet car and drove to the Trading Post. As I was walking around in a trance, Marty asked me, "Do you know what you are doing here?"

"No," I answered.

He took my arm and led me to the car. As we headed up the road he asked, "Where to now?"

I happily said, "To the Grand Canyon."

"Jeri," he said, pointing to the sky, "Do you see those black clouds up there? That is a blizzard."

I looked at him and asked, "Marty, do you really think the Gods that be are going to get me all the way to the medicine man and not let me see the Grand Canyon?"

As we started up the mountain, the snow got heavier, and soon there was no more traffic. I found myself praying, "Please don't let us get stuck, he will kill me." Soon I saw the sign with an arrow: South Rim of the Grand Canyon, and the words "Turn here" fell out of my mouth.

"Jeri, do you see how deep that snow is? We don't have chains."

I convinced him it would be okay. We pulled up in the parking lot, got out of the car and the clouds parted. I have the most beautiful pictures of the Grand Canyon with the sun peeking through on the snow.

By the time we drove to the main lodge of the Canyon it was beautiful, sunny and warm. We had lunch and continued down a different road to leave the Canyon behind us. A few miles down the new road the skies opened, and it poured rain so hard that we almost had to pull over because we couldn't see.

When the rain stopped, Marty put his arm around my shoulder and said, "One thing about being married to you is, it is never boring."

It was late and dark when we decided to stop and get a room. I took an offramp and there were many motels. The farther up the street we drove, the motels got cheaper. I went all the way to the end.

"Are you sure?" Marty asked.

I replied, "Why not? We're only going to be here for a few hours."

The price was good, but the next morning we could see sunlight through the holes in the drapes. We were cold: no heat. Time for a shower: no hot water. We got what we paid for, all fourteen dollars' worth. We threw on our clothes and left quickly to turn the heater on in the car. After a day of driving we arrived home, mission completed. I could tell Marina I had found the Indian. In a couple of months, she would be here.

I was busy at home working on my book, *The ABC's of Never Having Another Bad Hair Day*, and keeping all the balls in the air. I was always asking the Spirit to confirm if I was going in the right direction, to send me a sign.

After asking again, I got the message loud and clear. It came in the form of an email asking if I wanted to attend the first class that Michael Newton was teaching on his Life Between Lives. Oh my God, yes. I had heard him speak many years earlier and couldn't get an appointment with him, nor could I have afforded one. Could this be my next step in my hypnotherapy that I loved so much?

I was excited about life and setting up a trip to Arizona with Marina. I had to find a date that the Indian would see us, but they didn't answer their phones. Marty was skeptical when I picked the dates for Arizona and then left for Los Angeles for the Life Between Lives class.

When I got to Los Angeles, I called Marty. He was excited to tell me that the Indian's granddaughter had called to check on me. When he told her I was coming back to see them, she told him that the day I had picked to see them was the only day they would be home in two weeks. Again, my husband was amazed at how things fell into place for me.

After days of training with Michael Newton, we started to do sessions on each other. That afternoon half the group gave a session, then we would switch of the following day. When it was my turn to receive my session, I wondered what I would get out of it after years of sessions, healings and realizations.

After a longer than usual induction of being taken deeper, we started through this life, stopping at a couple of ages and working towards finding happy, positive or neutral memories. At one stop I found myself as a little girl down by the creek that ran behind the Big Red Barn on our farm. It was peaceful, and the pollywogs were my friends. I felt safe.

*Although it takes days, weeks, even months for all the information in a session to be integrated into our lives, I knew I finally felt safe as that little girl. If that little girl felt safe, I knew that the older version of myself felt safe as well.*

The second part of a session was going back into the womb. *I had always loved doing womb work with clients but had never experienced being there.* Suddenly, I could feel the warm, moist environment I was floating in. With continued questioning, I could hear my mother's heartbeat. *For that time, my mother was alive again and with me.* I could feel some of her emotions. She was happy to be pregnant. *I think for the first time in my life, I knew my mother wanted me. I knew my mother loved me. Those were some of the most precious feeling and memories I had ever experienced.*

The third part meant going to the most recent past life. This life opened with two cowboys walking out of their western town. They were leaving their families to go teach others something. Investigating this, I found that these two men were me and Sheila, the friend I had done that first session on when I started in this work. *The interesting thing was that when we met in this life, we lived on a street called Wagon Trail Lane. We had both left the men we were married to and now we both teach various parts of healing work.* That night after class I called her to tell her what I had learned.

I do not remember the fourth part of this session, the death scene. *This is also where we find out how we felt about the life we had just lived. How we felt with people in that life, our successes and regrets and we make sure we feel complete before we move on.* After a death in that life it is time to proceed to the afterlife.

Leaving the earth there is a feeling of calm, quiet and peace to total bliss. *Every client and story I have heard of all describe the same experience.* Coaxing from my facilitator had me start looking for my guide to meet me and help me move onward. At first, I could feel him but could not see him. I found him behind me. She asked me to ask him why he was behind me. He told us, "That is where he stays because I had never asked him for help." *Now, I knew I had more help. He helped with leading me through various places but advised me not to get too dependent on him, that I should learn to use everything that was available to me.*

He had me go to a healing place for souls when they return "home." For me this was a beautiful beach with a peaceful waterfall. *I could feel a different type of healing deep within my body. The information in a session is phenomenal.*

Towards the end of the session we went to the Life and Body Selection room. There were bodies hanging (this is not scary or morbid). I walked in and grabbed the first one. (Others telling their story that morning had spent a lot of time in that room finding the right body for their soul for that life.)

The facilitator stopped me and asked why I was in such a hurry. I told her, "I gotta go, the numbers are running out."

"What numbers?" she asked.

My response was, "You know numerology, and if I don't hurry and be born right now, I will have to go back to my council and set up a whole new life. I have so much to do in this life I don't want to set up another one. So let me go."

With that we ended the session. As always it is after the session that everything settles in and the answers really start flowing. Here are a few of my greatest revelations:

- *Finally, so many questions were answered. I now know who these Guides were that everyone talked about. I knew my Guides. I knew I had to ask them for help.*
- *I knew how Jack and my mother heard me talking with them when they were in the hospital and how my mother heard my thoughts asking her to wait until Saturday if she had to die.*
- *I could stop disliking that my birthday was so close to Christmas.*
- *I realized why I was so different from the rest of my family.*
- *I knew that during that car accident, when my father was motioning me to come to him in the bright light, I DID have a Near Death Experience. When my daughter said I could not go with him, I came back. That is when I heard them say, "We have her, let's transport." I now knew how we can decide to go or not.*

- *I could see some of why my life was the way it had been. I set it up. That was the good and the bad news. I set it up but with every decision I made I paved the way to the next step.*

- *I could believe more that my mom and dad are always with me. I knew that was my father who came to see my baby when Loni was born. I knew how he did that. I also knew he was the mysterious man who picked up my motorcycle the night at the hospital.*

- *Other emotions started up within me: an overflowing love for my mother, guilt for hating her for so long for what I thought she had done to me, wishing she were still here so I could show and tell her how much I loved her, sorrow over her life that I know was hard for her.*

- *I realized why my mother had all those unworn expensive clothes and the raggedy clothes she wore most of the time. I understood that the expensive clothes and belongings were for the person she would have liked to have been, but the self-worth or deserving part of her kept her wearing the raggedy clothes.*

- *This is how various parts of self plays out in our lives. For myself, I understood at another level what was going on that day long ago in the bathroom. When Jack tried to hold me, my heart was screaming, "Hold me!" and my head and mouth were yelling, "Leave me alone!" The little girl inside wanted to be held and protected, another part of me wanted to be left alone: the part that hated and feared men.*

- *For most of us there is an internal battle going on, be it nice versus angry, sad versus happy, guilty versus deserving, love hate relationships, the list goes on. This is usually when we begin the "blame game." We blame others because something they did or didn't do upset us. Few go inside to find out what we are really feeling and where that feeling came from. (One example of this is the night I came in to see Marty's daughter sitting on his lap and I ran upstairs crying. We took the time to find it was my feelings of not having a father like she had. That was not the adult me crying, it was my Inner Child crying.)*

- *From this I also realized that it was at my birth that my sisters started resenting me. They did not do or know it on a conscious level. I was born on December*

*20th. Back then, new mothers stayed in the hospital for a week, and my sisters missed Christmas. At four and seven years old, missing Christmas was important. They had been separated, staying at different friends' houses while mom was in the hospital. The doctor did not let her go home until the 26th.*

- *Also, because I was born on December 20th I had to hurry from the life and body selection room. I was born at 10:30 p.m. so, if it had been a few hours later I would not have been a Sagittarius. The numerology would have all been different. I just made it.*

- *After years of feeling bad and guilty for always moving, changing and doing everything I did, I was at peace that I had set it up this way and was just checking things off my list. After so many years of allowing others to give me the ammunition I needed to make me feel bad about my life, I could stand tall and know I had a lot of things to do in this life. I had already accomplished so many of them and had to get going on the rest.*

- *Feeling that I had a safe place on that farm was reassuring to me that I was okay then. Even with the fear, molestation, losing my dad, loneliness, I now knew I had friends and was safe.*

- *The vision I had of "choosing" my body so quickly in between lives answered questions about why I do some of the things I do. When I am shopping, I can walk into a store and take the first thing on the rack. Looking around isn't my thing. If I find something, I would like to wear I buy one of each color, so I don't have to take the time to go again for a while. I also knew why I liked brightly colored clothes.*

The whole experience was life-changing for me. I couldn't wait to get home and do more sessions. Marina was coming, and we would go to Arizona. Life was exciting and there was always something to look forward to. I thanked the Universe, God, the angels and now my guides for being with me in this wonderfully huge healing process that I call my life.

I loved doing private sessions with clients, being with them as they journey through this life, into the womb, to a past life on to the death scene of that life and then follow them through their journey into the between life. Being the facilitator of a group was an amazing experience, and watching the faces of the individuals as they felt the support of each other's energy and stories made me the happiest person around. It still does.

Yes, I do have an essence for my life.

Like Mark so eloquently began teaching me on my first day on my journey, "I cannot tell you how you should deal with your issues, but now I can help guide you on your spiritual inner journey."

## Chapter 18

# Another Trip to the Indian and a Ph.D. for Me

During this time Marty started to get very involved with a body movement/dance class that I'd introduced him to. It is a way to move pain and emotion from one's body. He was going a couple of times a week and I was going when I could. There were also weekend classes that he wanted to do. One night I was sitting on the floor at a class and I realized that most of those people sat at desks all week and were ready to move. I stood behind the hairdressing chair ten to twelve hours a day and I was ready to sit. I began staying home and he went alone to dance.

When Marina arrived I picked her up at the airport in San Francisco. Watching her reaction to America's excessive abundance was life-changing for me. I had seen how well they live in Greece, with what we believe is so little. She could see no reason why we need so much. (After she left I began cleaning out unneeded items from my life. This is when I got into clearing more clutter using Feng Shui. I began finding out how good it feels to have less.)

We left for Arizona the next day. We flew into Phoenix and drove up to Sedona. We went to some of the power vortexes and channeled. When we went to the Grand Canyon, I saw a different canyon through her experience. We drove down to Cameron to spend the night.

That evening, Marina began feeling sick. She was shaking, and even with all her clothes, coat and blankets on she felt freezing. I tried to convince her that her body was reacting to what it knew was going to happen tomorrow with the Indian, but she was not buying it. I eventually went to sleep, knowing she would be fine in the morning.

In the morning, she tried to eat but couldn't get much down. Off to the Indian we went. This time I got to watch what he did, and she also had an amazing healing with him.

We drove back to Flagstaff for lunch. On the way Marina started taking off sweaters and shirts because now she was hot. By the time we got to lunch she was feeling much better and could eat. It was a quick trip and we headed back to Phoenix for our flight back to my home.

We had the next week to explore California. We channeled, did sessions, went to the healing expo that was in town that weekend. From psychics and readers, there was more confirmation of our past lives and our future.

When she left, it was time for me to get busy. We were looking for a house that had a bedroom downstairs for Grandpa.

We took a trip to Chicago so Marty could do a long weekend dance/body movement class. One of the nights in the hotel room we decided to do a process to create what we wanted in a house. We got more specific than ever before and we had a lot of fun.

Back home, we looked and looked at houses. Finally, we put my condo up for sale. That meant we had to get serious about where to live. Marina channeled one night on the phone for me because I was getting stressed about not having a place to move to.

She said, "You will find a place when Loni's baby is born."

Okay, then, that wasn't too far off.

A couple of nights later, I got a call from a lady hoping that the condo was still for sale as she wanted to buy it sight unseen for the full asking price. Unbelievable, but now what? We had nowhere to go.

Driving down a main street one day, I was talking with my angels and anyone else that would listen to me, begging for a place to live *now*, when

## Another Trip to the Indian and a Ph.D. for Me

I noticed a FOR SALE sign. That was not the house. As I pulled away I noticed another house with a sign. I went to the door to have a look. The owner was a contractor who had just remodeled the whole house. As I walked through the main part of the house and looked out to the backyard, somehow, I knew it was mine. (Just like when I was selling real estate and showing places to a buyer, as we walked into a condo, I heard, *You are going to live here.* It took a little convincing by my boss to put in an offer. When I did it was a great deal and I moved in.)

Out in the backyard was an old, beat-up garage. I asked the owner if he would build me a beauty shop. He said, "You can't put a beauty shop there." When I asked him why not, his response was, "Because it is a garage."

As we walked around I kept working on convincing him it could be a beauty shop. I felt the energy there and knew. But when I showed Marty and our agent, they didn't think it was right and they kept looking.

A couple days later, I found out the house I liked had dropped in price. Our agent, who was annoyed that I didn't like anything she showed us, wasn't talking to me, so she called Marty. Marty told her we already knew that, and they set up a meeting for Saturday morning.

Friday night I was on the telephone with Marina when Loni and John came by to get my video camera. They were going to the hospital because Loni was in labor. They didn't ask me to go with them, though I had been there when the other two were born. I was upset and crying, and Marina was holding me together. Not being able to go to the hospital and not going to have somewhere to move in twenty-six days when my condo closed escrow had me stressed. John called later to say that they were sent home because she was not far enough along in labor. I went to bed exhausted.

In my dream I heard a baby crying. I woke up to a call saying the baby had been born early that morning. We had to meet the real estate agent at the house she and Marty liked. I told them again I wanted the other house on Harmony Lane, and we went there. The seller was there and within minutes the deal was signed, sealed and delivered to his agent.

The baby was born around eight a.m., the house was signed around ten a.m. and I was at the hospital to see my new granddaughter by noon. It had happened just like Marina channeled: I would find the house when the baby was born.

We planned the closing for twenty-five days later. My agent kept saying, "We can't get this closed in twenty-five days. This is a three-day weekend, that only leaves twenty-three days."

I told her, "If you wouldn't spend so much time saying what you can't do and begin planning how you are going to get it done, it will work."

We started packing. I was tackling the upstairs closet when I found the papers from my first weekend seminar. Included was the drawing Jack had laughed at, the one of me flying on the airplane to an island around the world with people waiting for me, a two-story house, a book I had written and the happy couple holding hands.

Yep, that was me. I was moving into a two-story house, my first book was ready to be printed, Marty and I were very happy and held hands all the time, and I was flying around the world to an island with people waiting for me. They all wanted sessions.

*Oh my God, this stuff really works. It may take a long time, but it does happen. I love it and want more.*

Work it did, and twenty-five days later we moved into Harmony Lane. I had ten days to work, get moved in, draw up plans for the beauty shop in the garage and then I would leave for Greece. The seller would be the contractor for the build and do the cement work around the house for the driveway.

In ten days everything was done, and I got on the plane to Greece. Marty would oversee everything and take care of Grandpa while I was gone.

When I talked with Marty, I felt that something was wrong. He kept telling me it was nothing, but the day before I left to come home he admitted that he hadn't wanted to worry me. The morning after the concrete was poured, he discovered that it had buckled and had to be taken up and be poured again. It wouldn't be done until I was home.

I channeled with Marina to ask why this happened. What I felt was, *There had been so much activity around the house, with all the new energy, that the ground was vibrating at an abnormal speed, which made the new cement wavy.* This made sense. The house had sat vacant for some time. We were bringing in so much high energy, moving, building, motorcycles, cars and people, I could feel it vibrate as I channeled.

I returned home to bring more high energy. The next couple of months were busy with building the salon, landscaping and putting everything together for our business' open house. My birthday, the open house, and Christmas were thrown into one big celebration. About one hundred fifty people came through the doors that day.

Marty and I were both busy showing people around the property and the new building that would be the salon.

I heard Marty in the kitchen saying, "Jeri, come here." When I told him I would be there in a minute, he said, "No, now."

As I started up the three stairs into the kitchen I saw my sister Billie and her family walk through the front door. As stunned as I was, I began introducing them to my friends. I hadn't seen her since our mother's funeral six years earlier. Just six weeks before this we had gone to my nephew's wedding but we had no idea a reconciliation was in the cards. I was overjoyed that Billie had taken this step to rebuilding our relationship.

One Sunday morning two months later, Grandpa did not get out of bed. I went into his room, took one look at him and immediately called the ambulance.

A few days later, we met with the palliative doctor. He asked me, "Was your mother Mildred?"

I thought Marty was going to fall off his chair. He had heard the stories of what I went through with my mother but to have a doctor remember me all these years later was a little unbelievable even for me. Was it because I was that bad or that determined?

Yes, that was me. I told him I had learned a lot since that time, and I was here to do the best for Grandpa and the one who had to be at peace with today was Loni. The tension in the room went away.

As he turned to look at Loni, the doctor asked, "What do you need from me?"

Teary-eyed, she asked, "Can you make Grandpa well?"

He looked at her and said, "No, I can't. Our oath is to do what we can to keep someone alive, but I can't make him well." *(Think about this if you have aging people to take care of. Are you making them well or keeping them alive? If the answer is keeping them alive, ask yourself who are you keeping them alive for and the reasons for that decision.)*

This amazing doctor asked Loni what she wanted to do, as Grandpa could not stay in the hospital any longer. When he told her he could go home to die, she told him, "No, Mom and Marty just bought a new house and she did not want those memories there for us."

He then suggested that we move him to a convalescent hospital. She told him no because Grandpa didn't want to be where Grandma had been. He looked at her and said, "Well then, that leaves the back of my pickup."

That broke the ice and changed the mood of the day as we all laughed.

We settled on moving him on Monday because Sunday was Easter. When I went to the hospital on Saturday, Grandpa and I had the best conversation ever. It was like the floodgates had opened and he told me things he had been holding in most of his life. He talked about Mom, my sisters, and how dear Loni was to him, especially after losing his own little girl. He also talked about me, and what I had brought to his life. As I listened to him, I thought, *Why can't people do this before they're on their deathbed? Get things out in the open. Heal their bodies with relief.* Monday morning, I moved him into the same convalescent hospital Mom had been in. After he was settled in I told him I would be back at seven.

When I walked into the hospital at about five after seven they told me he had died about fifteen minutes earlier. I knew he didn't want to be there and he did not want me there when he died. All my training came in to play and I was at peace with his death.

After his service, I knew I had to take him back to Montana. I was not looking forward to visiting that town again.

## Another Trip to the Indian and a Ph.D. for Me

Marty couldn't go with me, so I said I would go alone.

"No, you are not going alone."

He never told me no about anything so I knew he was serious. The problem was I didn't know who else I would want to spend sixteen hours in a car with. Just then I heard a *bing* from my computer; Marina had signed on. I whipped around in my chair and typed, "Will you come here and drive to Montana with me?" Her answer was yes, and not much later, we were off to Montana. Marina could not believe that so many miles could have nothing but sage brush.

We picked up a friend in Idaho and the three of us went merrily down the road. As we crossed into Montana it began to close in on me and I told them that when I said, "I have to go" the day after the funeral, it would mean I had to leave immediately.

We stayed up most of the night talking, then grabbed a few hours of much needed sleep. The service, which had been completely planned by Grandpa's sister, was very nice, and at the gravesite it was snowing and beautiful. Afterward, she had lunch set up at her house, complete with Jell-o salad. All of sudden I looked at Marina and said, "It's time to go."

Before I knew it, we were at the front door, with all my belongings gathered together, saying goodbye to all those people surprised at our speedy exit. Marina and my friend were saying, "It's snowing and time to go."

We went down to the spot where my dad had been killed to say goodbye, then to the cemetery where he and my mom are. About ten miles down the road, I pulled over and told my friend to drive. I woke up a few hours later when we stopped for dinner and noticed broken glass beneath me on the back seat. One of the picture frames had broken; I had laid on it for hours.

Another trip was complete and a success. I was sad that Marina had to go home quickly but in another couple of months I would be back to Greece to work.

My life with Marty was busier than ever, with working on our new home, putting in landscaping and sidewalks, family on both sides, and his daughter every other weekend. Four months after moving into the new house I had opened my salon and hypnotherapy office and was thrilled to be booking more hypnotherapy sessions. The salon was busy too, and we were getting more involved with the rapidly growing crossdressing community. In the middle of this I also had hernia surgery. One of my girlfriends moved in with us for a couple of weeks, which turned into a couple of years.

At this time, I fell into going to college. I intended to get a bachelor's degree. I don't know where I found the time to study. I loved it so much I couldn't wait to get off work to study more. I was so excited to finally get my degree that I was in the master's program before I knew it. This took a couple of years while going to Greece, working full-time and everything else. The thought that I would be the first person in our family with a master's degree kept me going. I got that degree and before I could take a breather I had signed up for the Ph.D. program. On to a couple more years of study. I was so engrossed that nothing else mattered.

During that time, Marty had become the president of a newly-formed crossdressing organization. As I supported and congratulated him, I had no idea what twists and turns this would take us through.

My girlfriend eventually moved out and different kids and grandkids moved in and out. I didn't realize how crazy life was. Marty often changed jobs or was between jobs.

A sad day came when he sold his motorcycle. Then he sold mine. He said we didn't have time to ride and they were just going to fall apart with no care. That ripped my heart out. Was he right, or could we pull this together and make time?

Life was changing and somehow I felt I had no control over it. The only thing I felt I had control over was getting my Ph.D. I wrote my dissertation on Death with Dignity. It took months of combing through the grueling memories of my mother's death and the lessons I had learned from it. Years later, these lessons informed my decision to take Grandpa off everything so he could die with dignity, rather than putting him through everything I'd put Mom through to keep her alive.

## Chapter 19

# Climbing the Mountain

Time for a little rest? Nope, not yet. There was a dance/body movement class on Maui that Marty wanted to take. At the same time, I learned that a teacher I'd been trying to meet up with for a few years was having a class on Oahu. Yep, we did it. We flew to Hawaii and spent the first night together on Oahu, then the next morning he flew to Maui for his class. After my class was over, I would go to Maui to spend the last few days with him.

The energy within me grew deep to heal the residue of the last few years.

The first days were group participation classes. Someone asked, "What is the difference between faith and trust?" I blurted out, "*Faith is what one has, and Trust is what one does.*" That came out so fast it embarrassed me. The teacher didn't miss a beat; she just agreed and thanked me. After class I wanted to apologize, but she was busy.

The last day I had made an appointment with her for a private session. The apology didn't happen until the middle of my session when we were meeting with my guide, Herold. *"No need to apologize,"* he said, *"because that was me speaking through you. At times when a point needs to be made I do that. From now on know that at times when appropriate I or my helpers will do that. You have known for some time that we help you in sessions and classes."*

In the womb part of this session I felt my mom being nervous and I tried to help but it made me sick. I just wanted to start this life because

I was full of love and it was going to be a busy one. My soul connection was easy, though I found out my body was going to be hard to maintain. At one point, I heard my mother's heartbeat. This was an exceptional feeling because at that moment she was alive again and I knew she loved me. *This is where we can find out about our soul connecting to our fetus. How we felt about coming into this life. What our mother/father was feeling about us coming into life. Different decisions we made about the information we took from our outside circumstances. This part of a session has been life-changing for me, many times. In some sessions, we can find out more of why we came here.*

Also, in the womb, I heard, *Stay small and not seen, you won't get hurt.* That was a lie because I stayed small and still got hurt. This is how beliefs get started that shape our life. That may not have been what was meant when I heard it in the womb, but it was how I interpreted it at the time and then continued staying small throughout my life.

*(Early on in my journey, a teacher told us, "We would rather be right than happy. That took years for me to grasp. We make decisions, early in life or in the womb, and then live our life making that decision "right" for us. Many times, I have learned and seen that those decisions I was making right really harmed my life. Yet, I maintained those beliefs. Usually what we say to self and others is, "That's just me, my personality or who I am." Those beliefs have been with us for so long we believe that's who we are.)*

*Do you know where your beliefs came from?*

The Past Life part of this session was earth-shattering, as I found I had lived in Hawaii, right at this site of this hotel, in 1292. (When I booked this hotel for the class I was upset because it wasn't on the beach. As usual, the Universe/guides will set things up before we know we need it that way.) I saw a little village with grass huts, canoes pulled up on the beach, men pulling in fishing nets, women doing work around the huts while children were playing. Two of these little girls were mine. When the pirates came and killed many, I escaped into the jungle to my sister's house. My two little girls and my husband were killed, and my sister was the woman doing my session with me now. *That explained why I was so connected to her from the first time I met her. I knew these two little girls were my twins I lost in this life.* More healing was done on me losing my twins. I died early in that life, frozen in grief and guilt. Before leaving this part, more healing was done on my grief, guilt and feeling responsible for everyone. *This also showed me why I love to go to Hawaii and lay on the sand.*

In the Soul state, I found out more of why I lived this life the way I have. Always in a hurry and never staying long enough to get the job done. Herold came to me and explained so much of my life and told me he didn't come too often because he did not want me to become dependent on him, but do it myself. He even explained why I like to wear bright colors. While Herold and five other guides were there they explained that I was the only one holding me back. The information they gave me went on for a very long time. (I still listen to this session as often as I can to reclaim the information and energy from it.)

*I always tell my clients that a session does not end when they walk out my door. In fact, that is when the session really begins. It is up to the individual how much they work with the information, to what they will get out of it. One must also take action on the information.*

*This was also reconfirmation of why my mother never changed her life, even after paying psychics, numerologists and anyone else she could find to go to. She never did anything about what they told her to change. I knew I had to work to make things happen for me.*

I went to Maui for a few days of rest. I had been to a different class the Sunday before we left, so I had processing on the beach to do from that class. I had been told to take little pieces of paper and write issues I wanted to release, tie them on a string and then burn them. As the flame moved up the string it burned the issues, releasing them to the Universe. Picture me, standing on the beach on Maui, burning a string with papers on it. I did it and felt relief and release. During the evenings Marty and I rekindled some of what had been absent.

It was about this time that Marty was offered a job by one of my friends. He had been out of work for about eighteen months and his unemployment was about to run out. It was a great job with unbelievable benefits, and one of our biggest miracles in a long time. We were rejoicing that we would be alright again.

When we got home, a hypnotherapy client said after her session, "I am taking you to India to work in the ashram I go to."

At the time I was skeptical, but soon she and I were on a plane.

On my first morning there, I walked into their meeting hall and found about a hundred people waiting for me. As I began the class, I thought, this will be easy because these people grow up knowing about guides, spirits and past lives. After the group past life regression, I asked if there were any questions. The first lady asked, "Is this real?" I almost dropped the microphone. When I regained my composure, I replied, *"If it comes from inside you it is real to you. No one put those thoughts or realizations into your mind."* As we discussed this I saw many relieved faces.

I was never comfortable at that ashram, but the week was such a whirlwind. After doing groups and many private sessions I had a day to explore Delhi before I boarded my plane that night. It was a short visit, but I loved the city, the culture, the people and the sights.

That trip allowed me to reflect on many magical events that had happened in my life. I needed that because at home feelings were changing and I didn't know what to do about any of it. The part that was changing was Marty. As he had become more and more involved with the crossdressing group, he had become less emotionally involved with me. Whenever I tried to talk to him or pull him back, he would get defensive and close up more. I felt I was no longer needed in his life. For the first time he had friends who understood him. He had always said that no one knows what a crossdresser goes through, and I could understand that, but I also had issues that I felt no one understood either. It did not matter what issues I brought up or told him about, he believed he was the one not understood or accepted. We would fight, make up, and finally retreat within ourselves. All he wanted to talk about or be involved with was his club.

I would go to the activities with him and spend most if not all of the time alone. When there were activities at the house, I felt totally left out of the planning and setup, until the work needed to be done. Since I was the only one left, I did it. Of course, I could not get him to see that part. It became a vicious circle in our lives.

I buried myself in work. At one point, looking back over a year, there were only three days that I did neither beauty work nor hypnotherapy. I knew this had to stop, for me and my body. Marina was always talking to me about this.

I was still going to Greece, Norway and England with her to work. Marina had become my anchor, and she considered me hers as well. Finally, she was coming back here. I would take her to my favorite place in the world, Hawaii. I was excited to show her what I loved. As we walked into the hotel room and out the sliding glass doors, I saw Waikiki and the ocean. I took a deep sigh of relief and relaxation. I realized then that this sight would not mean the same to Marina as it did to me. She looked at the sea every day from her home, right outside her door and windows. I was disappointed about that, but we had a fabulous time there anyway.

It was getting easier for me to leave Marty and travel because he was happy that he could dress and be what he wanted. I felt he was recreating what he had lived during his other marriages. I knew he'd lived a life longing for time alone so he could dress. I knew and had heard enough stories about how crossdressers live a life of hiding. Only I didn't understand this with us because with me he could dress any time he wanted to. I came to believe that hiding was also his way of protecting the female side of himself.

Back home I would work at being in Marty's life. All he would say was, "If you want to come, I would love to have you." Then I would go only to be left alone again. Emotionally, he was nowhere to be found.

In the salon, it was getting harder to maintain my disposition. Everyone thought I had the life to live. Everyone would tell him how good he was to me, how much he did for me and how lucky I was. Yes, in some respects he was good to me and I was extremely lucky to have my life. I had also worked very hard for it, both externally and through the deep inner work I had done. Yet a constant battle raged inside of me between the gratitude for my life and the depression I felt because the love of my life was slipping away.

One of my girlfriends invited me to her timeshare in Mexico. In this beautiful resort, where we ate the same food, drank the same everything, I got sick, very sick. The second day I ended up in the hospital.

When we got home I asked myself why I had gotten so sick. The answer I received was, *You got sick to show your friend that she could travel by herself.* That made sense because she had told me how nervous she was going back to the hotel and spending the night alone. Since then she has traveled alone.

It was time to go on another journey with Marina, and this time her sister Aleka would join us. I would meet them in Mexico City. I was torn about leaving Marty, Loni and even my dog, but I was off for the adventure. In the air I fell asleep reading an article on how fear stops us. My flight was delayed due to weather and we waited on the tarmac in Puerto Vallarta. I could see, smell and feel the sea air that I loved there. After that delay, we were off to Guadalajara to change flights to Mexico City. Guadalajara was total confusion. Helpers appeared at the right place when I needed them to translate information for me and direct me to the right gate. I offered them some of the homemade chocolate chip cookies I was taking for Marina.

During landing in Mexico City, I saw a big pink hotel building and wanted to stay there. After hugging Marina and Aleka, off we went to the pink hotel. They already had a room for us, and we went to get massages, then a great dinner.

I was relaxed and tired and soon drifted off to sleep. Suddenly, I woke up and told Marina, "I just got slapped across the face with a big branch of a bush."

"What?" After I repeated what I had said she asked, "Why?"

I didn't know why until morning. Then I told them, I had heard, *The slap was to wake you up and make sure you grasp all the information available to you on this journey.*

As we headed south to Cuernavaca, I called Marty, who told me of his vision of us being on the old Mexican bus with the chickens and pigs. I reassured him we were on a first-class bus with refreshments being served and a movie screen at each seat!

I spent part of the time on the bus thanking the Universe for what I have. Thanking them for bringing me and Marina together, as well as all the experiences we'd had and those that were to come.

When we arrived, we got a taxi to a village in the mountains where there was a pyramid. Aleka spoke Spanish as well as English and Greek, and somehow through all the translating I began to understand this was a very powerful mountain. The driver continued to talk as we climbed in altitude, going through quaint little villages. Suddenly, the look on Aleka's face changed and she turned and looked at us, telling us we had to have a question for the mountain. The driver, she said, was adamant that it had be the perfect question, or the mountain would send you back.

"What is the question of your soul?" he asked, then went on to say that he had lost a very good spiritual teacher when he was younger because the man hadn't asked the right question.

At our little hotel on a side street of one of those quaint mountain villages, we sat on the beds talking about the mountain and the question. It was like, if you were going to be in front of God and had one question, what would it be? The air was getting tense among us as we tried to come up with our question. We decided to go eat dinner. This turned out to be a tense experience as well, and after an unsatisfying meal we started walking and looking around.

I decided to treat us all to massages, which were about ten dollars. As we entered the rooms our jaws dropped in shock. Just a board to lie on with a dirty towel over us and half walls between us so we could hear each other. It would be my first hot stone massage. Well, the stones were either burning hot or cool. Obviously, none of these people had ever been to a massage school. It was totally unbelievable that we didn't get up and run out the door. For some reason, we persevered. When it was over, and the massage people left the rooms, all three of us began laughing and couldn't stop. Marina and Aleka told me what the people were saying during our massages. It was hysterical and broke the ice of solemnity that we had been in since we found we couldn't come up with the right question.

Back in our little room with no heat, we got ready for bed. I was in one bed and they were sharing the other. Aleka asked me if I would sleep with them one night so it would be like when she was a little girl and cousins would come over and they would all sleep together. I told her I would do so before the week was over.

It was Marina's turn to channel so we could see about the next day and what to do. The channeling was all about "the question." The question had to be a soul question because if it was frivolous or meaningless the Spirits would be upset and not communicate with us.

She channeled it was to be our own journey. We would probably end up going alone and each end up at different points. We were not to judge our journey, or the others'. We should each stay focused on our own journey.

After she finished channeling we talked about our questions and going deep into our souls. Suddenly, the to-do list I had written on the bus felt so unimportant compared to a true soul desire.

Marina had mentioned the word *resistance*, which struck a chord within me. I had been working on the realization that "nothing was holding me back" but me. Now I saw it was my own resistance. Some questions began to come: What is my fear? What am I running from? What does my physical body need? These questions seemed unimportant but that was all I could come up with. We were still talking when we drifted off to sleep.

We all had different dreams, some we remembered and some we couldn't. Waking up to chilly water in the shower and a plugged toilet was the highlight of the morning. We just got dressed and checked out, leaving our luggage until we came back from the pyramid. We found a cute little place in a courtyard for breakfast and spent the meal talking about our question.

Finally, we started up the path to the pyramid. It was very peaceful with little tables set up that we knew later would have all types of items for sale. We had figured out that this whole little village was set up for those who come to climb the mountain and see the pyramid. Soon the path turned into stairs with nothing on the sides; then there were no more stairs, just stacked rocks or boulders to climb.

Suddenly, I looked around and couldn't see Marina or Aleka. I was alone. I remembered the channel that we should each make our own journey and that the bet was I would be the one to not make it to the top. Only I had no idea where or what the mountain was. I kept climbing little by little. Watching others drop off. Trying to stay connected to the deeper part of me, whatever that was. This far up the hill I wasn't sure about anything. I asked different people who were coming down how much farther it was. They told me about an hour. Then about a half-hour. Then fifteen minutes. There were only more boulders to climb on. Looking up, I couldn't see the top of the mountain yet. Looking back down the mountain and seeing part of what I had climbed was unbelievable to me. There was something inside that just kept saying, "You can do it, keep going." It was a miracle that I found the stamina.

So many thoughts and feelings were running through me that it was hard to concentrate on them and keep climbing. I had the urge to pull out my little notepad and write. I wrote what came to me.

*Everyone is doing their path. You open the door and show your path. They do the same. Then each chooses. Question is, can you love and accept totally without judgment of their path?*

I reread this a few times but the meaning didn't come to me. I took another small sip of water and looked up the mountain. All this climbing and I hadn't even drunk half a bottle of water. I couldn't because there was no place to go to the bathroom either. I had thought about that a few times and quickly chased it from my mind.

Everyone kept telling me the top was close. Okay, if it is why can't I see it? This made no sense at all. Why hadn't I found out what this was about before I agreed to do this? Shoot, I don't remember agreeing to anything I just did.

Around one more bend over a few more boulders, I looked up and saw the top of the mountain with the pyramid on top. Oh no, between me and the top were metal stairs straight up. About one hundred fifty to two hundred stairs, oh my God. Something from somewhere made me start climbing those stairs. Almost at the top, I looked up and saw Marina coming down.

When she saw me, she threw her arms around me, yelling, "You made it, you made it!"

"No, not quite," I answered.

"Close enough," she said. "I will show you pictures of the top."

As we turned around and started down my legs began shaking. I thought going down would be easy. Nope, it was almost harder to reverse all those muscles.

She and Aleka hadn't seen each other since the bottom. I had thought they were together and she thought we were together. Marina was so excited that I made it she even took my phone and called Marty to tell him.

A little farther down the path was Aleka. We talked for a bit but knew we couldn't let our muscles tighten up or we wouldn't make it. When we stopped, I told them about what I had written. Marina told us about what she had remembered, and she knew it was her answer.

*Marina heard the story that there was a king who had a garden and he planted one cypress tree, one lemon tree and one little pansy. The king went away for a trip and when he came back both trees were dried and dying while the little flower was blooming in full color and beauty. He asked the flower why the trees were dying, and the flower explained that the cypress tree got very sad and depressed because it could not offer beautiful lemons to him and so it was dying. Then the lemon tree was sad and depressed because it couldn't be as tall as the cypress tree, so it was dying. The little flower told him that since he had planted a pansy that is what he wanted, and it did the best it could and bloomed for him.*

Even though we did not have the question, there was the answer. *What we did do was go with a completely open mind and heart. We kept asking, what is the question? As we got lost in the climb our minds became more open and the answers could come through because we were listening.*

At the bottom, we celebrated by buying each other little gifts from the vendors and drinking water. As we walked and talked about our experiences we stopped for a little street lunch. I said, "Oh my God, I want a good massage."

Marina said, "I would love a hot tub to soak my body in." (We now knew why there were so many massage places at the bottom of the mountain. We didn't want to go back there.)

We retrieved our luggage and caught a cab to another small town. Aleka was looking through a travel book while they talked in Greek and I rested and enjoyed the view. We pulled up in front of a building with big wooden doors and very tall stone walls that went on for so far I couldn't see the end.

They said, "Let's go see if this is a good hotel."

A man in a suit opened the door for us and we went into a beautiful lobby. Aleka told us to follow as we were going to look at the room. We followed the clerk out the glass doors into the most beautiful garden I had ever seen. Down a few stairs, we saw peacocks, parrots, beautiful flowers and an immense green lawn; to the right were dinner tables with linens, beautiful china and crystal, candles, and to the left were rooms for relaxing. Through a door to a hall and into a patio that led to our spacious room. A huge fireplace, then windows that led to another patio with chaise lounges and a table and chairs. There was a sofa and stuffed chairs with end tables and a coffee table, and behind all of this was a huge, king-size bed that led to the dressing room and on to the bathroom. It was absolutely incredible.

"I will show you the spa areas now," said the desk clerk, then off across the lawn we went into the outdoor pool area. Waiting pool attendants put out towels for us. To the right was a footbridge leading to the entrance of the spa. As we entered, we saw more beautiful peaceful marble-walled rooms, then continued past the treatment and resting rooms and into the hot and cold pool with wet and dry steam rooms.

We went back over the lawn to the reception area, where Aleka said," I think this will do." She booked our room for the night with spa treatments and we laughed all the way back to our room.

After changing and going to the spa for our hot tub and steam room experience we were shown into the relaxing room to lay on white suede lounge chairs and be served mineral water, dried fruit and nuts.

As we were lying there enjoying this beautiful room, Aleka said, "I feel like a hypocrite. I have always judged rich people for their extravagant lifestyle and now I find I could actually like it."

Laughing, Marina said, "Well, I think we passed the test on the mountain. To be led here to paradise I think we passed."

After a relaxing massage, we changed for dinner. When we got to the lawn the candles were all lit and our table was ready. We had the most amazing dinner ever, with drinks. Every so often one of us would say, "Climbing that mountain and passing the test was so worth it for this."

We sat outside in the garden and took it all in, then it was time to call it a night. It had been a big day, starting in a hotel with chilly water and plugged toilet, climbing the mountain and then on to paradise. Was that only one day? Before we went to bed we had one of us channel to see what to do the following day. Aleka wanted to go to another museum and some ruins. She promised there was no mountain to climb. I channeled, and they said that was fine to do. We did not have to spend a lot of time anywhere to gain the energy of a place; however, we should sit in a circle with our backs to each other, as those were the energy points that would connect the easiest and one of us would channel again.

That night, all three of us slept in that big king size bed, just as Aleka had asked. We got my wish for a massage and Marina's for a hot tub. All of us had gotten our heart's desires and so much more delivered to us. What an incredible day.

The next morning breakfast was served on our patio, wonderful food and so much of it. While we ate, Aleka announced that she was not leaving here. We were staying in paradise for another day.

She would get no argument from me.

We hired a taxi to the museum that was about an hour away. Marina and Aleka walked to the top of these ruins but I was going to sit on this rock and wait for them. I knew they wouldn't be long as we had the taxi driver waiting for us. When they returned suddenly, I found we were in a circle on this rock with our backs to each other and I began to automatically channel. Then Aleka channeled and then Marina. Each of us had incredible insight that was meant for all of us.

My channel was: *Time is an illusion – stay focused and listen to us. Guilt only slows the process down. Guilt takes away from enjoyment. Guilt is a useless feeling as no one else knows your feelings. The focus and accomplishments produce more interaction with us and more results.*

Aleka's channel was about Heraclitus, the dark philosopher. Heraclitus abstracted stress and then had the passion and desire to go through or penetrate the superficial visible world and look for the transition to a higher sphere of knowledge. Heraclitus was also the first one to use physical procedures to get to the outcome.

Before we left, Marina made an offering to the mountain. On our taxi ride back to paradise, I was given information on resistance. *Resistance is only in my head.* I asked for help removing it from me so I could do what was needed.

Back in paradise they decided we needed to go to the spa again. More hot tubs, steam room, relaxing in the white lounges and off to the massage. Another dinner that spoiled us for all other meals.

The next morning, we hopped that great first-class bus to head to Mexico City so I could fly out the day after that. Our hotel there was quite ordinary, though after the last two days nothing would even begin to compare. But being in normal surroundings helped me to come back to some type of reality and begin my journey back home. That night we walked around the city, stopping at a couple of bars for drinks and appetizers. Back in our room, Aleka channeled about the past week, then the three of us talked about our amazing experiences and accomplishments. We talked about everything from the power of the mountain to our own intimate thoughts.

In the morning, we went to the main shopping center to buy typical Mexican souvenirs and just be with each other before I left. As always, Marina and I parted knowing the Universe would provide us with our next adventure. In the meantime, I had enough newfound information to keep me going for months.

One day while driving to the dentist, I had an asthma or panic attack. Every time that I went to the dentist my body would tighten up and my throat would begin to close, and I would start coughing. While sitting in the chair it was hard to not cough so the dentist could clean my teeth. During that episode, I decided that I needed to call my girlfriend from hypnotherapy school who was also a dental assistant. I called her that evening and asked her if she would go with me to my next dental cleaning and do a session while he was working on me.

She agreed, and four months later we went to my dentist. We told him what we were going to do, and I was sure he had no idea what we were talking about. As he started the cleaning, she started talking me down into a light trance. My body already knew what was going to happen. I closed my eyes and as she talked, I felt the first tear slide down my cheek. I was feeling being held down, though I was perfectly aware that no one was currently doing so.

I held my hand up for him to stop and told my girlfriend that I felt trapped. She asked me how old I was when I was held down and trapped. I told her three years old. The poor dentist was trying to do his job, but I kept stopping him to tell my friend it was when my uncle was molesting me. I felt trapped, held down and he was trying to put something in my mouth. I felt more tears trickle down my cheeks while I was too scared to cry out. Then, when we knew this was figured out, we healed all that could be healed at that time. She asked me if I was alright and could go to a dentist without panic from now on. She then brought me out of the session so he could finish his job. I just wanted out of that office. He did not ask me to reschedule.

In the days that followed I dealt with the anger, sadness and other feelings that went with this additional information. I also had to deal with the loss of some teeth that I had had pulled over the years instead of filling them because it was faster.

Every time I thought I had healed all the molestation issues, something else would crop up. I believe this is true for anyone who has been molested; these are the issues that they can never put together. As much healing work as we do, the residue of being molested remains.

Before my next appointment I found a new dentist down the street from my home. The first visit, I told him what had happened. He was very understanding. His niece, who worked with him, told me that they now teach classes in dental school on how to deal with survivors of sexual abuse. Since then I love my dentist and have no problem going.

That problem was solved but there was still an ongoing saga at home.

It was Christmas again. The house was decorated, the presents ready, work was done for a few days and we were getting ready for the traditional Christmas Eve at our home. Since we moved into the new house, our Christmas tradition involved taco soup, salad and garlic bread. When my youngest granddaughter was done with dinner, her way of getting down was to go to the bathroom. As soon as she and her dad went in the bathroom, I would jump up, go into the living room and take the stockings out of hiding to put up. On my way out the front door I would jingle the bells hanging there. I would hear her yelling, "Daddy, it's Santa Claus!" As I came in the back door they would walk into the living room. Then, with her eyes wide open in surprise at the stockings, she would say, "Oh no, I missed him again!" It was a wonderful tradition.

As this dinner started my son-in-law announced that they needed to talk to me. Loni said, "No, not now," but he insisted, saying he had already started.

"I braced myself and said, 'Might as well go ahead.'"

He announced that this was going to be the last Christmas like this; he was tired of buying presents and from now on it would just be their family.

I was speechless, but my mind was racing. *What? Really? Your family? Then what am I? I thought I was family.* What could I say to that? Nothing.

After they had left to put the kids to bed I did my final drive over there with an SUV full of presents and breakfast for the next morning. We would fix all the presents under the tree, sit by the lights and have a drink. Then I would go back home sleep for a couple hours, and when they called we would go over and spend the morning opening presents and having breakfast. Later, we would have dinner together again.

Over the next few months I slowly came out of shock, the anger, sadness and every other emotion that was happening inside me. By about June I decided I had to make this work for me. *I could stay mad and bitter and that would only hurt me.* They were doing what they wanted to.

An idea came to me. For years everyone had been telling me I should go on a cruise, but I had been against it. Now I decided to make reservations to sail on the Christmas Day. That would give me something to look forward to that did not include Christmas. My clients who went on cruises were so happy and now they could tell me all about it.

On Christmas Eve Marty and I drove to Los Angeles to set sail the following morning. It was a week of bliss, even better than anyone had described it to me. I loved every minute of having my husband with me, and he was there in every sense of the word. We had a Christmas dinner to die for. All week in the sun, sightseeing, experiencing all assets of the ship, dressing up like we hadn't done in a long time, dancing, making love and just enjoying each other. We had New Year's Eve on board and disembarked on our anniversary.

The year had started out on a high note, though it had brought with it some changes. Marty's daughter Karen, a little six-year-old when we met, was now eighteen and had moved in with us. It was fine, she was working and dating someone. She and I spent many nights in the hot tub talking about her different fantasies. We were all busy.

One day she and her boyfriend told us she was pregnant. The baby was due around December 15$^{th}$. I immediately said, "Nope, it will be born on my birthday." They insisted it would be early, but something in me knew it would be on the 20$^{th}$.

I was whirling with memories of when I was single and pregnant, and my mother was screaming at me and furious with my situation. I sprang into action for Karen. She needed to be protected and have what she wanted for herself and her baby. Her boyfriend was leaving for the service in a couple weeks.

When she told me they had an appointment at the Justice of the Peace to get married, my heart sank. I knew she had dreamed of being married in our backyard. She had told me so once in the hot tub.

That wedding was what she was going to have. In nine days, I pulled it together.

It was beautiful. Our backyard was full of spring blooms, and we had it all set up with tables and chairs, flowers, an arch with more flowers, a white runner over the grass, food, a beautiful cake made by my sister Billie, the white dress Karen had already picked out, the veil I found to match, decorations, and music. Everything was ready, so now we had a few minutes to relax before Karen's mother arrived.

After a couple of drinks, my sister started interrogating me about why Bobbie would still not speak to me after about twenty years. In fact, both of my sisters had stopped talking to me when our mother was sick, and though Billie and I eventually reconciled, we had never spoken about "real life." I was not in the mood for it now and told her we would talk about it later, but she kept asking.

Finally, I said, "I think she won't talk to me because she knows it was her husband that molested me for many years."

I thought she was going to tell me I was crazy and not believe me. Instead, she jumped out of her chair and exclaimed, "Me too, me too!"

I sat there in a haze of disbelief, anger and sadness. I was also ashamed that I had never considered the possibility that she too had been molested by him. I had suspected other family members had been molested, but had never thought about her.

Another huge emotion I felt was validation. I wanted to hug her. She just kept asking me why.

"Why am I having all these memories now? Why, Jeri, why?"

As I sat there, the first wedding guests arrived. I had to pull this together fast.

I thought I could stand so I did. I greeted them. More people came. My sister and I acted like nothing had happened on the outside but on the inside, we were a mess.

I was called out to the beauty salon to help there. Soon Karen's mother showed up and everyone's stress level zoomed through the roof. Somehow, I had to get this wedding started. I had Marty start the music and ask people to be seated. The wedding day went off and was beautiful and fun.

We got Karen married and settled in her little apartment and her new husband left for the service.

Now there was time to go to lunch with my sister and talk. She asked me again why she has these memories now. *I explained to her, when we get older and lives slow down, our children move out, our minds and bodies now have time to reveal some of what it has been holding for years. With molestation issues sometimes our repressed memories come through as our children become the age we were when we were molested.* It is difficult to explain all the ways being molested affects someone.

Since we were being more open with each other than ever before, I told her about Marty being a crossdresser. With her religious beliefs I wasn't sure how she would take it, so I was relieved when she told me she believed God loves everyone and he would love Marty also.

It was time to finally ask the burning question that had been inside of me for years. With fear in my heart, I asked, "Did you have a baby when you were in high school and give it up for adoption?"

She said yes, then it was her turn to ask me how I knew and when I found out.

In a class years ago, the discussion was about a woman who was healing herself from giving up a baby for adoption. While she was doing her healing, I had the visions and memories of being in the fifth grade. Mom had moved us to another town, and I was told my sister was sick and had to stay in bed. One night I looked under the bedcovers and saw she was pregnant. Another night when they thought I was asleep, I peeked while my sister was walking to the bathroom and saw that she was very pregnant. I was excited because I loved my other sister's boys. I was going to be an aunt again.

One day I came home from school and found a note my mother left me. She told me to stay in the motel and she would be back soon. The next thing I remembered, she had taken me back to our hometown and told me to wait in the apartment until she got back. After she left I called my other sister Bobbie and went to her house. Boy, did I get into trouble when Mom got back. Billie came home too, but there was no baby. None of it made any sense to me.

After Mom died I cornered Grandpa and asked him if my sister had had a baby. I thought he was going to fall off the sofa. I told him I would stay up all night until he answered me. I reminded him that Mom was not around any longer to strike him down if he told me. He confirmed my memories.

Billie told me she had been looking for this baby for years. We are still looking for this baby because neither of us have any more memories or details than what I described above. We learned a baby boy was born in a Catholic hospital in Helena, Montana, in December 1959. My sister believes it was the 12th. If anyone has any information on a baby boy born in December 1959, please contact us.

With this out in the open we became closer than we had been in years, maybe ever. I had more compassion for *us* than ever. I began to comprehend how much of her life and our life she had no memory of. I remembered how little I remembered until I began my journey of healing. Eventually, I stopped trying to talk her into a session of any kind because her religious beliefs prohibited this.

We talked about her having colon cancer and a heart attack during the time we were not in contact. We would meet for lunch and cleared as much as we could, given her limited memory.

All the time this was going on I was working, writing, doing sessions, holding a couple of day classes that were a big success and of course always working on my relationship with my daughter. Marty was maintaining his life with his club. Karen had moved back East with her new husband and they were waiting for their baby.

It was time to get away from it all for another cruise. I loved the first one so much I could not wait to go again. This time we did the Eastern Caribbean. Another dream come true. Ten days with the sun, sea and Marty. Again, we partied, loved, laughed and truly enjoyed each other.

The baby's due date was coming up. Her first due date passed, then the second due date. As the dates became closer to the 20$^{th}$ I knew it would be born on my birthday. The morning of the 19$^{th}$ she went into the hospital to be induced. My prophecy did not falter. The night of the 19$^{th}$ my girlfriend came to give me a massage, and by ten p.m. we hadn't heard anything from the East Coast so we knew the 20$^{th}$ would be the date.

About five the next morning I heard Marty on the telephone, telling them congratulations. I took a deep sigh and wondered what this meant. I heard, *I picked your birthday to get your attention, so you would know it was me.* Who is this? I asked, and immediately knew it was the soul of my father.

I called my girlfriend to say, "You won't believe what I just heard." Her response surprised me: "That is why I saw your father around you last night during your massage."

I had to just let some of it go as I was busy with Christmas, and Marina and her girls were coming for the holidays. (I had gotten close to them during all of my trips to Greece. The one who was twenty months old the day we met them was now twelve years old and her sister was fourteen. It was time for them to come to my home in America.) I hadn't decorated since our Christmases were cancelled, but I did this year. We had a couple of great weeks doing holidays, then spent New Year's Eve in Reno with friends from India and Nepal. We had an international event going on.

When they left we had nine days to get ready to go back East to visit Karen and the baby. The day of our trip, Marty dropped me off to check the luggage and check in while he parked the car. As he walked into the terminal, I was putting the paperwork into my computer case when I notice my ring lying on top of it. As I picked it up thinking, shoot how did that happen, I heard, *Put it in your purse so you don't lose it.* But I slid it back on my finger, thinking that I would curl my finger around it to keep it on.

Not long afterward, I noticed that my ring was no longer on my finger. Out loud I said, "Oh no, my ring is gone!" The TSA agents came over and asked me about it. Because the airport was not busy at all, they started looking on the floor, through the buckets and all around. They reran my suitcase and computer case through the x-ray. I searched through the top items in the suitcase. I went back downstairs and retraced my steps looking carefully everywhere. My ring was nowhere, but we had to go get on plane.

During the flight I kept asking myself, *Why didn't I listen to the voice? Why didn't I put my ring away? What is the lesson in this?* I asked as many questions as I could to help ease my sadness. Finally, I just gave up; it was just a ring.

We arrived at Karen's house to see the baby. I knew I wouldn't walk in and see my dad sitting there, but what would I see or feel? When she handed me the baby, I looked into his eyes and thought, *Is this really your soul?* I felt or imagined that he looked into my eyes saying, *Is this really you?*

I started to cry, and Karen looked at Marty and asked, "Dad, what is wrong with Jeri?"

The question brought me out of wherever I was. They would think I had lost it. We had a few more days with them, and all the excitement made me totally forget about my ring.

One day, I was walking down the hall when I heard the little quiet voice ask, *Have you learned to listen to the quiet little voice that talks to you? Have you learned to listen to us?*

Stopped in my tracks, I answered, "Yep, I will do my very best to listen to you and carry out what you say."

Many thoughts ran through my head and I was sad that I hadn't listened to them and put my ring away. Part of me hoped that the airport would call and tell me they found my ring. The other part knew this was a lesson.

After a few days with them Marty and I went to Graceland for the day. It was somewhere I had always wanted to go, and we had a wonderful time.

The next day I heard, *This is how fast it can be taken away if you don't listen and do.* That rang through my whole body. I went out on their balcony and my thoughts were on that statement for quite a time. What can be taken? Is that why things really do just show up in my life? Is that why sometimes I work hard at something and it never comes to fruition? Do "they" really control so much in my life? No, *I control my thoughts and actions.* Okay, I'm getting somewhere now. I control my thoughts and actions, but they tell me what to do. Then I make the decision to do it or not. REMEMBER, *making no decision is a decision. When we procrastinate, we are making the decision not to do anything.*

With that thought, I decided I must follow through and go to Hawaii to work on my book. I had to write and accomplish everything they had told me to do. Chills ran through my body. There was fear, fear that everything would be taken from me if I didn't do what I was supposed to do. Excitement that there was help and a push to get it done. Finally, I knew help was with me. All I had to do was focus and move ahead. My feelings were mixed. Fear kept taking over my thoughts. Fear was familiar to me. I know that fear was what kept me from forging ahead.

Marty called me in to get ready to leave, so I went to the bedroom to get my cigarettes. I leaned over to pick up a pack next to the suitcase on the floor and *right there in plain sight, lying on top of the Levi's that I had worn the day before, was my ring.* My ring, how can that be? After all these years of my new beliefs, I am always surprised how "they" work. I ran out to the living room to surprise Marty.

As I put the ring in the zippered pocket of my purse I thought, I got the lesson and that is why it was returned to me. Then the thoughts began flowing in about the lessons and now I must listen and make things happen. Everything "they" have told me over the years, I must do.

## Chapter 20

## *Return to Panama*

Once we had returned home I was determined to get busy with this book like "they" had told me to. I went to Hawaii to be alone and write. The first part of the week, I realized how stressed my body had been and how exhausted I was. The last half of the week I got a lot done.

At home, I always had high hopes Marty would come around and be the husband he had been before he had his club. Instead, he kept pulling farther away, as the club grew more determined that the world would accept them. Anyone they felt did not accept them fully would be blocked out. This part was becoming more confusing to me because I did accept him as transgender. Yes, now they no longer called themselves crossdressers, they were now transgender. I likened it to something I had written about in the *ABC's of Never Having Another Bad Hair Day*, I have been called a beautician, a hairdresser and a hairstylist, but I am the same person doing the same thing. I could not figure out the difference.

I think the part he didn't like was that I also wanted him as a husband. This was one reason our cruises had become so important to me. Then I did not have to feel guilty for wanting my husband and we always had a special closeness.

I decided it was time to plan another one and chose the Panama Canal Cruise. I had always wanted to go back to Panama and see if what I remembered was correct.

Back in 1961, when I was thirteen and Billie was seventeen, our mother married John. Looking back now, I could see what a mess we were. Our mother wanted to get us away from our current boyfriends and I am sure she also wanted to spend some stress-free time with her new husband without us running amuck.

She decided to send us to the Panama Canal Zone and stay on Albrook Airforce Base with her sister and brother-in-law, who was in the U.S. Air Force. Her sister had seven boys ranging in age from six months to twelve years old. First she sent us to Chicago to see her brother and family for a week, then it was off to New York City for a week by ourselves before heading to Panama.

I had reflected on this period many times and remembered it as one of the best times of my childhood. But, think about it. Our mother had sent two out-of-control teenagers from a small town in Montana to New York City, then to an Air Force Base for three months with a woman who had several young children and a husband who was always off flying somewhere. Mom probably thought we were safe and out of town. Yes, we stayed safe but, a lot of the time we were a menace to ourselves. Yep, we had an enjoyable time on the Air Force Base.

I had always wished I could go back and see if there was really a place we went to watch the ships go through the canal. If the mountain we climbed, cutting through the jungle with machetes, was there. I wondered if my memories were accurate.

Now was the time. I knew I could only see it from the ship, so I booked a balcony room on the port side. I was so excited when the day came to sail out of Miami. Three days at sea ended with a beautiful trip to Columbia, followed by another day of sailing.

One morning I jumped out of bed and put on my swimsuit and cover up.

Marty rolled over and asked, "What are you doing, Jeri? It is still dark."

Excitedly I said, "Oh my God, we are here. Look at all the ships out there."

He could not believe I was awake and getting dressed before five a.m. I ran a comb through my hair and told Marty I would meet him up on Deck 12 when he got up. Then I was out the door.

I had no idea what to expect but I was going to be ready. It was hours of running up and down stairs to see everything from different perspectives. Part of the day we were on the bow of the ship with the crew. Some of the time I was in our room hanging over the balcony and listening to the television give the history of the place.

The middle of the day, there it was, the remnants of Albrook Air Force Base and the "mountain." Well, it was actually a hill, but it was there. I also saw where we must have sat to watch the ships go through the locks. (The Pacific and Atlantic, which the Canal connects, are different levels; the locks are structures that help the ships get through the Canal by lifting them up and dropping them to the level of the water on the other side). As I took in the view I wasn't sure what was going on in my body, but it was incredible. Almost like confirmation of my past.

After the amazing day in the Panama Canal, it was sailing for the rest of the cruise. Two weeks went quickly, and then it was home to reality.

Again, it was the holidays with no family to celebrate with, though it was getting a bit easier. Knowing it was not my choice helped, and besides, I did have the memories of the big Christmases we used to have. I was also looking forward to Marty's family reunion in Massachusetts towards the end of the summer. As long as I had something to look forward to, I could always maintain my life.

A few years earlier I had taken Brittany to London, Paris and Greece for her eighteenth birthday and graduation. Now we decided to invite her younger sister to go with us for her graduation trip.

This granddaughter had always wanted to walk the Brooklyn Bridge, so we would go to Massachusetts first then to New York City. When I asked her what else she wanted to see she replied, "Everything," and what better way to do that than a helicopter ride? The look of pure excitement on her face was worth the whole trip and we still had four more days.

As soon as the helicopter ride was finished Marty left for home, and she and I were off to make the most of our time sightseeing, shopping and having dinner at a friend's home. Another week of my life to cherish forever.

## Chapter 21

# See Your Power and Keep Your Light On

*If you don't change your beliefs your life will be like this for forever. Isn't that good news? What you focus on expands!*

~W. Somerset Maugham

As the next year began, I was searching for answers as to what I should do. I had been unproductive in reaching my goals. I just wanted change. (I do know that when I ask for change I should be specific. Nope didn't do that, I just asked for change.)

I had a kidney infection in January. I knew this meant something big was going on in my body. I had lost myself again. I had no motivation, energy, life or anything in me. Writing this book seemed totally impossible and that was very depressing. Marty and I had grown farther apart than ever before. All he ever wanted to talk about or be involved with was his club and his people. I got another bad cold and then another bladder infection. I had so much going on inside of me I knew I needed help from someone or somewhere.

During one of my many doctor's appointments he reminded me that I needed a mammogram. A few days later I got the dreaded call that they had to recheck something they saw. Of course, I was standing behind the chair working and was booked the next day when they wanted me to come in. I told them I could do an appointment on Monday, but after I hung up the thoughts of the devastation a diagnosis could mean began racing through my mind. I was so angry at myself for putting my clients before me again.

To say it was a long four days was an understatement. I went through the memories of every client who had come in and told me about their experience. I tried to focus on the ones that said it was nothing, but the ones who did have breast cancer kept pushing their way to the forefront. The fear of what I would do if I had to take time off work kept screaming through my thoughts.

What had I done to my body? Through my journey I had learned what we do to our body through our concise and unconcise thoughts and beliefs; in fact, I believed that my hysterectomy at age twenty-six was a result of being molested so many times as a child. (Many of my hypnotherapy clients who have been molested have female problems). I believe that molestation victims disassociate with various parts of our body during and after the molesting, which later causes disease.

I also knew that my relationship with my body had changed. I thought I had always been (mostly) happy with the way I looked. While going through the work around the molestation I had acquired an appreciation for my body and what it had carried me through. I had thought doing my experiment with Marty the first night he dressed would be the end.

Now I had to look at what I had done to my body while being married to a transgender man. When we first started going out together I felt I didn't look as good as "they" did. I didn't take two hours getting ready to go out at night. I didn't have the clothes some of them did.

Soon my feeling became personal. I remembered one night as we were in bed, he was rubbing my body, and said "God, I love your body." Suddenly, I felt priceless to him. He loved me and my body. Then he followed that up with, "You don't know how badly I would love to have your body."

It was like a giant slap to my self-esteem. I thought, *Oh shit, he doesn't love me and my body, he just wants it for himself.*

I changed forever.

At least, up until now I had changed. My body could have cancer and I had allowed something he said to me to start it.

I remembered my hernia surgery and the outcome of that. It was to be an outpatient surgery, but I ended up in the hospital for three days. The pain never went away. Doctors researched why the pain was so bad – even worse than before the surgery. For a few years I was always in and out of the ER and doctors' offices.

After giving a talk at a Healing Expo, I was stopped by one of the healers. Soon he had me on his massage table, in the middle of a huge room with hundreds of people walking around. As soon as I was in the session, his hands went right to the spot where my surgery had been. As I cried, I knew the pain was all about the night I'd learned about my molestation issues and Jack had been so out of control. It was then, as I sat curled on the sofa with my knees under my chin, that the hernia was created. The healer began moving the energy out of my body, and as he did the pain disappeared. I stayed around for a while to fully come back into my body and be present before I drove home. The pain has never come back.

Amazing what happens to our body during trauma.

Now, as I waited out that agonizing weekend to see if a malignancy had been created, part of me wanted Monday never to come and another part just wanted to find out the results and at least know what I was dealing with. Marty and I spent most of the time talking, sometimes very loudly, about my feelings. As usual, Marty just could not comprehend them. As always, he had it the hardest and I didn't understand.

Finally, Monday came. Marty took the morning off work to go with me.

At the hospital, I was given another mammogram, then asked to dress and go to a room to wait. As I walked into a small room lined with chairs around three walls, there were two scared-looking women sitting across the room from each other in silence.

As I walked across to the farthest wall, the woman to my left said, "Oh, you brought your angels with you."

I stopped in my tracks, looked at her and said, "What?"

She repeated herself with a smile.

"What made you say that?" I asked.

"I can see them around your shoulders, there are more than four of them."

I was so stunned I went and sat down. Now my head was really spinning. *Are the angels really with me? How does she see them when I certainly can't feel them right now? Who are they? Who is she?*

Before I knew it, we were talking about my angels, my hypnotherapy and my channeling. She was Asian and began telling me about her beliefs. We were deep in conversation when the other lady said, "I don't believe any of that stuff. My life was horrible as a child and it hasn't gotten any better."

The two of us were trying to talk with her and console her in some way when the door opened. The nurse called the woman I had been talking with and told her she could go. I asked her to tell my husband in the waiting room I was still here.

She looked at me and asked, "He's the good looking one, right?"

I grinned and said, "Well, I think so. How did you know?"

She winked and said, "I just knew."

The nurse immediately called my name. As I stood up, she said, "You are free to go."

I was so relieved I thought I might pass out, and before I could even utter the words thank you, she had called the other woman's name and told her to follow her to the biopsy room.

Out in the waiting room I went to see Marty and tell him the news. The ride home was interesting as I recounted the story in the little room. My mind was going over every word the Asian woman had said; I couldn't help but feel for the poor lady who was sent for a biopsy. Were the angels really with me and how did she see them? Did the angels really make this whole experience work out the way it did? I knew if they had done all of this for me then I had to do something huge for me, and for them.

What could I do that would show the angels my appreciation and gratitude for their help? Nothing I could think of was good enough. I knew I had to come up with something.

Again, a magazine that I had had since October suddenly showed up on my desk. I thumbed through it and found several ads for the same person. Perfect. I wanted someone who did not know me.

After a few days of emails back and forth I had an appointment. I ended up going to this woman four times. She worked on emotional issues and did a lot of body work. So many of the old issues came up again to be cleared in a different way. My body was feeling so much better. I felt there was hope again.

During that time another book came my way. As I read this book more connected within me and I knew I had to see the author, whom I had heard about for years. I made reservations to go to San Diego for a three-day class with her. A little research revealed that she too had been married a few times. This was a boost and confirmation that I could help others even though my life wasn't perfect.

I arrived in San Diego and checked into the beautiful resort where the class was being held, then went for a massage and had lunch by the pool. As I walked into class that afternoon, I felt so at peace and excited to come together with seventy-five other souls who wanted to work on their lives.

Friday evening began the unraveling of my emotions. On Saturday, a couple of hours into the class, I had that feeling again of foggy mind, so sleepy, numb and just plain out of body. I talked to the teacher, who confirmed that I was releasing and downloading information so quickly that my body was readjusting.

I also asked her a question in class, and in response she turned to the others and said, "She just doesn't see her power." The class all agreed with her. This was hard for me to take in. Could everyone else see this in me? If they could, then why couldn't I?

Sunday there was a drawing exercise, which for me started with confusion. The confusion upset me because many years ago a process like this had changed my life and now I couldn't do it.

Finally, I told myself, "Jeri, forget what she is saying. Go inside and just draw what needs to be drawn."

I closed my eyes and drew. When I opened my eyes I was shocked, I had drawn my inner belief of my father's casket, all the flowers around it and a little girl (it was stick figures) standing in front of it. As I looked at the little girl, I knew it was me. She was begging her father, "Please don't leave me, I don't know where you are going."

Shocked and crying, it took me awhile to come out of the process. As I sat there waiting for instructions as to what to do next, I thought that by now, with all of the Life Between Lives sessions I'd had and all the client sessions I had led, I did in fact know where my dad had gone. I thought about all of the experiences I'd had with my father since he died and my knowing that he was always around when I really needed him.

Then I had a terrifying thought: *Oh my God, is my work with doing sessions over? Now that I know where my dad is, am I supposed to quit doing sessions? Was all this work so I would know where my dad went?*

Fear continued to run through me as the teacher gave us the next set of instructions. As I was doing that exercise I heard, *You are here to help others find out where they are going in this life.*

Wow. I better get going and make that happen.

All too soon the class came to an end and I found I didn't want to leave this space. Everyone was walking around hugging, some laughing and some crying, but all were happy. Suddenly, a man I hadn't even spoken to all weekend came up and wrapped his arms around me.

"Don't let anyone put your light out," he whispered, "You need to shine that light and help others."

With that I fell into his arms and sobbed. "What made you say that?"

"You just do not see your power. I have been watching you all weekend."

He then led me over to a chair and we sat and talked for a while. I found out he was a doctor from the East Coast and we said we would keep in touch. I left the room aching for sleep but with a new lease on life.

I was only home for two days when Marty left for Oregon to see some of his children. This gave me time alone to think about all that had transpired the weekend before. Then it was time to get busy, as Marina's daughter Christina, now fifteen years old, would soon arrive from Greece to play soccer. She had come the previous summer as well, but then she had been playing for a few different teams and had little time for anything else. This year she was only playing for one team, so we'd have ample opportunity to do other stuff as well.

I picked her up from the San Francisco airport and we spent the drive talking about what she wanted to do over the next seven weeks. Everything she wanted to see was in the Los Angeles area; now all we needed was a free weekend so we could head south.

We left on a Thursday afternoon and had a wonderful drive – talking, eating, singing along with the radio and playing with the truck drivers. Christina also captured our whole excursion down the interstate through pictures and videos on her new Go Pro. We stayed at the top of the Grapevine, so she could see our approach into L.A. in the daylight.

Friday morning we drove down into the city and found the first sight: The Hollywood sign. I was surprised by how happy and excited she was to be there, even though she'd been telling me for days she couldn't believe she was going to Los Angeles. After seeing the sign from a couple different vantage points it was time to move on.

Down into Hollywood we went. We walked along the Walk of Fame, looking down at all the stars, then found an open-air van to go on a tour. I called my cousin and told her where we were and when she could meet us, then we climbed into the van for a fun and exciting ride through the Hollywood Hills, Beverly Hills, and Rodeo Drive. After the tour, we met my cousin and her husband for more sightseeing and dinner, then Christina and I set off to find a hotel at the beach.

The next morning as we were dressing and packing I heard on the television that the beaches were closed because of lightening and high surf – remnants of a hurricane that was coming up the coast from Mexico. I thought, *That can't be around here because Los Angeles doesn't get hurricanes*. Sure enough when I looked out the window the sun was out, as usual.

After eating we went to see the beautiful beaches of Southern California. The first stop was Venice Beach, and I was surprised at how few people were there. We even found a parking spot. Then it started sinking in that the lightening and high surf were here. We walked the pier for a little while and watched the few surfers, then decided to go up to Muscle Beach where the action was supposed to be. It was only a few minutes away, but by the time we got there it had started to rain so we kept driving up to Santa Monica Pier, which I had always wanted to see. By that time it was pouring and everyone was running for cover.

Up the coast to Malibu we went, only by the time we got there it was raining so hard we could barely see the ocean. It was time to head inland. I found a road that would take us up to San Fernando Valley, from there we would contact my cousin again and go see my other cousin's daughter. By the time we got up in the Valley the streets were flooding, and it was still pouring. We saw my cousins for a bit but it was getting late and dark so I decided it was time to get out of LA and start home. We had heard that the next day was supposed to be even worse.

As we set off toward Interstate 5 it was raining harder than I had ever seen it and wind was whipping around in great gusts. The streets were so flooded that oncoming cars threw enough water up on my windshield to stop the wiper blades. Every couple of miles we saw another collision.

Things only got worse when we got onto the interstate. I kept saying to myself, *Just get us out of here safe*. We could see that westbound traffic was stopped because of multiple accidents.

Christina finally asked me, "Jeri, how can you see?"

I told her I couldn't, I was just following taillights. Gripping the steering wheel so hard my hands hurt, I just kept asking for us to get out of there safely.

At one point Christina said, "You are going sixty miles an hour."

I looked down at the speedometer and thought I should slow down, but somehow I couldn't take my foot off the gas. At that moment I couldn't think about it. Suddenly, I realized I was stopped and in front of us was a three- or four-car pileup in the fast lane. There were a couple of men out there in the driving rain helping people out of the wrecked cars.

I sat there trying to look out the rearview and side mirrors and could not believe my eyes – there was no traffic coming around the corner! I knew I had to get out of there without hitting those men helping the people out of the cars. Suddenly, I heard *Go!,* and my foot pressed on the gas pedal. A moment later, there was traffic all around me again. How had I gotten out of there without getting hit? My head was spinning.

A little while later Christina said she needed to go to the bathroom, so I turned off at the next exit. We soon found ourselves at a motel, asking a couple of men standing out front if there were rooms. They didn't step out of the doorway, as it was still pouring, but they told me there were no rooms anywhere. So it was back onto the freeway and off at the next exit. The first motel we found was also full, but they told us go across the road because that place had had rooms twenty minutes earlier. Now dripping wet, I went into the other motel to find a line had formed.

I was fourth in line when I spoke up and said, "I don't mind standing in line as long as there is going to be a room when I get my turn."

The poor woman looked up from her computer screen, counted the people in line and said, "You will be the last room except for the ones with reservations."

I later found out Highway 15 was closed because of the fire that had swept across it Friday night and burned up many cars, and that now the floods had washed out the bridges. Highway 20 was closed because of mud slides. It was so unbelievable, especially since California was in the fourth year of the drought.

By the time I got to the counter to check in, people with rooms were offering to share with those who didn't. *I thought, Wow, this is how people help each other in times like this. You see it on television but now I am witnessing it in person.*

I ran back out to the car to let Christina know we had a room. By then we were starving and miraculously found an open hamburger place. We arrived back at the room drenched but grateful that we were finally safe and sound. Looking outside it looked just like the visions I had seen on the news when we watch the hurricanes blow through other towns. I watched the bands of wind and rain blow across the parking lot.

I laid down in bed, but my body would not relax. I feel asleep feeling stiff. All too soon I was awake with the light streaming in the window. Shocked that it was not raining, I got up, showered and dressed, then woke up Christina. It was time to officially cut our trip short and head home.

As we got into the car I was amazed at how clean it was. All the bugs from the ride down were gone. It had rained so hard it literally washed my car sparkling clean. As I started the ignition Christina asked if we could go back since it wasn't raining. At the exact moment about twenty drops of rain fell on the windshield.

With this blank look on her face she said, "Nope, let's head for home. I don't want to go back there."

On our way back to Sacramento we talked about all that we had seen. About six hours later we were home, and not a moment too soon. I was completely exhausted. Thank God, I thought. I fell asleep before my head hit the pillow.

The next night I was drifting off peacefully to sleep when I felt someone tapping me on the shoulder. I raised my head to see what Marty wanted and saw he was sound asleep.

*Hummm*, I thought as I comfortably settled back down on my pillow, *What was that?*

Then I heard, *It's us.*

There was a part of me that knew who "us" was, but I asked anyway.

*Your angels*. I had such a feeling of total peace and comfort. One voice spoke up and said, *Remember when you heard 'Go'? That was me*. Then she giggled.

All at once the whole drive in the pouring rain came flooding back to me. I knew I hadn't been driving the car that night. I felt how perfectly it had been set up so we could arrive safely. I kept thinking about every moment of that trip as I drifted off to sleep in extreme gratitude. In the days to come at random times I would think of the whole experience and say thank you again and again.

## Chapter 22

# Miracle on the High Seas

*Change of thought makes your behavior change. Change of behavior makes your habits change. Change of habits makes your personality change. Change of personality makes your destiny change.*

Finally, April 15th arrived. The next day I would be flying to Tampa to catch a fourteen-day transatlantic cruise. Two weeks to write! Between clients I went to print out my boarding pass, only to find that my flight had been cancelled because of bad weather in Denver. I called the airline and was told the only airport I could get out of was Oakland. Though I knew Marty would drive me down in the morning, I wasn't excited about flying out of Oakland. I had never been there, but just thought it wasn't going to be good. I told myself that at least I had new flights, going through Dallas.

Friday night I finished packing and printed out what I had completed of my book to date. Then I threw in a copy of my first book, *The ABC's of Never Having Another Bad Hair Day,* into my bag, checked to make sure I had everything, and went to bed.

For weeks I had done every modality I could think of to set up this journey. I had prayed, channeled and asked my guides, angels and spirits to please just set up everything I needed and or wanted.

I knew Marty was going to be okay; actually, he'd be happy he could do what he wanted and dress when he wanted, though for the life of me I still could not figure out why he couldn't dress at home, and when I was there. I was also still dealing with the shock of him telling me that he was tired of going on cruises, as I thought we'd always had a great time. How does someone get tired of having a good time on vacation? He said he wanted to do other things. Despite this, I had arranged for one of his coworkers to surprise him with a gift halfway through my trip. I'd always loved surprising him, and despite my hurt over the distance between us this time was no different.

Saturday morning we drove to Oakland and to my surprise saw that the airport was rather nice. *Again, I had drawn conclusions based entirely on assumption, rather than true information. How could I continue doing this when I teach not to do it?*

While waiting for my flight I met a woman who was just coming out of rehab for drugs and alcohol; we talked and she told me I helped her a lot. Then, when it was time to board my plane, I learned that there was no pilot and we would have to wait about thirty minutes. Oh great, I only had about thirty minutes between flights in Dallas and I knew how big that airport was. The pilot did get there and we took off. As we were landing in Dallas I discovered that we were landing at Love Field, not Dallas/Fort Worth. Shoot, now I didn't even know where I was going. When I walked out of the plane I found my gate was only two gates away and the airport was really nice. I even had time to grab food for the next leg of my journey. *Lesson Two, and I was only a couple of hours into this journey. I had again made judgments without any information to base my thoughts and stress on.* After a smooth flight into Tampa, I was off to my nice hotel for the night.

- Have you made decisions based on no information?
- Have those decisions turned into something good?
- Take a minute and reflect on how you make decisions.
- Take a minute and feel how or what helps you make those decisions.

- Do you check inside you to know if your decision was a head decision or a feeling-based decision?

Sunday morning after breakfast it was time to head to my ship. The good part was Marty and I had been on this ship twice before so I was familiar with it. The bad part was there were memories everywhere. The other two times we were on this ship it was decorated for Christmas, so it looked pretty plain by comparison; that was okay, though, because it took some of the sting from the memories. I decided to go up to Deck 12 and get some sun, a drink and relax until I could go to my stateroom. As I sat there I remembered the sail-away parties Marty and I had gone to and how he was always a main player at them. As I finished my drink I thought, *I don't want to stay here because I will start crying.* I also noticed that something was telling me to go down to the Customer Service Desk. Down I went, knowing there would be a long line as others entered the ship. Oh well, I didn't have anything else to do.

I got in line and soon the lady behind me started talking to me. The usual questions began between us, including "How many cruises have you been on?"

I told her this was my fifth but the first one alone without my husband.

She looked at me sadly and said, "Oh, did he pass away?"

"Oh no, he is at home."

I could tell from the look on her face that she was surprised, so I added, "I am here alone so I can work on writing my second book."

Her eyes brightened. "What kind of book are you writing, because I am an editor." She then told me her name was Pamela.

Immediately the questions began. *An editor? Really? Oh my God, now what? How do I ask her for help on her vacation?* Suddenly I heard someone say, "It's your turn"; it was the woman behind the counter, waiting for me to go up. I'd almost forgotten what I was going to ask them about my Internet Package. They told me what I needed to do, but my mind was spinning so much I didn't even hear. With a muttered "thank you"

I started walking away. Then I heard Pamela say, "Wait a minute for me so we can talk."

I called Marty to tell him, and he chuckled and said, "Jeri, for anyone else that would be amazing, but for you it is normal. Go get 'em, girl."

I told him I had to go because now that lady was again standing in front of me. We set up lunch the following day so I could meet her partner and talk about my book. I told her I would bring what I had already written and a copy of my other book.

*Now, why did I bring a copy of my book? I had never done that before and why did I print out everything I already had on my computer? Really, why? Even as I asked the questions I realized I already knew. Thank God I had listened to my guides when they prompted me to do that.*

I had also taken with me a large folder with notes and everything I had saved through the years that I had always wanted to go through. I started that task that night.

After getting into my stateroom and getting everything set up for my next fourteen days at sea, I was in heaven. I went to dinner and found out what was going on, on the ship. I found out it was a solo cruise and there were more than one hundred thirty solo travelers aboard. There were many activities set up, plus tables in the dining room at specific times so one would never have to eat alone. Although I knew there would be times I just wanted to be alone to think and write, this was comforting. I met a few of these people at dinner that night, but mainly I just wanted to go back to my room and open the door, smell the ocean and begin to rest. I also figured out my internet so I could call Marty anytime I wanted. The whole time, my mind was going crazy about the possibilities of working with an editor and at the same time trying not to get to excited in case she thought my book was not worth taking on.

The following afternoon I found myself sitting across the table from a professional editor. Two hours passed quickly and then it was time to say "good day" and give her what I had. It was time to go to my room and get busy. That was the easy part. I was alone with my thoughts, good and bad. I began getting organized to write. Before I knew it, it was time to go to dinner and socialize a little. When I returned to my cabin there was a message on my phone. When I heard the message was from Pamela, my heart sank and my mind made all the decisions on how she was going to say that the book wasn't for her and I should have a nice cruise. Instead as I pushed nine to hear the message she said, "I just wanted to tell you, I have only read part of your first book and some of the new book. I also wanted to tell you to never doubt yourself again. I like where you are going with this."

Oh my God, I couldn't believe my ears. I listened to it a couple times to make sure I'd heard her correctly. I had. She also told me she wanted me to check in with her each evening and that we would meet again soon.

The next day she came to my cabin to return my material and we talked about her suggestions. I was off and running. Now I had to stay focused.

*My angels, guides and spirits had certainly gone above and beyond this time. I knew they were going to be with me, give me ideas and help. But, an editor, really? I still couldn't believe this.*

A couple of days later I was walking through the ship when someone stopped me and asked, "Are you the author?" This stopped me in my tracks. *How do I answer that one?* While I was fumbling for words, he told me he'd had dinner with a couple the previous night. She was an editor and said she was working with an author on board. Okay, then, I must be that author. I told him I was. *Later I realized I had become that author, sadly, not because I believed it but because someone else believed in me.* There was a part of me that knew I had to live up to what she believed.

After three glorious days at sea we came to Bermuda, another place on this planet I had dreamed about seeing for as long as I could remember. I spent most of the day touring the island with one of the women from the ship, and it was everything I'd always thought it would be. But a bigger part of me wanted to go back to the ship and write.

Over the next four days, I spent some time with the others I had met but I told them, "Please don't take it personal when I just leave and go back to my room to write." I went to one show Marty and I had seen before on another cruise, but my heart really wasn't in it that night.

The cruise also went to the Azores, islands off the coast of Portugal that I had wanted to see for about twenty years. They were nice but the weather was cloudy and I wanted to go back to the ship, and to my room. I now had only four more days on board and a lot of work to do.

Pamela and I did have a few more meetings and phone calls. She always built me up and kept me motivated.

All too soon it was time to say goodbye to the ship in Copenhagen. I had been there once before with Marina, but didn't get to see much because we were rushing to catch a flight. Now I had a full day to explore the city before flying to Frankfurt, where I would meet Marina the following day. After landing in Germany I had a great night's sleep, then lunch by the river the next day in the beautiful sun. There had been snow before I got there but now I sat by the river thanking the Universe for giving me great weather once again.

Marina and I had the best time we had in years. I was rested, feeling good about myself and loving life. For the next couple of days, we went sightseeing, had great meals, talked a lot and laughed more than we had in a long time. I was sad when it was time to split up and go home, but a smile lit my face again when I was upgraded to business class on my flight back to San Francisco. *The Universe surely knows how to do everything up right. Thank you, thank you and thank you.*

At home Marty was getting ready for his own adventure – a three-week trip to Europe.

I thought I was going to be lonely when he was gone, but instead it went so quickly and I found I had another three weeks of heaven in my own home. In fact, I had a hard time readjusting to him being home. *As soon as he did get home I recognized an energy in the house that I had always thought was mine. I now recognized that feeling was not mine but I felt the energy he carried.* He was more distant than when he left. I was so sad and didn't know how to reach him.

Soon I recognized it was an energy of agitation. The energy was here now. I felt it and took it on as mine again. I worked on everything I could inside of me.

At this time the world was reeling when Bruce Jenner announced his decision to transition from man to woman. He/she was on every magazine and they were all the talk in the salon. As each client made their comments I would casually begin talking about something else. Then one evening, as I was mixing a client's color, she picked up one of the magazines, marched over to me, stuck the picture in my face and exclaimed: "Jeri, oh my God, have you seen this, what would you do if Marty told you he wanted to be a woman?"

This is just awful. All I could do was lead her to my chair, take the magazine out of her hand and work as good as I could to change the subject. It didn't work, and it was all I could do to maintain my composure as she continued to carry on about this.

How just how could I confide in someone this opiniated? This brought up some of what I wrote about in *The ABC's of Never Having Another Bad Hair Day*. One is opinions – everybody has them. I have learned after over forty-five years behind the chair to keep mine to myself. One never knows what someone else is going through.

- What do you do with your opinions?
- Is it kind or cruel to share your opinions unsolicited?
- Is it withholding information to not share your opinions?
- Do you watch the reactions of others when you offer your opinion?
- Do you change your opinion based on what others say or do?
- Do you think about your opinion before you share it?

Right then Marty walked in the door. I rushed him out as quickly as I could so she wouldn't catch him off guard and say something to him. When I did come into the house he asked what was wrong with me. When I explained what had happened, he thanked me.

That night I got to see again how many of my feelings I kept from him so as not to hurt him. He had no idea what I smoothed over while standing behind the chair.

A couple of weeks later I drove to Arizona to see my granddaughter. We spent a peaceful long weekend camping in their fifth wheel camper, then I was home again. That's when I found out where some of the agitation Marty was carrying was coming from. He wanted to retire. Only he didn't have a monthly retirement to draw on so I called it "quitting his job." The fight was on, though we agreed to put it on hold while Christina was visiting for another summer of soccer.

Three days later I picked up Christina at the airport in San Francisco. The next seven weeks were so busy I almost forgot about what was going on at home.

During this time there was a situation involving my car and my daughter. I left totally hurt and in disbelief. Christina was with me and didn't understand what had just happened. I didn't understand it either. As I pulled away from her house, I realized I hadn't stayed to fight with Loni. That feeling was so good. Whatever changed in me I knew was good. I decided I would send Loni love every time I thought of that situation and see how it played out.

For the first time in almost fifty years I did not feel guilty that Loni was mad at me. Usually, as soon as something like this happened I immediately went into "I have to fix this, I need to be better or different so she will love me." As I reflected on this over the next couple of days I began to realize I couldn't be good enough to make anyone love me, no matter how many classes I took.

It was harder when two days after Loni yelled at me I found out on Facebook that her father had died. She told Marty she wasn't ready to see or talk to me. There wasn't anything I could do for her except send her a text and a card. I had all my feelings to deal with. *I knew that someone dying doesn't make them go away inside of me. In fact, in most cases it amplifies the buried feelings. Plus, I was writing this book and already bringing up many of those feelings. Even as my heart was hurting for my daughter, I was reliving many of my memories of the last fifty plus years, including those with him. I was in and out of every emotion I had inside of me.*

Christina was my saving grace. I was working all week, taking her to soccer practice two nights a week, and taking trips with her every weekend for her games, which didn't leave me much time to dwell on anything. Those seven weeks were wonderful and flew by all too soon. We had worked out our differences and talked about everything. Though I really didn't want to see her leave, I did want to get back to my life and my writing. I had a newfound burning desire inside of me to finish this book.

Somewhere in those weeks I had a new feeling of wanting; specifically, I wanted a new car, I had never liked the one I had since the day we bought it. Plus, if Marty did decide to quit his job, or retire as he continued to call it, I didn't think we could qualify for a loan without his income. We did go look at a couple of cars, but they were all too expensive, not the right color or just didn't feel right. Before I knew it, I was looking on the internet and talking with a dealer who sold cars online. Bingo, he had one that looked promising. It was still too expensive, but while I was thinking about it and waiting for a call back from Marty to reassure me I was doing the right thing, it sold, so I knew it had to have been a good deal.

That night I had a dream. I wrote and told the salesman about the dream since he had seen my website and agreed with my beliefs. I knew why I didn't buy that one, there was a better deal coming. We didn't have to look for it because it would find us. I also realized I had an "independent dependence" on my husband. That was an eye-opener for me. I was an independent person yet I was so dependent on our relationship. I knew I had to figure that part out. For now, though, I was focused on getting my new car. In order to purchase one online, I had to deal with not seeing, feeling, or sitting in the car to smell the new car smell. *We are always using some or all of our senses. Especially, the new car smell, that one gets everyone for some reason.*

A couple of days later I was driving to Reno with Christina when the salesman called and told me the car had found him. It was a better price, the right color and had all the extras I wanted. I told him I was driving over the mountains and to call Marty and tell him to put the deposit down so we could buy it. Marty's sister was also visiting from Massachusetts and at the end of that week we all went and picked up my new car. I was in love, Christina was in love and we had her last three days to spend in my new car.

As soon as they both left Marty started in about leaving his job. Every time I thought I had him talked out of it for another year he came right back to it. Then one night I was sitting on the patio when he came out and announced that he had given his notice. He still called it retiring.

Everything in my body was screaming at me. Every buried feeling, I had came charging up inside of me. Everything I had consciously and unconsciously buried was in my face. I was so angry that I had allowed myself to be sucked in. Everything I felt I had given up, done for him or us, everything I had sucked up to keep peace, everything I had let go of that I wanted, and everything I had made excuses for to make things "okay" were shaking me to my core. Plus, I still had the incident with Loni simmering on the backburner.

After a couple of weeks I decided I needed help – not only physically, because my body hurt, but emotionally as well. The tug a war inside was so strong, and I thought that once again I had hit bottom and couldn't help myself. *I decided I had been living a spiritually paralyzed life. I realized over the last couple of years I had known the right spiritual sayings to keep me in check. I realized I had used my spirituality against myself. I realized I had used my spirituality to bury my true feelings even deeper.* My belief was that it wasn't spiritual to get mad or get what I wanted. I used my feelings of not being good enough to allow others to treat me badly.

At the same time, I knew I had felt trapped in relationships (i.e. Marty and Loni were the only two that meant my life to me). *And, I knew deep down that I couldn't be good enough for them to love me in a way that it would fill me up. I knew it was time for me to love me. I mean truly love myself. Be proud of myself. To fill myself up. Whatever they were doing they were going to do no matter what I was doing. In fact, neither of them really knew what I was doing, feeling or being. They were in their own lives.*

Then I read on Facebook: Spiritual Death happens *one compromise at a time*. There was that word again – compromise. I wrote about it in *The ABC's of Never Having Another Bad Hair Day*. So, what is compromise? How do I know when am I compromising, agreeing because that is what I believe, giving in or just readjusting my desires? How do we compromise so both people come out happy? Marty had always made it very plain to me that he did not like the word, and I knew I'd always worked my beliefs so he wouldn't have to compromise.

All of a sudden I was free of myself. I had hit bottom again, in a different way and I knew I had to save me. I had to be what I was destined to be. How do I do that with no energy, self-esteem, joy in my life or anything else? Marty had told me many times he did not want anything to do with anything I was working on, so I wouldn't be getting help from him.

*I knew I had a choice. Yes, I could stay mad and bitter, but that would only hurt my body and my life. Or, I could make this work for me. Immediately, I knew this was what I chose. I wanted to save me. But where should I begin?*

As I was working on doing this, I was going to healers, chiropractors and doing anything else I could think of to help me. I spent time out in my "she shed" writing, though I was still going through my "Am I really good enough to do this?" The part that kept me going was everything I had been told by healers and my channeling that this was what I was to do.

One night Marty yelled at me, "Why are you making me pay for retiring? What about me?" I didn't think I was making him pay for anything. I was doing everything I could think of to be okay with it.

I almost succumbed to his "you are doing this to me" and my feelings of not being good enough for him and guilt over not making him happy. Then, during that night, I thought, *Shit, what about me? I'm not making you pay for anything. I have feelings and beliefs too.*

It took me a couple of days to sort this all out. Then, one Saturday morning I had a sit-down with Marty. I had a client coming in five minutes so I knew I could say what I wanted and there wouldn't be time for it to turn into the usual debate, with him trying to convince me he was right and I was wrong. There was no right or wrong, there just was.

I said, "You made the decision to retire or quit a good job. Now you don't get to tell me how to feel, say, do or be after that decision. I'm not making you pay for anything. You have no idea the changes in me since April 16th. I am beginning to live the result of the last five months. You don't get to tell me how to feel."

As I heard my client go into the salon, I dried my eyes, bucked up and went to work again.

I am not saying any of this was easy. I was still confused and working on any part of me that came up. I began going out with a couple of friends to dinner. One friend who I hadn't seen in a few years came back into my life. I was also going to Bingo again. Loni and I started talking again. Part of me felt better and part of me felt so empty. I reconciled that my marriage was never going to be like it was the first ten years before the crossdressing club came into our life. I didn't know what was going to happen with that, but I knew I had to save me.

One evening one of his daughters was in town and stayed with us. She and I went to dinner and talked for a couple of hours. Of course, crossdressing came up. When I came home, I knew I had more reconciling to do around Marty's desire to spend more time as a woman. In the back of my mind I knew this was the main reason he wanted to not work. He had told me when he wasn't working he could be more of who he wanted to be. It wasn't just about work, however, because he still wouldn't dress and be home. He had many reasons why he couldn't and they were all my fault.

I had been put in contact with a new healer because the one I had been working with for a couple of months told me, "Whatever is going on inside of you is too complicated for me." Have you ever had a therapist tell you that you were too complicated for them? That one really made me more determined to find out what was going on.

The new healer did a session with me to find out what part of me was hurting. *As with all sessions it began as soon as I made the commitment to do it. So, the following information came to me before, during and after the actual session.* I found on a deeper level that when I met Marty I had put all my trust and love into him. I recalled the test the night we met, how I had wanted trust and he wanted love. When he began pulling away emotionally, when he found the crossdressing club, I was losing all of my security and most of my trust. I went back over all the times in our relationship when I gave my power to him. Believing I was not enough. *Because, I had made another wrong decision, I could not even trust myself. I lost all trust in everything. Oh, my God, am I at the bottom now or do I have farther to fall?*

*Plus, as he pulled away, trying to fulfill what he needed, he no longer felt the love between us. Neither of us was getting what we wanted most in life.*

As fall fell over the city, the rains came and the days grew shorter, I continued my quest in quietness. There was little to no conversation in the house; it was avoidance at all cost. This all led me deeper inside, where it was anything but quiet.

I remembered the channeling Marina had done at the beginning of the year. She told me, "Many things will be revealed to you this summer."

Whenever a new issue came up over the summer I would think, *Is this it? Oh no, this must be it. Nope, this one is bigger so it must be it.*

*Again, as in sessions, the results come in little pieces. We need to connect the dots. When I looked back on this summer, I realized there was no way these pieces could have been put in front of me all at once. One part had to show itself and be integrated before another part could be opened for me.*

There was a lot of uncertainty, but one thing I knew: this book was the most important thing I needed to do. As the holidays approached, I reflected on how I'd felt about holiday events the last few years, ever since my son-in-law had cancelled the holidays with us, and realized I did not want to do them.

For years I had listened to many of my hair clients complain about Christmas and all the work it entailed. They would look at me like I had two heads when I said, "If you don't want to do them, then don't do them." Yet, even as I said this, I was doing the same thing. I did the holidays for Loni as she grew up, then the grandkids and husbands so they would have the holidays I never had when I was a child. All along I knew I was doing it for others, but I never realized the extent until now.

Then again, I also knew it had made me happy to be doing for them. I will say it again, *We never do anything that we do not get something out of.*

When my son-in-law cancelled Christmas with us years earlier, after months of being angry and in disbelief, I finally made that work for me. That was when we went on our first cruise. A life-changing experience for me.

Now I was going to make this year work for me as well. Instead of spending hours decorating, I spent it writing for me. *I quit saying "I don't care" and instead started saying, "I let this go for now; I can always change my mind."*

Decorating for the holidays just to look good or happy was not for me any longer. When people asked me why I wasn't decorating I would just say, "Didn't feel like it this year." Many were amazed. Perhaps this also presented an opportunity for some to analyze why they do what they do for the holidays.

Christmas was still coming whether it was wanted or not, just like the end of Marty's employment was coming. As I geared up for both events, my biggest question to myself, healers and Marina was, where is the fight, passion, determination and perseverance that I have always had? Never had I not had determination and motivation. Somewhere inside I knew this was not me and I was not going to go down like this. Period.

Then the astounding remark came out of his mouth: "I did not marry you to make you happy. You even said it in our wedding vows."

I couldn't talk or think at that moment. I went and looked at a copy of our vows. What I had said was, "I promise to always look inside of me to make me happy so it will not be your unending job."

Wow.

In the coming days I would roll those words over and over in my mind. He had carried this with him for seventeen years. No wonder a lot of this happened the way it did. I took it as he had lived the last seventeen years not caring if I was happy or not, while I felt I spent seventeen years working and trying to keep him happy. Oh, my God. I had said that in our vows, only I didn't realize that meant not caring about each other's feelings. Again, I thought about how he felt about the word compromise.

He believed that compromising meant "Giving up everything to keep the peace."

So now how much of my giving in to his wishes was based on that discussion we had way back when? Was I subconsciously trying to be the good wife and not make him compromise so he would love me?

Then, during another discussion we were having about all of this, he said, "Jeri, when I met you I fell into your life because I didn't have one. Then I found my people and developed my life. I am going to have it and you can't stop me."

Wow, another huge eye-opener. I began to look at many parts of our life together from a different perspective.

He also believed that since I had the home with the beauty shop and hypnotherapy office I should be totally happy with my life. He was going to be happy with his life and quit his job.

I kept trying to explain to him that he had been on a twenty-year adrenal high with his crossdressing. That adrenal high was slowly going away. There were no more firsts. Or at least I prayed there were no more firsts. In the beginning, we did all the firsts together – when he dressed on trips to Las Vegas and San Francisco, played golf as a woman, and marched in the Pride parades and held crossdressing events at our house. He had gone anywhere he decided he wanted to go while dressed and had even told people about himself, something that would have been unthinkable when we met. Then when he helped form the new club there were many more firsts, but most of those were without me by his side because he had all his new friends.

I felt he needed another adrenal high, so he was going to quit his job. Of course, he didn't see it that way. He had his had his money and his budget, so he was okay for now. Great, where does that leave me? I had to remember that he hadn't married me to make me happy and obviously not take care of me either. Then again, I had always taken care of myself anyhow. I just hadn't realized it or put it together until now.

He would tell me, "I'm tired of working and I need to be me." I would ask, "What does 'being me' mean?" He didn't know, all he knew was he couldn't 'be me' and work any longer. Since he wouldn't or couldn't tell me what that meant I had to assume it meant being a woman more of the time. What would that mean? What would I do or feel? For now I decided I would ride the wave and pray it didn't crash.

There was so much going on inside of me most hours I didn't know what to think. Then I would realize that I had been pretty much crazy inside of me for a few years; I just didn't know it.

When I saw a Facebook post that read, "Well that didn't go as planned," my first reaction was to laugh. Then reality set in. Nope it hadn't, so now what?

In the middle of this, one of my closest friends became ill and died within a week. We had told each other everything for almost forty years. Standing by her side in ICU, seeing her hooked up to life support, brought up so much inside of me. What does life mean? What does it matter, our battles in life? Everything we work for – belongings that control our lives, loves we had and maybe lost, children we want to love us and believe we were good parents – all gone with one pull of the cord. She told me she was "tired of the struggle." Of those who'd left me, I would miss her the most.

Again, I went over many of my battles, the hurt when a client left or died after years of my working to keep them happy. It seemed everything, including writing this book, was bringing up the good and bad of my life.

I found myself fighting back tears most of the day, then would wake up crying in the middle of the night. Can't say I ever remembered doing this before. Something was wrong and I was just going in circles. I prayed, asking "them" for help, to please help me find my fight. By fight I meant my inner fight, inner power, and inner strength.

I would remind myself about the channeling I had done with Marina about a month earlier, when I was told, *What you are going through now is going to bring you to a new type of core inner strength. You cannot find that true inner strength if you have independent dependence with your relationship. Go deep within to feel that core strength. Use this experience as a gift that he is helping give you.*

Again I heard Mark's words echoing through my mind: "There will always be someone to help you with your lessons."

Working with my thoughts or emotions helped me feel better each day, and talking with Marina would always lift me up. Each night I fell asleep praying, asking for help and sending gratitude to all of my unseen friends and helpers. I had faith that they were there, I just had to find the way to hear them fully. I took herbs, vitamins, essential oils and had all types of body work done on me.

Then it happened, I had a dream that my insides were like the Jenga game. (This is the game with the blocks of wood that are stacked and each player pulls one out and places it on top of the others until the lower blocks have no stability and fall over.) As I saw the stack of blocks falling in my dream, each block was an emotional hurt, each time I was hurt one block got pulled out, as these blocks were falling through space I could read some of the writing on them as to what that hurt was. Finally, I could see that there were two blocks left to rebuild on. I was asked, "What are you going to do? How are you going to rebuild? What are you going to do with all of these blocks?

At that point I knew, from deep inside of me, I had to rebuild these blocks. I asked for help on how to do this. Then I felt my heart pounding, I started forgiving my heart and asking my heart to forgive me. My inner child was there also. I asked her for forgiveness. She just wanted to hug. I could feel my heart expanding, I could see my heart getting bigger and bigger. I asked for forgiveness for all the decisions I had made that ended up hurting me in the end. As I watched all of this and felt my heart growing, a few of the blocks began stacking up. I was told, *Don't be impatient, it will take a little time to rebuild all of the blocks. When they do rebuild they will be stronger and clean. Be kind with yourself.*

When I woke up in the morning I felt better than I had in a long time. It was a Saturday and I was going to get some things done. During the day, I stopped to check Facebook. One of my friends had posted an article about *Gaslighting.* (Google gaslighting and see if any of the definitions are a fit for you.)

As I sat at my computer and read the list of definitions and signs of gaslighting, my whole body knew this was for me. For each of those signs I was reading had been on one of my blocks. Oh, my God, my body was reacting to each sign.

Soon I could take a deep breath. I knew my next mission was to keep the forgiveness process going and keep rebuilding those blocks, however that was to happen. I was going to watch for each sign or signal that was sent my way.

Each day more pieces fell into place. No holiday decorations or presents at our house. Thanksgiving Day was spent at my daughter's. First Thanksgiving Day in years. Then the big one came and we were included in Christmas Eve and Christmas Day. Plus, she and I spent about three hours alone while the rest went to a movie. We talked as we sat on the patio and while we were preparing dinner. I was so thankful for these days. More things were moving and changing.

Happy New Year, our seventeenth wedding anniversary and on to the year I would turn seventy. One of my first resolutions was to take care of me and make me happy. Okay, I decided, I will go skiing after three years of missing that part of my life. It was a truly amazing day spent with myself and nature.

## Chapter 23

## *Seventy Unforgettable Years*

*"There are only two things you have complete control over: what you think and how you feel."*

When I first began my spiritual journey, I always heard, "Life is a journey, not a destination." Well, hearing is one thing and experiencing is another, and I have experienced that lesson more times than I can count. The takeaways: whether it is good or bad it is going to change, and enjoy the good and breathe through the not-so-good.

Now, as we headed into the new year, I decided I was going to make this one count and come out happier. Age had never bothered me, and turning seventy was no different. I did, however, have the feeling it was going to change me. It began when, while talking with a friend who had just turned seventy I heard myself say, "My mom died at seventy-five, my sister Bobbie died at seventy-six, and your husband died at seventy-four, so if we follow them we have about five years left."

I knew I didn't want to live the last five years of my life like this.

I continued going to healers and massage therapists; I continued channeling. And each time, in one way or another, I got the same message: finish the book. As if that wasn't enough, several clients, during their Life Between Lives sessions, announced, "My guides are telling me that you have to finish your book." After their session they would ask me if I was indeed writing a book. When I told them I was, they were amazed to learn that our guides talk to each other! Through their collaborative efforts our guides had provided additional confirmation for me and a deeper understanding of the spiritual world for my clients.

While I was being guided to buckle down and write, Marty was planning another trip to Europe for an early summer body movement/dance class. We decided I would meet him in Barcelona after the class, and oh was I glad I did. As we drove through Spain, there was a closeness between us I hadn't felt in years, and Gibraltar, where we ended up, was one of the highlights of all my travels. After a heavenly week of sightseeing, making love and romance, we headed to the airport to go our separate ways – Marty back to the States and me to Greece. After a few days of sun and sea with Marina I too went home to see if we could continue this reigniting of our relationship. God, I so loved it when we had that connection.

It soon became evident to me that these feelings were mine alone. I knew some of what I felt was based on memories of what Marty and I had shared, and that memories are, at the end of the day, only in our minds. Soon, friction began taking center stage again. I was working, and he was playing golf, pool, computer games and watching tv. Every time I returned home from the salon my feelings of sadness would surface. How could he watch me work all day while he played? How does one do that? He had what he called "his money," because he had worked for it. Now it was up to me to make mine.

My saving grace the rest of that summer was planning my trip to Africa with Marina.

I had been mentally planning this trip since October 3, 2001 when, while sitting at the Athens Airport I said to him, "Africa is calling me." I just knew I had to go there, and often visualized being with those animals, but in all the years that followed I never felt it was the right time. Now, as my seventieth approached, Africa beckoned again.

Once again, organizing a trip – and figuring out where the money would come from – occupied my mind and provided a welcome diversion from the confusion at home. Suddenly, a woman I had met in Los Angeles back in 2002 showed up on my Facebook page. When I saw that she lived in Johannesburg, I sent her a message asking if she knew anyone who set up safaris. She referred me to a couple of friends who were travel agents and I reached out to them.

Around the same time a hypnotherapy client who I hadn't spoken with in a few years called me. She was from Africa. Suddenly, information was coming from all directions.

I told the travel agent what we were looking for – about two weeks at the end of September or beginning of October; safaris were a must and massages would be a plus. And it had to be inexpensive, very inexpensive. Soon she was sending me ideas of different things to do while there. Some of those ideas were rejected and some were sounding pretty good. Finally, it was time to say yes to something.

A couple weeks before we left, someone posted an article on Facebook about Table Mountain and how powerful it was. As I investigated more about the mountain, I found out it was known as the "Mountain of Positive Energy." I knew that like our bodies, the Earth has chakras and lei lines, and when I found a map that showed where the mountain was relative to these powerful energy centers, my excitement grew. I began pulling its energy into me.

My flight went off like clockwork, and I landed in Johannesburg completely energized. I knew I wanted to continue to Cape Town that night, ahead of schedule. I changed my ticket and boarded the plane, not knowing what I would do when I got there. On the nearly empty plane, a woman sat next to me. As we started talking I found she lived in Cape Town. I asked if she would use her cell phone when we landed to call the hotel for me.

"Let's just do it now," she happily replied.

The concierge said the room I had booked was already vacant and she would send a car to get me at the airport. Everything was falling into place.

The bed and breakfast was perfect. I settled in for the night, enjoying the lights and sights of Cape Town from our balcony. The next morning was perfect weather, and after a wonderful breakfast off I went to get a massage and do a little shopping. I couldn't wait for Marina to arrive that evening and experience this.

Our first day we spent on Table Mountain. The power of the mountain was immense. We channeled, meditated as we walked, enjoyed the air and sights and began our processing together and internally by ourselves. All too soon it was time to board the tram and descend to the bottom so we could go to dinner.

On our way to dinner we passed by a jewelry store and stopped in. Before we left, I had read of the metaphysical qualities of Tanzanite and I wanted a piece of it. This powerful stone helps you look beyond limitations and know yourself deeper; raise your vibration; achieve financial goals; direct your energy; and open your third eye. It also relieves stress, strengthens the immune system and heart, and works with cell regeneration. The list goes on and on. After looking at several rings, necklaces, and bracelets, I found a perfect pair of reasonably priced earrings.

As I wore them out of the store, I heard, *These will help you see what others do not, help you hear what others do not and will help to open up your crown chakra to receive what others do not.*

*Okay,* I thought, *I'm good with that.* Off to dinner we went.

After another amazing day touring south of Cape Town and the Cape of Good Hope, with a stop to see the penguins, we rented a car and began our scenic drive along the Garden Route.

As I walked into the bed and breakfast at our next stop, it felt familiar and at the same time creepy. I knew this place had been built as a private home. After a couple of nights there, I finally asked one of the waiters if it indeed had been a house. He confirmed that it had and said there were pictures in the parlor. When I looked at them I immediately knew I had been there, not as a resident but as one of the workers. I don't believe it was a good life for me.

When we got back to the room, Marina had a birthday cake waiting for me. We ate and drank champagne while she sang Happy Birthday to me. My heart was happy. The next few days in the town was an idyllic mix of visiting with elephants, massages, delicious food, and of course channeling and processing. Though my real birthday was still a few months away, I knew this was the celebration I would hold in my heart.

Then it was time to fly to our first animal reserve for the safari drives. Oh, how my heart opened for all the beautiful amazing animals. Of all the pictures I had looked at over the years, not one had done them justice, and I realized this was as it should be. One must feel what they feel when they see them. One must be in their presence.

As I saw each animal I would thank it for being there and allowing me to see it in its magnificence. I would silently tell each one of them how I saw them. I would try to feel their power, strength, beauty or what they had to share with me. They all had something to share — sometimes it was a word, other times they communicated through a feeling or a glance — but I knew they acknowledged me and that I came away enriched by the experience.

I knew I had been processing inside of me the whole journey, though I didn't realize how much until one evening ride. We were riding down the dirt trail looking for animals when suddenly I began crying. By the time Marina realized what was happening my jacket was wet with tears.

She took my hand and whispered, "What is wrong?"

All I could do was shake my head and say, "I'm okay." With her acknowledgement the tears increased, and I started asking myself again, *What is this about? What is happening? Why now? I am loving being here.*

With that I heard in my head, *You are letting go of fear of losing. Fear of losing and/or not being loved by Marty, Loni, Marina, clients, everything and everyone. Let go of the fear around the book you are writing. Just let go of all your fears. You will be fine.*

That statement brought up mixed emotions. I know that when we let go of something, what it is replaced with doesn't show up like we think it will or how we wish it would. Where was this leading?

When the crying was over, part of my body felt weak and part of it felt peaceful, and I turned my attention back to the ride. It was getting dark now, and the tracker began using his light to spot animals. I was amazed by his ability to see what the rest of us could not.

We were tracking a leopard when the ringing of my cell phone shattered the stillness. I quickly pulled it out and saw it was Marty.

"Hello," I whispered, "I can't talk now, we are tracking a leopard." I started laughing and said, "How many husbands call their wife when they are out tracking a leopard?"

Marty chuckled. "How many wives answer their cell phone when they are out tracking a leopard? I'll talk to you later. I love you."

That laughter brought a lightness inside of me. The experience of the sadness and tears was over but not forgotten.

In between safari drives, massages and wonderful meals – including another birthday cake for me – Marina and I were both deep into processing information we were getting from our messengers or higher beings. We channeled and wrote down what we were getting, and it appeared information was coming from everywhere. I also noticed that despite my joy at being in Africa there was tension inside of my body. At times I didn't know if I was angry, sad, happy or everything all at once.

One morning we were preparing to head to our next destination, closer to Kruger Park, when I heard, *Your receptors are open.*

Okay, what are my receptors? I searched within and heard that they are like little points connected to your charkas. When they are open, you must guard your environment and the energies close to you. As we got into our van for the two-hour drive, I concentrated on staying positive.

I had thought I had seen all the beauty Africa had to offer until we arrived at our new lodgings – a tent tucked into the greenery with a river running below. This was no ordinary tent, however; there was a king-sized bed, more furniture than one could use, and a patio with a lounge chair and another chair to match. The bathroom was mostly outside and overlooked the river. A deep bathtub sat on the edge of the patio, the shower alongside of it that looked like a tree coming out of the wooden floor. There were double sinks and the toilet in a separate little room.

Wooden pathways lined with exquisite flowers, shrubs, bushes, lawn, trees and vegetables led us to the different areas of the compound. There was an amazing spa, a swimming pool with the river running past, a restaurant under the trees by the river, a bar and a reading room. There was another, more formal restaurant up the hill by the main house, and a shop where they sold items made from roses and macadamia nuts that they grew on the property. Most of the food that was served had been grown there as well.

The first full day there we left our paradise to tour Kruger Park. I could not get enough of seeing these magnificent creatures. Marina and I also bonded with our driver, though he seemed reluctant when we broached the topic of going to see a shaman.

Our second day we were to go on a Panorama Tour. When we got into our car, we found the same driver we'd had the day before. It was like meeting an old friend. We were merrily going down the road when we passed a little village. It bought to mind our conversation about the shaman the day before.

When the driver realized we were not going to give up, he pulled over on the side of the road to talk to us about it. I don't know whether he didn't want to deviate from the schedule or if the shaman was mystical to him, but finally he agreed to take us.

A few minutes later, Marina and I found ourselves sitting before a frail-looking woman. With the aid of an interpreter, she read each of us, focusing on issues we needed to know. I don't know who we were more grateful to – her or the driver for taking us off the beaten path.

After exploring this little village, it was time to continue our journey for the day. Since our detour meant we didn't have time to complete the scheduled tour, the driver took us instead to see some nearby waterfalls. They were beautiful, but as I looked at them I was experiencing feelings I couldn't explain, not even to myself.

We drove on to our next stop, a place called God's Window. As soon as the driver had mentioned it earlier in the day, I knew I wanted to go there. I just didn't know why.

As we walked up to the site, I saw several pathways leading to a lookout point. I went to the edge of the lookout and just stared out over the valley below. There was something magical about this spot. When I turned around, I saw Marina standing there and had the sudden impulse to hug her. As I did, I had a feeling of complete release and relief, then I heard, *You passed.*

I looked at Marina and said, "God, I wish all healing processes could feel so warm and fuzzy."

Indeed, we had been processing a lot these last days and many of the feelings I'd had as a result were definitely not the warm and fuzzy type.

All too soon, Marina and I were on our way to the airport in Johannesburg, our amazing journey at an end. After our *goodbyes* and *see you soons,* we headed off to find our flights, only I could not get on mine. I had to stay in Johannesburg another night.

After calling Marty to let him know I walked out the front door and immediately saw the hotel where I wanted to stay. With help from someone from the airline, I was checked in and ushered to a beautiful, peaceful room. It was as if the staff had known I would be there.

As I laid on the big comfortable bed, I asked my guides, "Why am I here for the night?"

*To decompress,* they replied.

As I thought about that, I knew they were correct. This extra night gave me the perfect opportunity to begin the process of rejuvenation after everything that had transpired during this journey. I fell asleep thanking the guides, angels and Universe for all that had been delivered to me.

## Chapter 24

## Seventieth Year

I knew deep within that this year had to be different; it was simply a matter of what I did to make it so.

It began in January, when Billie and I drove to Arizona for Brittany's bridal shower. My sister was going to make the cake. We were only gone forty hours, and most of it was spent in the car, which meant we had plenty of time to talk. We covered our past, present and future. I saw again how differently we looked at life and how differently we had lived it. In fact, I've always said if you talked to me and my two sisters about our childhood you wouldn't even believe we'd lived in the same town, let alone the same house. Hearing her talk made me even more grateful for all the modalities I had used to take the trauma and drama out of my memories. The memories were still there but they no longer bit me when I thought or talked about them. These modalities had also proven to be priceless to my hypnotherapy clients.

When I began going to classes I used to hear teachers say they were happy that they had gone through everything they had. I used to think that was nonsense. No way would I ever be happy with the things I'd lived through! These days, I still wouldn't exactly use the word "happy," however, I do feel blessed to be able to share my story and give hope to others.

The shower was beautiful, and we had such a fun time getting things ready and being there to support Brittany.

After another pleasant drive back home I decided to go to Loni's job and surprise her with the shower treats I had brought back for her and my other granddaughters. Only the surprise was on me. I found out that she had taken a week off work, then, after making several phone calls I learned she'd had major surgery and didn't even tell me. Obviously, she doesn't want me in her life. Okay, I got it.

A few more days passed before I finally got to talk with her. Some conversations were okay but most were not. I did my best to put it out of my mind, for the wedding was coming and I wanted peace while there.

The night before we were to leave for the wedding, I was standing behind the chair doing my last client when I heard, *What are we waiting for? We should leave.* I went into the house and told Marty and Christina, who was visiting us again, to pack it up. Within the hour we were on the road.

We surprised Christina with a trip to Las Vegas, and her face as she saw all those lights was priceless. We also ended up picking my middle granddaughter and her boyfriend up at the Vegas airport the next day, proving one is always in the right place at the right time. We even had time for a plane ride over the Grand Canyon.

The resort where the wedding was to be held was beautiful. In the days leading up to it, Marty, Christina and I relaxed and stayed out of everyone's way. I had no idea what was going on, but tensions were high and I was going to stay out of the line of fire. That is what I did, and it was the best time I'd had in years; the best wedding I had ever been to. Brittany was the most beautiful bride ever. We ate, drank, danced, laughed and I enjoyed every moment. I so loved being with Marty when he was with me in every way and that was usually while we were on a vacation.

Two weeks later, I had surgery to remove a growth on the bone of my toe. I'd had this procedure a couple times before over the years, and the doctors could not explain why it kept growing back. I would have to be off work for a week and would use the time to work on this book. One of my hypnotherapy clients was coming over with lunch and to help me build a blog; another friend was urging me to hold online classes. My plan was to be up and ready to go to the Healing Expo in South San Francisco in two more weeks.

While working on my computer I noticed that one of my teachers was in California, about two hours away. I had been asking the Universe and my guides for a Life Between Lives session and even thought about flying to her to get one. Instead, they had brought her to me! A few texts later I had scheduled an appointment. My guides had really set this one up for me. Thank you, thank you.

I then started making my list of questions I wanted answered during the session, and the people in my life I wanted to deal with.

As I still had stitches in my toe, was using crutches and couldn't drive, Marty agreed to take me so I wouldn't take the boot off and drive myself. It reminded me of the Sunday drives we used to take years ago.

After my teacher and I chatted for a few minutes, we got right down to it. Because we knew each other and had worked together so many times, it didn't have to be a typical Life Between Lives session. It opened with a man, standing on the side of a beautiful hill with only material wrapped around his waist. She asked me what he was doing and I told her, "Waiting." After a few moments, she asked what he was waiting for.

"He was waiting for his support team," I said, "He wanted to be supported." I knew this man was me in a life, probably many lives. He stood there for a long time, just waiting. Then she asked me again, "What is he doing now?" I told her, "He died. He died just standing there waiting for his support team." At various times during the session, I would say, "That was so weird, he just died standing there waiting." I couldn't believe it.

At one point she asked me if he had given up.

I said, "No, he never gave up. He just stood there waiting until he died." I moved on to a big glass and metal building; it was all glass, so I could see into all the meeting rooms. Even though I was paralyzed with fear, I went into one of these rooms. I knew I had to. There were two entities there. One was for my physical body, one for my emotional body; both were teachers. Then, with a series of questions and healings, the facilitator addressed my heart and emotions. We moved on to a couple of other subjects, then my toe began to throb. She asked me why my toe was hurting suddenly. I told her that was where I stored my anger. Also, my foot said the energy centers were not open to allow energy to flow out. This made sense to me since I had been so angry and confused the last couple of years. I decided that I was not going to allow my anger to make me grow this again.

During that session I was given an incredible amount of information; energy centers were opened, as did the energy channel to my heart. I learned that I had many contracts in this life, one of which was to terminate fear and to stop waiting to be supported. I get to be whole and not give up. There was more work done around my heart and the energy centers. Fear was draining down my left arm and out my fingers. Somewhere in me I knew I could no longer wait to be supported. I decided I could be my own support system.

I then went into another meeting room with five chairs on one side of the table and a chair for me on the other. There were only two entities there at the time; they said they were guides and were showing up as "Motivation" and "Super Action." Three other guides would show up in about three weeks and I would know. Motivation said he would help the process to "unstagnate" energy that had been stuck and transform it into what was needed. Super Action said he would help to get things done. There was more healing around my heart energy so I could help others grow.

Also, they said that belief seeps out of me all the time. They helped secure the place of the leak so it wouldn't happen again.

The facilitator then asked my guides, "Does Jeri's life need to be perfect or in total order for her to be able to finish her book, help others, do sessions and classes?"

Their answer was, *In the eyes of the Light, she is perfect.*

I left the session excited and looking forward to seeing how all of this would show up in my life. It was such a relief to know that perfection was not a requirement for me to do what I love.

Two weeks later, I was off to the Expo with Ronney and with no crutches or boot on my foot. As always, we had a wonderful time together, having healings done, getting readings and enjoying the community of likeminded souls. Ronney also found the time to network, spreading the word about her website, WorldWideWisdomDirectory.com, and meeting future potential clients.

Two weeks after that I headed to St. Thomas to stay with a friend. It was a good opportunity to heal my foot more and relax; however, whenever I tried to get information, all "they" would tell me was this was a time to rest and rejuvenate.

I tried to listen to the recording of my session and was disappointed when it wouldn't work on my phone. I know the guides can do a lot with electronics and electricity, so I kept asking why I couldn't listen to it. Again, I got the message that this was a time for rest and rejuvenation. All I could do was trust and work with what I remembered.

Within nine days of my return home, Christina went home to Greece, Marty went south to see a friend and I got busy cleaning the house and the salon. I cleaned closets and cupboards, washed bedding, and had all the windows washed and the carpets cleaned. I also did yard work, donated goods to charity, had items hauled away, did hypnotherapy sessions, cut hair, and worked on this book. Clearly, Motivation and Super Action had showed up!

Two of the other entities also showed up and took their chairs at the meeting table I had seen during my session. They were "Perseverance" and "Accomplishment." The fifth one reveled himself to me in the shower one morning as "Determination."

One night I was working on my computer when I heard, *You are okay. Quit feeling guilty for it.* I knew immediately that I indeed was okay, but I still quickly wrote it down so I wouldn't forget. I thanked whichever guide had said it, and I continued to read it often.

Marty was leaving for Europe for a month, and I found myself looking forward to it. I set a goal to finish this book by July 4. The exterior was already completed and I was now ready to work on the inside. The moment I dropped him off at the airport that is what I started doing. Of course, all my guides, angels and spirits were here to support me. They gave me so much new and enlightening information that sometimes I had to ask them to give me a rest. Everything began falling into place, plus my body was feeling so well I couldn't believe it.

That month was the most productive period I'd had in years. I even found time to reconnect with friends, sometimes having them over, sometimes going out. More importantly, I reconnected with me and the peace within.

At exactly eight-fifteen on the evening of July 4, I finished this book. All there was left to do was press send on the email to my editor, congratulate myself and go out front with the neighbors to watch the fireworks.

With all this peace within I had almost forgotten how sad things were around the house. One night, as I was Skyping with Marty, he said "Jeri, I have choices."

"Yes, I know you do, and so do I. But there are always consequences."

He told me no there weren't.

"Yes," I said, "It's called Murphy's Law. With every action there is a reaction. Sometimes they feel good and sometimes they don't."

Finally, he agreed.

Despite this unsettling exchange I still found myself excited that he would soon be coming home. I thought that after being apart for so long, and with my rediscovered peace, he would be happy to be home also, and to be with me.

Now, all I had do was wait and see how it all showed up in my life.

## Chapter 25

# *The Unexpected*

I was feeling great. I had met my goal. Now all I had to do was wait for what I thought was the last chapter to come back from my editor. I had no idea this book would have to be amended to include the biggest devastation of my life.

When Marty returned the tension around the house reignited. The peace I had felt was gone. My emotions were spinning. My motivation was nowhere to be found. It became a chore to make it through a day. Was it because of me, or was it his energy? Why was he so distant? The more I tried to get close to him the more he pulled away. I was so confused.

At the same time, Angel, my little Pomeranian, was getting sicker. I had thought her congestive heart failure was improving, but for the third night in a row she had been coughing and sitting up by my head, looking at me when she woke me up. It was more than I could take.

I had taken a day off, only to have my plans cancelled. That morning, Angel came halfway down the stairs and just looked at me as if asking for help. As I went to pick her up I heard, *This is why you have today off.*

Within minutes, Marty, Christina and I were headed to the vet. They took Angel from me as soon as we got there. When we were finally called back the doctor said she couldn't go home with us. They then showed me the x-rays they had taken and explained her heart was so big it was cutting off her oxygen supply. The prognosis was not good and I had a choice to make.

Someone led me and Marty to a room and they brought Angel to me. As I sat and held her, she melted into my chest. All too soon the doctor came in and gave her a shot. I now know I was out of my body in pain, fear and disbelief. As I watched her, I saw the little white puff, almost like smoke and knew that was her soul leaving her body. As the puff faded, she went limp in my arms and a warm liquid spread across my stomach. I knew she had peed on me. My Angel was gone.

I don't know how long I sat there before I stood and handed her to the doctor in her little blanket. I don't know how I ended up in the back seat of my car. During the long ride home, I heard Angel ask, "Mom, what happened? What did you do?" I told her she would have never gotten better and there wasn't anything more I could do for her. We talked as I cried.

When I walked into the house, I was possessed to remove everything of hers. Everything from the house, the salon, the backroom, the yard and my she-shed. I picked up and saved every puff of hair I found on the floors. About four that morning I got up and called the vet and asked them to cut a lock of her hair off so I could have it.

The next few weeks in the salon were torture as I had to relive it every time I told someone. We put a sign in memory of Angel on the door so it would prepare people before they walked in. She had been the mascot of the salon, and everyone greeted and petted her even before they said hello to me. It had always been the ongoing joke, that I was second. I never knew I could cry so much. Then the huge realization came: Angel's dying had allowed me to cry. I had discovered the sadness that I had been hiding deep inside of me for so long. Memories and situations involving me and Marty came flooding through me and I could finally cry about them as well.

Before, I always had to put on a happy face for my clients. Nobody knew the sadness and situation that was going on inside of our house or inside of me. Nobody knew about the last couple of years. Now if they saw me crying, they thought it was about Angel.

A few weeks later Marty left for another short trip. I thought I would have some alone time and be able to regain the peace I'd had while he was in Europe for that month. Nope, that didn't happen. Memories and sadness were all around me. All I wanted was that support team that I had felt and now was gone again. I vowed I was not going to die waiting for them as I had in past lives.

One day, as I was riding down a street, I suddenly pulled over, took out my phone and called a divorce attorney. The next day I was sitting in his office crying my eyes out. I didn't know if I was crying about my marriage or Angel.

Finally the attorney said, "I can sit here with you as you cry or we can fill out these papers."

The papers were filled out and I signed them. Didn't even know what they said.

A couple of days later, I was on my way to pick up Angel's ashes when Marty called to let me know he was almost home. He asked me why I was crying, and I told him, expecting to hear words of comfort.

Instead he just said, "Okay, I will see you when you get home."

Just like that, *I'll see you.* As I sped down the freeway I was once again struck by the fact that he was not my support system. He had already told me in many ways that he did not want to be involved with what I wanted to create in my business and book. In fact, each day he took another step away from our relationship. He was in his own world and I wasn't to be any part of that. He had his dance on Sundays that I wasn't welcome at because as, he told me, that was his and if I went I shouldn't expect to be a part of his experience. He had his transgender club and if I did go, he didn't have time to talk with me or be with me because he had duties to fulfill.

He didn't want to go anywhere with me, and we had little to talk about because his life was his life, his secret. Crossdressers grow up hiding themselves. He had told me the stories of his two other marriages and how he had hid everything, but I never thought that would happen to us because I already knew it all. I was the one that held him through so many firsts and lasts. But after he formed "his" group the secrets began again. I knew it, felt it and every time I would bring it up, he got more defensive and pulled farther away. He had a way of blocking anything and everything I brought up. Everything I did or didn't do upset him more. As time went on I turned more toward myself and my work just to keep me sane.

When I got home Marty was already there. Somehow, it made me feel lonelier. Lonely and wondering where my support system was. I think that was when I began asking for my support team to really show up. I heard, *It is within you.*

All I could think was, *Really? Where?* If it was inside of me then surely it was buried deep. I knew my purpose was to write this book and help others learn to love themselves. I knew I had to love myself. I knew that from hypnotherapy sessions, channeling and the first automatic writing I had done on that boat trip from Delos to Mykonos. I knew I had to go deep and find my support system. I had to love ME. But the question remained: How?

## Chapter 26

# Discovery

The next day I had Marty served with divorce papers. Shocked is not a big enough word to describe his reaction. That night we talked, fought, cried and felt everything on the emotional spectrum. Eight hours later we had reached a decision: we would see a counselor.

We went to a therapist I had known years earlier, but after just a few appointments Marty said he did not want to continue. I did. During one of my sessions the therapist told me that I had to either stay mad or resolve my issues around Marty not working/retiring and taking the money he had as "his money." It was his money because he worked for it and he deserved it. It would be "our" money if I would agree to sell our home, which meant giving up my beauty salon and my hypnotherapy business, moving into a cheap apartment and living, as Marty put it, "simply." His idea of retiring was to live life with no responsibilities.

It was hard not to stay angry, especially when I recalled how he'd told me that his not working would not affect my life at all. It affected it alright; it affected every minute of it. At the same time he kept telling me that my working controlled every minute of his day.

I had things that I loved to do and things I wanted to achieve. I wanted this book out. I wanted to build my hypnotherapy business again, as I had let that slow down. Whenever Marty heard that I had a session he would say something like, "Oh, if you didn't have that session, I was going to ask you to go somewhere." Then the guilt would set in and I would wish I didn't have that session. *The energy I was putting out on working was also stopping it, even as I continually prayed for more business.* I still wanted to travel and live my life to the fullest. Marty, on the other hand, said he was tired of going on cruises, which was one of the reasons I went on the fourteen-day transatlantic cruise by myself. Anything I wanted to do was placed on his backburner and then ignored altogether.

At one of my therapy sessions the therapist used EMDR. I didn't have a lot of faith in it, even after she told me it changed the brainwaves of trauma victims. As we finished the first session I felt something had shifted but I didn't know what.

The next day was Saturday. I came downstairs, already crying, and found him at his desk. We started talking and suddenly I felt hot; I could focus on him but couldn't see him. My hands were glued to the chair and I couldn't move. I heard Marty yelling my name, but it sounded like it was from far away. I could see his hand moving to my face, but I couldn't feel it on me. I knew he was slapping me and yelling my name, but I couldn't respond in any way. When he said he was going to call 911 I began coming out of whatever this was. Somehow I knew I didn't want an ambulance. I have no idea how long it took but eventually I began to feel my body. He was still standing in front of me with his face right in front of mine.

Oh my God, what had just happened? Marty was asking me if I could hear him. Yes, I could. Then he said, "You just scared the shit out of me." I just sat there feeling very weak, taking in everything around me. I wasn't scared, wasn't in pain, I wasn't anything at that moment. He asked me if I wanted him to help me upstairs to shower, but I said no. I was not going upstairs unless I could make it on my own.

It was quite a while later when I finally told him I could do it. Standing with the hot water running over my body felt like heaven. I started asking what had happened to me and was told, *That was a total rewiring of your electrical system.* Wow, I had seen that in sessions with clients, but I had never experienced it. Now what the hell was that going to do?

I began looking back at the last six months, five years and our whole married life. I began to see how and where I began and continued to give up on myself, my dreams, my power and everything that brought me joy... somehow our whole married life began looking different to me.

*Have you ever thought about what you have given up on in your life? If you have, do you know why? Was it a husband, children, parents, self-confidence, money, work? Take some time and write down your thoughts.*

Try as I might, I still could not wrap my head around him giving up everything we had in order to do nothing. I understood that what he wanted was to be "who he was more" with regard to his crossdressing and transgenderism, but he could do that and still work and be here. He didn't see it that way.

In his opinion, the only way to resolve things between us was for me to retire with him and live his life and be happy about it. I knew I could not do that. I did not want to be married to a man with breasts; I did not want to be married to a woman. That was no secret, as I had told him that from day one. I also knew that if I gave up more of me, I would die. I had goals that I had to meet in this life. I just wanted him to talk reasonably with me, to compromise some, but to him compromise was a loathsome word. It got to be that when I looked at him I saw another person; to try to feel him brought up empty emotions and energy.

I used all the information from every session, every channeling, every reading and every message I got from the guides and the Universe, trying to understand our relationship and how to resolve it. Rereading and editing this book brought up the memories, good and bad. I wanted the miracles again. I wanted to be happy like we were the first twelve years; I wanted my husband and our life back. I cried and begged for him to meet me halfway. I wanted a straight answer. But no matter what I did, I couldn't escape one simple truth: we were at an impasse.

I felt like every time I walked into the house he was placing another demand on me to do or not do something. I couldn't say certain words, I had to look at him in the correct way, I could no longer ask him if he had eaten so he wouldn't have to feel guilty if he had already eaten while I was working. He made it very clear that my working controlled every aspect of his life now. And, after almost twenty years my smoking bothered him. Suddenly, he couldn't be around it.

One dreadful morning he woke me up to tell me our house had been broken into during the night. The first thing out of my mouth was, "Did they take my laptop?"

No, they hadn't. I still had this book.

That was the only bright spot as I came downstairs and began the process of assessing what they did take: all my prized jewelry that was in a bowl on my desk; money in the desk drawers from Marina; my purse and everything in it; keys to everything; both of our cell phones and much more. The sheriff came to take a report, CSI came and got fingerprints, then the locksmith came to rekey the cars and all buildings on the property.

For the next month my life was consumed by making reports and dealing with the insurance company. As for Marty, once his phone was replaced he left the rest up to me. I recall one day while sitting outside of the sheriff's department, I had called home, crying so hard I could barely breathe or talk. I wanted a support system so badly and that call did not qualify.

During those days of reflection, I remembered how the voices had told me, *You should put your jewelry away. You should put that money in the bank and give it to Christina when she needs it.* Once again, I had not followed their advice.

*Once again I had learned the hard way: if I listened to those voices everything worked out. When I didn't listen, when I didn't act on what they told me, it never ended well. Those voices that scared me so long ago had become my closest ally.*

I asked Marty to go out with me and replace my wedding ring, which the thieves had taken. He did go physically but when I tried to get him involved all he would say is, "Whatever you want." He still had his. I just settled on a cheap ring. Something on my finger.

Six weeks later the insurance company reimbursed us. I had done all I could do and the matter was settled. But I still had no idea what I would do to deal with the immense emotions running through my veins. I was still grieving the loss of Angel and working on making some sense of my marriage and my life. I was no longer asking, "What is next?" Now I kept saying, "I have had enough, no more."

I turned my attention to Marina's upcoming visit. She was coming to see Christina and would stay for a month. We had a lot to do for soccer finals, plus there was much I wanted to do with Marina that would hopefully help me discover more about myself and move past some of this pain. Thankfully, Marty agreed to a truce; there would be no fighting until after she and Christina left in mid-December. That would be the only thing that went according to plan.

As soon as she got here Christina got sick, and I ended up in the emergency room with a cold and bladder infection. Christina's team lost in the third round of playoffs, and Thanksgiving weekend was nothing like the joyous occasion the year before. Marty's brother died, and he flew back East for a week. You could have cut the tension in the house with a knife.

When they left, everything went back to our new normal. Marty and I did nothing for my birthday, Christmas, New Year's or our anniversary. He wouldn't go anywhere with me because I might say something to someone if they asked him what he did for work. I embarrassed him, he said, because I was not happy about him not working. On our anniversary, I remember looking at him as he sat at his computer and thinking, *I am in shock*. That was when I realized how "in shock" my whole body was. It couldn't believe what was happening here anymore. I knew something would eventually reveal itself, but what? I just wanted my loving husband back.

The only thing keeping me together was an online class and community; at least they gave me something to concentrate on besides the meanness that was all around me. I was still going to my counselor. I cried all the time. I could not wrap my head around any of this. All I knew was that I had two choices: save me or die.

One Spiritual Counselor told me this was my time in life to "turn my knowledge into wisdom." I googled the definition of both and thought "Yep, it is."

I knew there were lessons to be found through this experience, but my God, what was I missing? The more I searched within the worse things got on the outside. The more I asked Spirit for answers the fewer I got. This was not really a surprise; my turmoil and devastation were blocking me.

One night I read on Facebook that Marty was returning to Europe in June for his dance class. When I asked him if he was going, he said "Yes, I told you."

"No, you didn't," I replied, "I would have remembered."

"Well now I guess you are mad."

It was yet another time I'd told him I was upset, only to have him make me wrong.

"Oh, no not mad, just hurt that the women from your dance class knew before I did."

By the next day, my hurt had to turned to relief. *If he goes,* I thought, *maybe I can find that peace again.*

Isn't that sad?

## Chapter 27

## The Last Hurrah

With no way of reaching my husband, I continued to turn within. I had my new online class to keep me busy, as well as other classes that I took through Ronney. I began finding friends to go to dinner with. I had also started going to bingo with a friend one Monday night a month.

After some time in the little bingo hall we graduated to a casino. It cost more to go but the payoff was larger. Our second time there I won enough to play on their money for months. I was excited to go back again.

The next time, we went as usual to get our bingo papers, claim our favorite table and then go have dinner. We ate and laughed and talked for over an hour; then, as we were walking back to the bingo parlor, I suddenly felt the floor begin to roll beneath my feet. I looked around and saw all the flashing lights were double, then triple. I knew I couldn't walk any farther and found a stool by a machine and sat down. When my friend asked, "What are you doing?" I told her I couldn't see and couldn't walk. At first, she thought I was kidding. Someone close to us told her she was calling security.

The next thing I remember, there was this medical team all around me. They had me hooked up to monitors, were pricking my finger and checking everything. They were asking my friend questions. Someone was saying to me, "We can't make you go but we suggest you go."

*Go where*, I thought, *I'm going to Bingo.* Then I heard my girlfriend say, "Well, I really don't want her in the car with me." I thought, shoot, it is my car. Nothing was making sense. Then I saw the gurney next to me.

*Oh, so that is where I am going.*

It was winter, and I remember being incredibly cold as they wheeled me outside to the ambulance. As we rode down the streets I saw headlights and wondered if that was my friend in my car. How can she drive my car? This and a hundred other questions swirled through my head.

When I next came to I was coming out of the bathroom and a male nurse was waiting to help me back onto a gurney. Though I still couldn't see much I could make out Marty and my girlfriend standing there. They looked as confused as I was. Where was I and how did I get there? How did Marty get there?

Once in my room the medical team started asking me all sorts of questions, but there was nothing I could tell them. They ran tests for everything – stroke, heart attack, high blood pressure – and found nothing wrong with me. During that time my vision started coming back. About five hours later they sent me home.

The next few days were filled with doctor appointments and whirling thoughts. Oh, my God, this is what I am doing to my body. I knew it couldn't take much more of the stress, disbelief and heartache every time Marty told me I was wrong, couldn't see things his way or make a decision.

One of the next doctor visits was to an ophthalmologist, where I was diagnosed with the beginning of Macular Degeneration. All I could think was, *What do I not want to see?* – that is what eye dis-ease is about.

Now I had more to work on. Correct, I did not want to see what was going on. I didn't want to hear anymore either. I just wanted it to all get better. I just wanted *US* back and in love.

I wasn't saying anything anymore. I was staying out of his way. He was doing what he wanted and when he wanted, and I didn't say a word.

All I had to hang onto was my planned trip to Phoenix for a four-day Mind, Body and Spirit class I had set up. I was going to stop and see my granddaughter on the way.

Not a moment too soon, I was in my car with twelve hours to myself. Or so I thought. Shortly after I hit the road I started getting messages from Spirit. *Have this class for YOU.* As I thought about that I realized that this would be the first class I'd ever done for ME. I realized that all the years I had spent in classes was so that I could *make me better so they would love me.*

If this class was for me then what would I work on? What do I want? How do I get what I want when he obviously does not want anything I want? What do I need to do for me? Questions, that was all I had.

Well, at least I had about ten more hours to work on that. Ten more hours to process and clear the feelings of being stupid, of having wasted all that time, money and energy. I knew I couldn't be good enough to make anyone love me. I knew *I had to love me.*

I thought back to that first automatic writing I'd done in Greece eighteen years earlier: "Learn to love self and show others how to love themselves."

Okay, that is what my goal for this class would be.

After a couple of great days with Brittany by the pool, I headed off to Phoenix. Driving into that town, I felt so peaceful. I loved it there.

This was followed by four amazing days of class. I came to several realizations about myself. I met new friends to go to dinner with. I cried a lot, but I also laughed for the first time in a long time.

The teacher had a labyrinth in the backyard. I had seen it as soon as I arrived and knew I had to walk it. She was of the same mind, and said during class that she wanted each of us to walk the labyrinth before the class ended.

The third evening I decided it was time. A lady was waiting for me to go to dinner with her, but I started it anyway and decided I was going to take my time. Halfway into the walk my feet began to hurt because the sand was in my sandals, and my hip was hurting because of the way I was walking to keep my feet from hurting. Still, I kept my focus on what I wanted to release when I reached the middle of the labyrinth. When I got there I did my little ceremony; I also thanked the Spirits, Guides,

Universe and anyone else that had helped get me here at this time, when I needed this so badly.

When it was time to turn and walk out my first thought was, *I don't want to walk all the way around and out. I can just step out the short way. I have done enough.*

I lifted my foot to step out and heard very loudly, *Stop! That is cheating yourself.* I looked at the labyrinth, shook the sand out of my sandals and took my first step, then another one. Before I knew what happened I was at the end of the labyrinth. Wow. How had that happened and with no pain? Then, as I stood there looking back, I heard, *This is how fast it can all go.* Wow. Okay. I went over to the firepit and burned my paper that I had written on all four days.

How fast can what go? My best thought was, it could go fast that Marty and I could pull this together and be in love again. Plan things for us. Work together to bring peace to our home. We could be happy again. That would be so amazing.

I felt so good I knew this could only mean good things. Now I was anxious to get home to see and feel what had changed. The next morning I rose early and began the long drive home. I didn't know if I was going to stop for the night or drive straight through, but I was looking forward to the time alone to just be with myself and go over the last four days.

I decided to stop for something to eat and pulled off the highway. While I was sitting at the fast food restaurant, I realized in was in Blyth, California. This town had had been in the back of my mind since my ex-husband Pat moved there right after our divorce. As I looked out the window, I knew I had the chance to do a final release ceremony. Quickly the memories flowed through me, and as I drove out of that town, I knew I had released many emotions I had been holding onto for decades.

Thirteen hours later I reached home. I had talked to Marty a few times during the day; I was feeling so good and relaxed and I just hoped that when I walked in, I would feel the love from him. I was tired so we talked briefly and went to bed. The next day while eating breakfast I asked him when he was leaving for Europe, as we hadn't talked about it since the night I'd read the Facebook post. I thought if he went away again with me feeling this good, I could finish this book again and get a lot of other things done as well.

Suddenly, his energy pumped up strong and he said he was not going. When I asked him why, he said, "You take away all the joy of me going away. I don't want to go and have to come home to this."

As I sat there in shock, he went on to say that this had to be settled once and for all. Once again, he said we needed to sell the house and I needed to retire with him and live his retired life. Once again I told him I couldn't do that. I wondered if my days away were a waste, as nothing seemed to have changed at all. For now I just had to be grateful I had plans in a few weeks to go see a friend and get my hair done.

The three weeks leading up to my departure were like nothing I had ever experienced. When I looked at Marty now it was like looking at a caged animal. There were times when the energy around here scared me. My body was so tight at times I didn't think I could move. I just could not understand any of what was happening. I had no idea what to say, how to act or what to do. He was totally untouchable. I stopped asking him for answers or to talk about it because every time he did answer it was another part of our marriage that had been wrong.

I flew out on a Thursday evening, with plans to stay at my friend's until Monday. Friday morning while I was showering, I heard, *Go home Sunday*. When I got out of the shower I told my friend I was leaving a day early. I had learned to listen to the voices. I changed my flight reservations and called Marty to tell him. He was a little surprised and really didn't want me to come home early; he had a hundred things he had to change, he said, in order to pick me up at the airport. I told him to never mind, I would either call someone or get an Uber, but he said he would do it. My girlfriend and I put our plan into action and got everything done.

I thought I knew why I was going home a day early. Nope, wrong idea again. When I got home, Marty told me he had rented an apartment and was moving out.

Shock, horror and disbelief ran through my body. After twenty years of marriage and all we had been together, it was suddenly over? His wall was so big, his emotions were totally shut off and there was no way to talk with him at all.

He told me getting married had been all my idea. When I reminded him that he was the one who came home from Massachusetts with an engagement ring, he looked down and said, "Ya, I did that deed." I had no idea what that meant. Nor did I understand why everything he said about our marriage was now so bad and how he had lived what he called "an obedient life."

In those weeks he put down everything we had done from the way we dressed to how we made love. Then when I would cry, he would say "Jeri, can't you just remember the good times and move on?" I was in such shock I couldn't even think.

He agreed to stay until Christina left the end of the month but he was going to keep the apartment. Money had always been the big issue, and now he was going to pay for an apartment that he wasn't yet living in.

He did continue to say, "Now we can build a better relationship than we have had in years. We will go see a counselor. It will be better now." Then he would tell me what we were allowed to talk about if we did go into therapy. We could not talk about the past, he said, only the future. The past was over; we needed to let go of it and move forward.

During the next fight he stated he just did not want the responsibility of this house or a relationship. He had worked all his life and now he deserved to be free and do what he wanted to with *his* money. *He* deserved? What did *I* deserve? What did a twenty-year marriage deserve? What is deserving, anyway? And how does one crush another on his way to deserving?

Every day I would think, well at least they'll be no more surprises, only to be shocked yet again by how much he already had planned out. He had already changed the bills to my name. He had also changed his passwords to both computers and blocked me from all his information.

The rest of that month, it was all I could do to hold it together until Christina graduated.

One night as we got into bed, he grabbed me and we had the most beautiful lovemaking session we'd had in months, maybe since Spain. All I could think was, he has changed his mind and knows he loves me. No one can fake this. Until... well, let's just say it didn't end well for him. I laid there, feeling like a failure and at the same time thinking that he was probably taking some kind of hormones that had affected him sexually. I had thought that for years, even as he continued to deny it. The next day when I tried to talk to him about it, he blamed it on me.

We made it until Christina's graduation weekend, then he started moving out. It was twenty years to the weekend since we'd made the decision to make our relationship work. Was twenty years all we had? I still prayed we could pull something together.

He asked me how I wanted him to move out. I told him I wanted to be there and see him move everything he was taking. I wanted some type of closure. Even this, he couldn't do for me. I would get up in the morning only to find he had gotten up in the middle of the night and packed his car. The next day, the same. Finally, Christina and I came home from a dinner he'd begged off from to find he had taken all of his computers. He was all moved out. The next morning, he came over to see Christina off. She was heading home for good, or at least until she left for college in Hawaii that fall.

After she left, he stood there holding me as I cried that my heart was broken. After all the crying I had done already I didn't know I could cry this hard. And all he could just say was, "I'm sorry, Jeri."

I knew that if he'd never gotten that money when he quit working none of this could be happening. I later discovered that he had been planning his departure for the last couple of years.

I remembered the day he was hired at that job and we were so happy. Now it was the demise of everything.

I also remembered him telling Christina one night, "When you have a goal, you have to be patient and take one step at a time. You do one part and then move on to the next step." Indeed, he had set his plan into for months, if not years, earlier and worked steadily toward his goal. Part of me had to admire that part. Now it was definitely my turn to put my own goal into action. But, where do I begin? What is my goal by myself? I had me, my work and my book.

They were gone. I had to get busy cleaning house to keep from thinking about how I could end it all. The days to follow I don't think I ever hit bottom. Every day was a new bottom. Every night I cried myself to sleep. I woke up crying. How could I go on? Was he right when he told me I could never make it here without him? Part of me agreed; the other part said, "Watch me."

I listed rooms to rent so I could make some money to make the mortgage payment. He did leave me some money but I knew that wouldn't last long. The people who called on the room were scams or people with no jobs. Who knew there were scams for room rentals? I kept asking "Them" why this was happening to me. Why couldn't I rent a room?

Finally, I was sitting at my desk when the answer came: *You need time alone to regain you. You need time to heal. You need time to find you again.* Okay, then I guess I better get busy finding me. I knew I missed that person for a few years. I knew she had gone into hiding.

I loved Marty and hated him from one minute to the next. How could he do this to me, to us? How could he leave our home and move into a tiny apartment filled with furniture from Goodwill and things given to him? He told me he had seen people in Europe in their little spaces with few possessions and they were happy so he would be happy also.

All he would say was that he'd changed and didn't need this stuff any longer. He wanted a life without restrictions. He wanted to be free and only surround himself with people who embraced him as a woman. Me wanting him as a husband and a man was not what he wanted.

I had thought I was the one person in the world who knew him. I was the one who had helped him leave "the Closet." I was the one who had gone with him as he walked the streets for all the firsts. I was the one who had stood and cried with him through so many obstacles. I was the one who had cried as he shaved his chest, on the broken promise that he would grow it back in the winter months.

Whenever we talked, he would ask, "Jeri, when are you going to see it my way? When are you going to realize I am right? You can't work more years doing what you are doing. You need to retire with me."

There were times when I would second-guess myself. Was I stupid? Was I selfish? Was I closed-minded, or what? I continued to push any bad thoughts about him away. I loved what we had those first ten or twelve years so much. How would my heart ever heal?

Memories surrounded me on every inch of this property. The home we had moved into and spent so many happy years was now the site of my worst nightmare.

I started to reflect on all of it. I started to look back at the many decisions he had made on his own, things I told myself to get over. Usually by the time he got home from work I was so happy to see him I just tucked my feelings away.

I could see and feel that my need to be loved by him and to able to love him filled every ounce of my body. Now every ounce of my body was in pain and disbelief.

I could remember and see how I'd continued to give my power up. Then it was back to my online classes to save me. That community saved me. I learned new ways to "Take my Power back." I did that process every night for weeks, mostly through the tears. I worked with the angels, my Guides and Spirits.

One day I was walking through the kitchen when I saw the numbers on the stove clock: 3:33. I walked into my office and picked up my phone and it was 3:33 in the afternoon. I looked up the meaning of 333. It read, *"The ascended masters are right by you, assisting you with whatever it is that you're currently working on. You're in great hands.*

I thought, *I don't think I have ever really worked with the Ascended Masters.*

I heard, *Write this down.* I grabbed a pen and my journal. *Now you are numb and blocked to us. It will take three days to begin to open more freely. Move through the pain and disbelief. You are loved and have so much to give. You have been giving to the wrong person. Like you were told before, Love self like you have others. You are important to mankind. The book will help thousands/millions.*

I picked up my Archangel cards and shuffled them, then picked four cards and laid them out. The first three were Make Commitment; Let go of Fear Now; Honor and Trust Feelings. The last card was the one I get every time: New Beginnings and a Fresh Start.

Okay, then. I guess I am on the right track.

First, I had to stop saying, "My heart is so broken." I really didn't need the heart problems these words could bring about.

The dreaded night came again, and I had a dream. I woke up knowing what this meant. Later, while in the car on my way to lunch with my daughter, I called Marty and asked the dreaded question.

"Are you taking hormones?"

He answered, "Yes."

I started crying and asking why. His answer was one I had heard before: "Jeri, we are not together so I can do what I want." He then went on to say, "You don't want to retire with me and live my life, so I am going to do what I have always wanted to."

What you have always wanted to do? This was news to me. Then I remembered the fight with his son years earlier, when he finally admitted he was taking herbs. He had told me he stopped and remained adamant that he would never go on hormones.

For the first time, it hit me: this was what his moving out had been about all along. He had to make our homelife seem so bad so he could justify leaving. Well, he finally had what he wanted. I began seeing the secessions of plans that were set into motion years ago. From selling/giving away all of his tools a few years ago to the changes he had made in our life. I could now begin to see it all.

By then I had arrived at the restaurant and told him I had to hang up. I dried my eyes tried to get myself together but Loni knew as soon as she saw me. We talked but she didn't know what to say to help me.

That night on the phone it continued. He tried to convince me that the hormones wouldn't change his body so he couldn't have sex anymore.

I knew that was a lie. How could someone who had loved sex so much and what we had just give it up?

"Marty," I said, "this is like a badge of honor with all of your friends. Now you can go brag that you are on hormones."

"Sure," he admitted, "there is some of that going on."

Oh my God, I was exhausted. How, just how, could he do this to us? How could he take away that part of our life as well?

When we finally hung up I went outside into the cool night air to water my plants. I kept my feet bare so I could feel the ground. Maybe I could get grounded. Suddenly, I felt this electricity go through my whole body. What was that? I heard: *This is what your body has been carrying for over ten years, the fear of him going on hormones. You just released the fear.*

I thought, *Oh my God, it is over – the fear and the marriage*. I did not want to live with someone who only thinks of himself, who not only doesn't want to make love to me but now will have no desire for sexual enjoyment.

I knew I had experienced yet again the same rewiring of my electrical system that I had witnessed with clients. It was an amazing feeling. Was a different type of healing for me about to begin?

Everything I had believed, thought or learned was haunting me to the core of my heart. The man I loved had moved out to make his new life with his money. The first man I ever felt safe with was gone. The man I'd thought supported me in my/our adventures had twisted them to be unrecognizable. I knew I had to come out of denial.

## Chapter 28

## The Healing Begins

*"Life is a journey, not a destination."*

~ **Ralph Waldo Emerson**

Gradually, I was led to the steps that would heal me. Knowing I had to connect with nature, on the night of the next full moon I went out and laid on the ground. I was doing a lot of processing and feeling stronger each time. I knew I had beliefs that had to be changed and I was willing to do what it took.

One night, I headed outside to water the backyard. It was a beautiful evening and cooler than it had been the past week. As I walked out onto the patio, I heard the hot tub running. Something sparked inside of me and I knew I had to get in it. I had not been in the hot tub for about three years or so. I knew it was because I got tired of hearing Marty's remarks about how much it cost to keep it hot. Plus, whenever he got in it with me, it never ended as I had hoped.

I stood on the patio, hemming and hawing about whether to water or follow the message to get in. Then I was taking off my clothes, grabbing the towel that was laying on the chair and walking toward the hot tub. I noticed I was fighting with the original decision I had made those years ago to never get in it again. It was one more thing I had given up to maintain the peace.

I swung my leg over and felt the hot water. As my body sunk in, it began to relax. *Awww, this feels so good.* As I talked to my body, telling it to relax, just relax, I felt the stress leave my muscles, then my shoulders, then my head.

I began talking with my Angels, Guides and Ascended Masters. What belief, I asked, do I have that has to be changed, released, or rearranged? After some contemplation, I heard *Doubt*. I broke into tears and I knew that was it. I did have doubt in everything since I'd realized months ago that I could not trust myself to make good decisions. All I could do at this point was ask them to help me and take the doubt away from my body and existence.

I could feel something leaving my body through my hands. I focused on every cell in my body, from the tips of my toes to the top of my head. Soon, the crying stopped. Now I knew I had to fill myself up with something.

The angels told me the opposite of doubt is belief, then they filled me up with the belief that I had given up and away so freely over the last few years. Belief in ME. I knew then that I had the strength, power, and intelligence. I knew that I was fearless. I had traveled all over the world by myself and now I was FREE to do it again. *Watch out, world!* I thought, as I was filled with love for those voices that had once scared me.

When I came into the house, I posted about my epiphany in a closed Facebook group I was in. The next morning, I read someone's comment, which they ended with, "You Deserve It." Chills ran through my body. I knew that DESERVE was my next step. I had struggled with that word ever since Marty had started telling me he deserved to take our money, he deserved the life he wanted, he deserved everything. I then remembered the life I'd had when I married him – a house I could afford, a good job, money in the bank, a motorcycle club, and friends. I had deserved those things, at least I thought I did. Now, in order to get what he felt he deserved, my life had to be destroyed. What did this mean?

The question, then became, how could I resolve this struggle within in myself? How could I make "deserve" work for me?

Again, for days I went over our twenty years together, sometimes day by day, event by event. Marty had told me he didn't marry me to make me happy. Okay, I get it. He married me because he didn't have a life then. I get it. Now you have your life, your money.

I would go over every class, every channeling I'd received, every message I had gotten. I knew what I needed to do, but how? How does one pick up from here? I knew I was going to do everything I could. No one was going to break me.

As soon as I made the decision to find out, miracles began to happen. First, I fell into a publisher through the online class I had been taking. During a dream it all came to me. She could take my first book and make it a success, just as I had been told for years. That first book would be a success when the second book came out. During the second class we had it was only she and I; I had a whole hour to be with her and set up a plan.

The next day, I asked Marty to come over and help me on the computer so I could send her the manuscript of the first book. During that time, he said he would do most of the work for me. When I expressed surprise, he asked me why.

"Well maybe," I said, "it's because the last few years you have told me you didn't want anything to do with the books or anything I was doing."

"Oh Jeri, why do you have to beat me up for things I said? Why can't you just let things go?"

I wasn't beating him up, I was just answering his question.

He was playing more mind games, but I realized it didn't matter any longer and I didn't have time to argue about it. I just said, "Thank you for doing this for me," and moved on.

Next, I received a call from the sheriff's office telling me they had the man who had broken into our house last October. When I called Marty from outside of the office, crying with happiness and relief, all he said was, "I know this is your deal, and sure I will listen to you, but I can't do anything about it."

In the past I would have been devasted by this response; now I told myself, *Okay, I will be happy about this and deal with it.* As I let go of the idea that he had to be my support system, many others, including clients and friends, stepped forward to help. I found I had counseling sessions available to me, free. I also found support from the District Attorney to help me through the process of prosecution. This is ongoing now, so we will see.

The counseling sessions have helped me deal with the tremendous losses I've suffered over the past year. They are also helping me with my feeling of being undeserving and unlovable, and that is just the start. There is still much more to heal.

One afternoon, my daughter asked me to go to dinner with her. Over the years, Loni had kept in touch with her half-siblings (her father's children with Rita). Now her half-sister had revealed that they had two more half-siblings – a brother and a sister. These siblings had been found after a cousin took a DNA test through Ancestry.com. The half-sister was only five months older than Loni, which answered many questions about the summer she was born. The news was a huge slam in the gut, but it also took so much guilt away from me; I think it also helped Loni understand why I left her dad. I believe we have overcome the storm pretty well.

And still others came into my life, people I never would have met if Marty and I were still together. One evening, during a very mixed up text, and not knowing where it came from, I ended up talking to a traveling nurse interested in renting my room. The next day she came over, fell in love with the place and moved in the following Monday. That was Angela, the woman who wrote the Forward for this book. What I had thought would be a financial arrangement has proven to be a truly blessed encounter.

As I worked on healing and loving myself, I found I had more motivation to finish this book than I'd had in years. I went from believing that I had to have at least a full day off or a weekend to write, to saying and believing, "Oh great, I have a half-hour between clients to write." Every spare moment, day and night, I wrote.

I still had my meltdowns, but most of the time they were not as severe. Yes, sometimes I would cry uncontrollably. When that overwhelming feeling from my solar plexus began to rise up, I would repeat, "My book is coming, my book is being written." Or I would quickly change my thought to something I was looking forward to. Again, I knew that *thought control* was my friend. I worked it sometimes through the tears.

Most importantly, I finally realized that I do have my support team within me. It had taken two years and a lot of trauma since I'd heard it during that Life Between Lives session, but for the first time I really knew it. I realized that even if I can't find them at a given time, I can talk to them and they will respond. I began seeing the little miracles each day. I began enjoying things I did. Everything was beginning to look different around me.

People, including Marty's friends or acquaintances, began opening up to me. They told me they were happy I finally saw what was happening. Apparently, they had seen the handwriting on the wall long before I did. They all told me their opinion of him over the years. Yes, the years. Sometimes I was left speechless. I fought the "I was so stupid" and I knew I had done everything out of love and in an attempt to keep our marriage together. When I began to question what that love was, I told myself I didn't have the time to spend going over all of it again. I was on to me. Still, Marty and I continued our nightly discussions on the phone and saw each other occasionally. With each conversation I would pick up another insight that, upon reflection, shifted my thoughts and feelings.

I knew I wanted to come out of this as karma-free as I could. I wanted to come out of this with peace and with no regrets. I didn't want to hate him, though that was a battle I sometimes lost. I knew I needed more forgiveness for myself and towards him.

I could see him as a soul, a soul that also had things to learn in this life. I could no longer try to change his soul's progression, no matter what it was. There were times when I looked at him and saw the scared little boy inside. There were times I looked at him and felt the scared man. Sometimes I looked at him and only saw the anger and rage that he tried to hide. I no longer had time to figure that out either. Sadly, I could no longer see the amazing man I fell so in love with. I was not hurt by him being transgender, because I supported that part of his life. The hurt came as he pushed me away and finally left the way he did. I still could not understand why we couldn't have done our individual soul journeys together, like we had the first ten years of our marriage. Maybe our limit in this life was twenty years, and that was what we got, right down to the weekend.

Then I had a class called "Are You Waiting for an Apology?" My first thought was, *Hell yes, I am!* As I sat with that, I remembered all the *I'm sorry Jeri's*, and I got pissed. That was his way out. As long he said he was sorry, then I didn't have the right to hurt. Move on, that's the past. "It is easier to ask for forgiveness," he quoted to me one day, "than it is to ask for permission." He had said a mouthful there. I had always thought we had a marriage based on consideration for each other, not on asking for permission. Apparently, this was just another thing we saw very, very differently.

I couldn't even take the time to figure out if I could stay in this house or not. I couldn't spend more time worrying if I could save my salon and healing room. I stopped worrying about money as much. I set an hour each weekend to worry about the bills. That's it. This is the money I have now. If it spreads over the bills, it does. If it doesn't then we will see next weekend.

Mark, my first teacher, had told us, "If you are going to be sad, then set an alarm for ten or fifteen minutes. Be as sad as you want. Same thing with anger; take fifteen minutes and beat a bed or pillow. Then go on to something else. Do not stay there."

That is what I was working toward doing now.

One day, while walking from the salon to the house, I heard the voices say, *I am so lucky*. I sat down at my desk and thought about that. Yes, I am lucky. Then they said, *Write this down*. Again, I grabbed my journal and wrote, "*Yesterdays are sad right now. The future brings me stress. Right now, I am lucky.*" Oh my God, I finally figured out what Living in the Now means. I had heard that for years and didn't quite get it. Now I know.

I had fought journaling for years; now it had become my best friend. I guess I was turning my knowledge into wisdom and I couldn't wait to see what happened next.

Most nights, I could go to bed and have my body relax. Instead of crying myself to sleep, I could plan my tomorrows. Once, a few years ago, I'd thought I knew what the tomorrows would bring, but that had been an illusion. Now I wasn't sure at all, yet I still could look forward to them. One thing's for sure, good or bad, I know it will change. I tell my clients, "Everyone wants things different, but many do not want to change."

Change is in the air, and with my Support System with me I have faith it will be good. I do have an essence for my life. Somedays, I have to trust, minute by minute, my faith and the messages I had gotten from Spirit.

Marina came for my birthday. We had a great time together – wonderful dinners, shopping, and massages. We also talked more than we had for a long time. We channeled each night. She asked me as I was channeling: "Should Jeri rent the upstairs bedroom?" They answered: *If the person comes to her it will be the right person.* I was already renting one room to the nurse, but I hadn't thought I wanted to give up my privacy upstairs. Then, the very next day, a man fell into my lap to rent the bedroom. I was surprised and at the same time, not. I knew it was set up the right way. He moved in on Christmas Eve morning. He has been a blessing in so many ways.

As the new year and our twentieth anniversary approached, I knew I did not want to be home. I knew I wanted to be on an airplane, my safe place. I can still fly for free, so my plan was to go to the airport, get on the first plane going anywhere, get off and get on another one, for most of forty-eight hours. Then one of my girlfriends offered me a free condo on Maui for two weeks – definitely a better option.

Still, I meditated on that one, because Maui was my least favorite island in Hawaii. I was told I needed the feminine energy Maui has. I had suppressed my feminine energy for years, first because of the molestation issues, then again as a result of everything that had gone on with Marty over the last few years.

Timidly, I accepted the challenge. Off to Maui. This book came back from editing while I was on the plane there. Thankfully, I could concentrate on my book. But my body had other plans. I had massages to calm down the pain that it was releasing. I slept, rested and relaxed. I walked on the grass and the beach barefoot. I laid in the sun by the pool and soaked up the energy of the island. Ten days later I was back home, feeling really good and ready to go.

Two days later I was cut down as Marty's next plans were revealed to me. Again, I was back to climbing out of my hole. After numerous conversations and oceans of tears he finally gave me something I was looking for. He gave me some truth from deep within him.

Finally, I knew I hadn't been losing my mind. I wasn't the wrong one. Things I had seen and pushed aside were justified. I had done everything I could have done, I had been fighting a losing battle. Mark, had taught, "If you want to play the game you have to have a player." I hadn't had a player for years.

Am I now free? Free to move on? I hadn't looked at another man in twenty years. The girls used to laugh at me when they said, "Oh, God did you see that guy?" and I would answer, "No, Marty is my world." Can I now believe that I am Loveable? Can I ever love and trust again? I now understood the women who said they never wanted another man, ever, and just lived the rest of their lives alone. I understood it, but I knew I didn't want that.

Am I now free to be strong, motivated and resilient again? Am I now free to allow me out of my corner that I so willingly backed myself into? Am I free to just breathe?

I realized that somehow I was losing weight. Actually, I had been eating out and more food than I had in months. My clothes were loser. My stomach was going down. How can that be? Then I received my answer: my body was releasing emotional weight. My body had been holding onto something to protect me. By something I mean I don't think it was fat but an energy that I needed for protection. I stood up straighter than I had in maybe years. I had a glimpse of brightness inside.

Even though some mornings were still tough the darkness didn't last as long. I knew I had at least one more hurdle to jump. I had faith I would be okay somehow.

Now that you have come to the end of this book, I have a few final questions for you:

- Do you have faith and trust?
- Do you know your Inner Child?
- Where you traumatized or abused as a child?
- Have you been abused in a relationship, mentally, physically or sexually?
- Do you know your soul?
- Do you know your purpose in this life?
- Do you know the Guides, Angels and Ascended Masters that work with you?
- Do you listen to your voices and know who they are?
- Do you have a Support System within?
- Do you feel safe in your body?
- Do you have health or weight issues?
- Do you have to forgive yourself or others?
- Do you know your chakra system and how it works?
- Do you have transgender issues in your life?
- Do you know how your past lives are affecting your life today?
- Do you know the decisions you made about your life in the womb?
- Do you know what decisions you have made about how your life is today?
- Do you know what your children are teaching you? And why?
- Have you been molested? Or raped?

- Have you had an abortion?
- Have you lost someone close to you?
- Have you had a miscarriage? Or lost a child?
- Have you been hurt when it seems not to be your fault?
- Do you know your Soul Journey?
- Are you feeling lost or seeking your direction?
- Can you breathe? (I mean *really* breathe.)

If you have answered "yes" to one or more of these questions you may be guided to contact me. Of course, there are multiple other issues or reasons that may come up for you.

One morning I was driving to Starbucks when I heard the voices say, *Back From the Brink.*

"Oh, wow, what does that mean?"

*That is the name of your next book.*

"Really, is there a third book? This one took so long, I'll be ninety years old by the time that one comes out."

They laughed and said, *No, you won't.*

## Chapter 29

# A Pandemic, A Broken Arm and Jack's Back

Whatever my hopes and expectations for 2020 were, they were shattered when the pandemic spread across the globe like wildfire and changed life as we knew it, almost overnight. Suddenly, businesses were shuttered; many lost their incomes; and we couldn't shake hands with a friend or see our families. For a while, people didn't even know where their next sheet of toilet paper was coming from. Everyone kept talking about a "new normal," but there was no normalcy to be found.

The world went into fear and that fear energy could be felt by everyone on the planet. How are we going to survive? When can I see my daughter and grandchildren? It wasn't until politicians and scientists called for us to protect the elderly that I realized I was the elderly. In an attempt to maintain some humor, Loni would call each day and say, "Check. Okay, Mom, I am checking on the elderly." It was the only giggle I had all day.

Then, with one phone call, the Universe answered many of my prayers.

That day, instead of her usual joke about protecting the elderly, Loni said, "Guess who I just talked to?"

A couple of names went through my mind, but none struck me as particularly remarkable.

"No clue, sweetheart…"

"I just got off the phone with Jack."

That news might have shocked me more than the pandemic. I hadn't spoken to Jack since the beginning of my relationship with Marty more than twenty years earlier.

After a lengthy conversation in which Loni told me how this had come about, and some of what was said during her hour-long talk with Jack, it was time to call my sister Billie. Apparently, she was the one who had initiated contact with Jack. She hadn't said anything because she thought I'd be upset about it.

I wasn't. I understood that Billie's life was also at a standstill because of the pandemic and that she just needed someone to talk to. Eventually the topic had turned to me, and Billie mentioned my divorce and that she thought I needed help. Once he hung up with my sister, Jack went into action and contacted Loni to see if I needed help.

The next day I sent Jack a text, and before I knew it, we were having one of those marathon phone calls, just as we had when we reunited all those years ago.

We had been speaking regularly for a few weeks when one evening I fell in my living room and broke my arm. If I thought I wasn't doing much before, now, with a full cast, I really had time on my hands. Most of it would be spent on the phone with Jack.

Seven weeks later, as businesses finally started to open, we decided it was time to come face to face. Since he was in Denver and I was California, we chose Reno as a meeting place. As I made that drive, nervousness, excitement and every other emotion was running through my body. A few minutes outside town, I called Jack, who was five minutes ahead of me, and asked him to pull over and wait. He told me he was pulling into a gas station.

My stomach was in knots as I turned into the parking lot. What would it be like to be together after all these years? Before I could even put my car in park, he had opened the door and was pulling me out. He wrapped those big arms around me, and I knew my body was no longer afraid of his strength and size.

We were barely checked in at my favorite hotel when some local friends were texting me to see if we could meet them for dinner. Jack and I reluctantly broke the hold we had on each other and went to join them. All we could say to each other was, "Can you believe this?" It seemed like some kind of dream.

That night we returned to our room, where we would spend the next forty-eight hours. Most of the time we talked about everything and anything – the good times, the bad times, and a bunch of things we had never talked about in sixty-one years of knowing each other. Maybe we had grown up? Or maybe at this point we had nothing to lose so it was time to bare our souls. Besides, I figured he would read about it all in this book anyway.

As was always the case when we reunited, we shared past events, each from our own perspective. There were things he remembered that I didn't, things I remembered that he didn't and things we both remembered, though quite differently. The box of pictures and letters Jack had brought provided some evidence, as well as memories of the great times we'd had together.

Before we left, Jack pulled out the black velvet box with the beautiful engagement ring he had put on my finger in May of 1992. He had held onto it for the two decades since I gave it back to him. Though we were not ready to talk marriage or engagement, he slipped it on my finger as a symbol of our commitment to work on our relationship. That's where we are as I conclude this writing – taking it day by day as we rediscover the bond, we have shared for most of our lives.

Thank you for finding me, sweetheart.

The story's not over, so stay tuned, folks!

Always, remember the darkest days can lead to the light. The light days can turn dark in a heartbeat. Work on resolving the past, plan for the future and LIVE IN THE NOW.

# About the Author
## Jeri Brown-Roraback Ph.D

Jeri wears many hats —author, teacher, hairdresser, and healer. For more than twenty-five years she has extensively studied the holistic world, taking countless metaphysical classes and earning her PhD in Metaphysical Sciences from the University of Metaphysical Sciences in Minnesota. Jeri is certified in various healing modalities, including *Mind-Body-Spirit,* and is always on a quest to learn additional techniques for restoring the mind and body to a state of peace.

Jeri specializes in Life Between Lives® Hypnotherapy sessions, in which she leads her clients beyond their past lives to the place the soul resides between earthly incarnations. There, they can access answers to their questions about present or past lives, their time in the womb, and their soul journey. The information that can be obtained in these sessions is truly monumental and life-altering.

She has travelled the world, from Italy to Africa and from Panama to Peru. She has held classes and private sessions in Greece, Norway, England and India, always taking time to explore and immerse herself in each country's rich culture.

Jeri has also been a practicing hairdresser for over forty-five years. These days, she can still be found serving her loyal and much-loved clientele in her salon on Harmony Lane in Sacramento, California. Connected to the salon is a sanctuary where she works with her hypnotherapy clients.

Jeri is also the author of *The ABC's of Never Having Another Bad Hairday*, a compilation of the insights and wisdom gained through her tragedies, her studies, her travels and of course, from "Behind the Chair."

Now over seventy years young, Jeri wants others to know that we are never too old to begin or continue your Soul Journey. She is currently creating a new and different life on almost every level, and is in the process of writing her third book.

# Acknowledgments

*"Even the Olympians need a coach."*

The day I heard this message was a game-changer for me. Like so many survivors of trauma, I had always been determined to do things on my own. Now Spirit was teaching me that to seek help is not a weakness, but a symbol of strength and the desire to improve or change.

A coach can show up in many forms, but they tend to show up when we need them most. The following are some who through their love and support, helped me discover my strength, clarity and purpose.

To my darling daughter, Loni, thank you for choosing me as your mother and for blessing me with three beautiful granddaughters. You have saved me many times, and though our journey didn't always look perfect, you made it a journey worth taking. I am so proud of the woman you have become, and I love you more than you will ever understand.

Thank you to my family, friends and lost loves who have supported me along my soul journey. To Ronney, creator of WorldWideWisdomDirectory.com and EvolvingHealthEducation.org and the former owner of Inner Words Magazine. How grateful I am that you answered the phone that day thirty years ago. That call started me on my healing path, and us on some of the best adventures of my life. I cherish every moment, from the beaches of Hawaii to our nightly Zoom calls, sharing beers, fears, accomplishments and tears. Thank you for your support, laughter, and always pushing me to "get it done." I love you.

To Marina, my soul sister, who always loved me even when I couldn't love myself. We have laughed and cried together, supported each other in so many ways. Thank you for trusting me with your journey, in and out of sessions, and thank you for sharing your family and your wisdom with me. We have climbed many mountains together, both literally and spiritually, and I know we have many more miles to travel. See you at the next airport!

Christina, you were only twenty months old when we met, and since then I have watched you grow into an amazing woman with many accomplishments both behind and ahead of you. Little did we know the night you asked to take my picture for your photography class that it would be the cover for this book! (it is no longer the front cover) I miss you every day – especially our trips to Dairy Queen and those long road trips when you navigated, took charge of the dash controls, sang with me and kept me laughing. The Angels are with you in your journey through life.

Angela Murphy, in our short two months of living together, we have connected on a level that is unexplainable to most. What began as a business arrangement has turned into a deeply treasured friendship and a learning experience for us both. We have reminded each other that broken hearts can heal and that we should never judge anyone's life because *You don't know that you don't know what you don't know.* Thank you for trusting me with your life during your sessions, and for writing the Foreword to this book. I am so grateful for our nightly Zoom calls. You help keep me full of love and laughter. I love and appreciate you.

To my amazing friend, Kathy A., you came into my life many years ago, staying on the sidelines until I needed you most. You gave me strength and a belief that I was supported. May we keep yelling "BINGO!" for many years to come!

To my other friends, oh my, your names alone could fill a book! You know who you are, and my heart knows every one of you. Thanks.

To Pamela Carson, my first book editor. Since that first miracle meeting, you have supported and empowered me to keep writing. I cannot thank you enough for your time, expertise, and confidence in me.

A very special thanks to the many clients I have worked with throughout my career. To my hair clients, thank you for your support and friendship during my forty-five years "behind the chair." Each and every one of you entered my life for a reason. To my spiritual clients, I am humbled and honored that you trusted me with your lives, past, present and future.

With each healing you have received, I have received. You have been a constant source of information and learning for me. Each of you has given me the opportunity to do what I love.

To all my Spiritual teachers along the way, thank you for being there and doing what you loved. Each of you, in your own way, has been my inspiration to keep going. Above all, thank you for teaching me that no matter what I have gone through, there is a blessing and lesson to be uncovered and appreciated. Those experiences have taken me to where I am today, and has provided me with the wisdom to help others.

To Jennifer Rogers, of A Place In Time Photography in Kihei, Hawaii. Thank you for the great photoshoot at the beach. I was amazed by your expertise and grateful for how easy you made it all seem. (For anyone who would like lasting professional memories of their time on Maui, Jennifer is your lady!)

Thank you, Shanda Trofe of Transcendent Publishing, for quite literally showing up with a miracle. You walked me (and sometimes pushed me) through the publishing of *From Behind the Chair: A Soul Seeker's Journey to Freedom* and the relaunch of *The ABC's of Never Having Another Bad Hairday*. I cannot thank you enough for your knowledge, expertise and love of books.

Dear Jack, as I wrote this book, I never dreamt I would be proofreading it with you. But here you are in my life again, 61 years strong. Since I was 12 years old, you have loved me. Our years in the '90s now look totally different to me since we have spent hours talking about and dissecting what happened. Thank you for stepping up and finding me this time. Thank you for every encouraging word and belief you share with me, and especially when you look into my eyes and touch my soul. Thank you for allowing me to feel love and trust again. I love you as we stay determined to make it work this time for the rest of our soul journey.

And last but certainly not least, to the second "Marty" in the book, thank you for sharing the last twenty years with me. Though I'm not sure what lies ahead for us, I will be forever grateful to you for allowing me to love deeply, helping me survive betrayal and, in the end, forcing me to feel my own strength. Because of you, I realized I could feel safe in this life and that I could feel unimaginable hurt and pain and still survive; because of you, I was able to find my support system within. And, I am sure that through this experience I will learn to trust, feel love and feel safe again. My daily desire is that one day we can both come to a place of peace with our new, independent *Soul Journeys*.

To connect with or learn more about Jeri
and what she offers, visit:
**JeriBrown-Roraback.com**
Sign up for her newsletter and receive a free gift
Read Jeri's Blog
Have Jeri come to your city
Dates of classes, either in-person or online
YourInnerPower.com
Learn more about Jeri's Hypnotherapy
Or email Jeri at:
powrnu@gmail.com
To find availability of services
Facebook:
JeriBrown-Roraback
To order Jeri's first book
*The ABC's of Never Having Another Bad Hairday*
Amazon Contact Jeri through her website.

www.ingramcontent.com/pod-product-compliance
Lightning Source LLC
Chambersburg PA
CBHW071342290426
44108CB00014B/1418